DISTANCE LEARNING
MAKING CONNECTIONS ACROSS
VIRTUAL SPACE AND TIME

Anthony G. Picciano
Hunter College
City University of New York

Merrill
Prentice Hall

Upper Saddle River, New Jersey
Columbus, Ohio

Library of Congress Cataloging-in-Publication Data

Picciano, Anthony G.
    Distance learning: making connections across virtual space and time / Anthony G.
Picciano.— 1st ed.
        p. cm.
    Includes bibliographical references and index.
    ISBN 0-13-080900-4
    1. Open learning. 2. Distance education. 3. Instructional systems—Design. 4.
Educational technology. I. Title.
LC5800 .P53 2001
371.3'5—dc21

99-089132

Vice President and Publisher: Jeffery W. Johnston
Editor: Debra A. Stollenwerk
Editorial Assistant: Penny S. Burleson
Production Editor: Julie Peters
Production Coordination: Carlisle Publishers Services
Photo Coordinator: Sherry Mitchell
Design Coordinator: Diane C. Lorenzo
Cover Designer: Jeff Vanik
Cover Art: Image Bank
Production Manager: Pamela D. Bennett
Director of Marketing: Kevin Flanagan
Marketing Manager: Amy June
Marketing Services Manager: Krista Groshong

This book was set in Palatino by Carlisle Communications, Ltd. It was printed and bound by R. R. Donnelley &
Sons Company. The cover was printed by Phoenix Color Corp.

Photo Credits: NASA Headquarters, 1, 185; Anne Vega/Merrill, 21; Jet Propulsion Laboratory/NASA, 43;
Anthony Magnacca/Merrill, 65; PH College, 89; Photo Courtesy of Ventana Corporation, 109; Scott
Cunningham/Merrill, 133, 159.

Merrill
Prentice Hall

10 9 8 7 6 5 4 3 2 1
ISBN 0-13-080900-4

To my students

About the Author

Anthony G. Picciano is the author of two books on education and technology, most recently *Educational Leadership and Planning for Technology* (Merrill/Prentice Hall, 1998). He is a professor in the Education Administration and Supervision Program in the School of Education at Hunter College. His teaching specializations include educational technology, organization theory, and research methods. He also has been a faculty fellow since 1994 at the City University of New York Open Systems Laboratory, a facility dedicated to experimenting with advanced uses of instructional technology and to providing staff development programs for organizations such as public schools, colleges, and private businesses.

Dr. Picciano has served as a consultant to a variety of public and private organizations, including the Commission on Higher Education/Middle States Association of Colleges and Universities, EDUCOM, the New York State Education Department, CITICORP, and the U.S. Coast Guard. He has received a number of grants and awards from the National Science Foundation, the Alfred P. Sloan Foundation, the U.S. Department of Education, and IBM. His articles on educational technology have appeared in journals such as *The Urban Review, Journal of Asynchronous Learning Networks, Journal of Educational Multimedia and Hypermedia, Computers in the Schools, Equity and Choice,* and *EDUCOM Review.*

Preface

The purpose of this book is to provide the theoretical framework as well as the practical considerations for planning and implementing distance learning programs. Fundamental concepts of distance learning, planning, program development, and the basic technologies used are presented. Emphasis is placed, throughout this book, on the distance learning application and program development in total and not on any single component. Most important, this book is meant to provide a foundation from which educators throughout the world will view distance learning as an appropriate approach for meeting the ever-expanding needs of students. As the information age progresses, as demand for highly skilled workers and professionals grows, and as lifelong learning is routinely accepted, distance learning will proliferate and will eventually become a necessity for meeting these needs.

The material is designed for administrators, managers, teachers, distance learning coordinators, chief information officers, and media specialists who are involved in initiating and supporting distance learning in schools and private businesses. This book is also appropriate as a text in a preservice or in-service course on distance learning.

DEFINITION OF TERMS

The term *distance learning* will be used throughout this book to refer to any type of instruction in which the teacher and students are physically separated. This appellation is preferred over *distance education* because of the increased responsibility placed on the learner in most distance learning applications. An extensive definition of the term is provided in Chapter 1.

The term *virtual* is used frequently in this book and means being functional and effective without existing in a traditional mode. Virtual learning, for example, is learning that can functionally and effectively occur in the absence of traditional classroom environments. Other uses of the term *virtual*, as in virtual systems or virtual space and time, will be defined where appropriate in the text. The adjective *traditional*, used in this paragraph and throughout this book to describe a classroom setting, refers to the common format of an instructor conducting a lesson, delivering a lecture, or leading a discussion with a number of students physically present.

Organization of This Book

This book is organized into nine chapters, plus a guide. While each chapter can be read independently, the material is presented in a logical sequence. Chapter 1 is an introduction to distance learning. Chapter 2 provides a review of planning and applies a modified social process model to planning for distance learning. Using this planning model, Chapters 3 through 7 explore the components of the model including distance learning technology, instructional development, student perspectives, faculty development, administrative support, facilities, and finances. Chapter 8 brings some of the material in the previous chapters together and explores the evolving Web-based virtual model that relies extensively on digital and computer networking technology. Chapter 9 gives a brief glimpse of the future. While this last chapter reviews some of the material covered in previous chapters, it is not a summary of the book but rather a discussion of the dynamic nature of distance learning, especially with regard to the evolving technologies. Following the chapters is *A Guide to Designing a Web-Based Distance Learning Course*, which illustrates the features and components of a typical Web-based course. This guide can be used in conjunction with the material in other chapters, especially Chapter 8. A glossary and an appendix, "On-Line Sources of Information on Distance Learning," are also provided.

End-of-Chapter Activities

Each chapter concludes with a summary of the material covered in the previous pages. One or more case studies designed to stimulate thought and discussion on the material are also provided. The case studies reflect situations that exist in many educational environments and allow readers to make decisions about planning or implementing a distance learning program. Each chapter also has its own reference list that facilitates pursuing citations for further reading.

Website

The website provides material designed to assist in using this book for instructional purposes. The website is organized by chapter and includes:

- a summary of the main concepts of each chapter;
- additional information and insights for using the end-of-chapter case studies for in-class activities or for student assignments; and
- links (URLs) for additional on-line resources and materials pertinent to the subject matter.

Other materials will be added in the future as the distance learning technology evolves and changes to keep this book current and up to date.

ACKNOWLEDGMENTS

I gratefully acknowledge the guidance and assistance provided by the staff at Merrill/Prentice Hall, especially Debbie Stollenwerk, Penny Burleson, and Sherry Mitchell, and to Amy Gehl at Carlisle Publishers Services.

I would also like to thank the following reviewers for their valuable feedback: Andrew J. Brovey, Valdosta State University; David G. Gueulette, Northern Illinois University; Kay Persichitte, University of Northern Colorado; Farah Saba, San Diego State University; and David VanEsselstyn, Teachers College of Columbia University.

In addition, I have benefited significantly from my professional associations with a number of colleagues: the faculty in the Department of Curriculum and Teaching at Hunter College; Janet Patti and Marcia Knoll in the Administration and Supervision Program; and the faculty fellows, staff, and administration, especially Mike Ribaudo and Colette Wagner of the Open Systems Laboratory at the City University of New York.

I am most appreciative of the support of the Alfred P. Sloan Foundation for my work in distance learning, especially Frank Mayadas who has been gracious in sharing his guidance and insights into this dynamic subject. This work was also funded in part by the generosity of the Hunter College Presidential Scholarship Awards Program, David A. Caputo, President.

Lastly, Michael and Dawn Marie have made me a better person. And what can I say about Elaine, who supports me in everything I do.

Anthony G. Picciano

Discover the Companion Website Accompanying This Book

The Prentice Hall Companion Website: A Virtual Learning Environment

Technology is a constantly growing and changing aspect of our field that is creating a need for content and resources. To address this emerging need, Prentice Hall has developed an online learning environment for students and professors alike—Companion Websites—to support our textbooks.

In creating a Companion Website, our goal is to build on and enhance what the textbook already offers. For this reason, the content for each user-friendly website is organized by topic and provides the professor and student with a variety of meaningful resources. Common features of a Companion Website include the following:

For the Professor—

Every Companion Website integrates **Syllabus Manager**™, an online syllabus creation and management utility.

- **Syllabus Manager**™ provides you, the instructor, with an easy, step-by-step process to create and revise syllabi, with direct links into Companion Website and other online content without having to learn HTML.
- Students may logon to your syllabus during any study session. All they need to know is the web address for the Companion Website and the password you have assigned to your syllabus.
- After you have created a syllabus using **Syllabus Manager**™, students may enter the syllabus for their course section from any point in the Companion Website.
- Class dates are highlighted in white and assignment due dates appear in blue. Clicking on a date, the student is shown the list of activities for the assignment. The activities for each assignment are linked directly to actual content, saving time for students.

- Adding assignments consists of clicking on the desired due date, then filling in the details of the assignment—name of the assignment, instructions, and whether or not it is a one-time or repeating assignment.
- In addition, links to other activities can be created easily. If the activity is online, a URL can be entered in the space provided, and it will be linked automatically in the final syllabus.
- Your completed syllabus is hosted on our servers, allowing convenient updates from any computer on the Internet. Changes you make to your syllabus are immediately available to your students at their next logon.

For the Student—

- **Topic Overviews**—outline key concepts in topic areas
- **Electronic Bluebook**—send homework or essays directly to your instructor's email with this paperless form
- **Message Board**—serves as a virtual bulletin board to post—or respond to—questions or comments to/from a national audience
- **Web Destinations**—links to www sites that relate to each topic area
- **Professional Organizations**—links to organizations that relate to topic areas
- **Additional Resources**—access to topic-specific content that enhances material found in the text

To take advantage of these and other resources, please visit the *Distance Learning: Making Connections Across Virtual Space and Time* Companion Website at

www.prenhall.com/picciano

Brief Contents

Contents

Chapter 7 Administrative Support Services, Facilities, and Finances

Chapter 8 Web-Based Distance Learning: The Virtual Model

CHAPTER ONE

Introduction

In April 1997, educators from twenty-two countries met in Salzburg, Austria, to attend a nine-day seminar, the focus of which was planning and implementing distance learning projects for teaching English as a foreign language in their countries. Participants shared the experiences of their homelands. In Iceland, radio transmission and the Internet are used to provide instruction to fishermen who spend weeks at sea. In Indonesia, television is used to provide basic language literacy to inhabitants of the hundreds of islands that make up this country. In Pakistan, a combination of mail and satellite television was being considered to improve English language skills in villages in the remote northern mountain provinces. These images of great distances, geographic obstacles, and scattered populations are frequently invoked as the basic rationale for distance learning programs or courses. At this same seminar, participants from Great Britain and the United States also described programs for students leading busy lives in large metropolitan areas such as London or New York City. These students take courses "at a distance" within a mile or two of their schools for the convenience of studying in their homes or places of business.

Educators throughout the world, whether in rural or urban areas, increasingly are considering developing distance learning as part of their academic programs. For rural and isolated communities, distance learning can be the vehicle to conquer geography and space between teachers and students. In populous metropolitan areas, distance learning is sometimes seen as a mechanism for fitting education into the busy lives of older students who struggle to find the time to balance careers, family responsibilities, and schooling.

While distance learning through the mail, radio, and television has an extensive history, newer technologies such as digital communications and networking have begun to emerge that make it much easier for educators to provide some form of distance learning for their students. Conquering space and time, a daunting venture in the not too distant past, is becoming more commonplace as computer, communication, and video technologies are being used to bring learning virtually to any place on Earth and at any time.

THE QUEST FOR VIRTUAL SPACE AND TIME

Historically, humankind has been on a quest to conquer new frontiers and to find new places: Phoenicia, Carthage, Greece, Rome, the Ottoman Turks, the New World, the American West, the ocean depths, the galaxies. Once new places are discovered, we make every attempt to shorten the time it takes to travel there, to find the best route, and to make our travel as convenient as possible. We have been obsessed with what some refer to as the tyranny of geography (Auletta, 1997, p. 305). And we are obsessed with reducing that tyranny by improving our vehicles or methods of travel—faster ships, faster trains, faster cars, and faster planes.

We have studied the Age of Discovery, the Age of Flight, and the Space Age, and much of our historical study has centered on military conquest and commerce. What has sometimes not been given enough attention is the search for knowledge and information that underscored many of these enterprises. The emperors, kings, and queens who financed expeditions and exploration wanted to know about new lands and peoples. What is there? Who is there? What are they like? How do they live? Alexander the Great, while recognized as one of the greatest military tacticians of his time, also established the Library and Museum in Alexandria as the scientific and cultural center of the Mediterranean. Kublai Khan was as interested in learning about Western culture as Marco Polo was in learning of Eastern culture. Napoleon, in his expedition to Egypt in 1798, took with him approximately 150 scientists, artists, and other scholars. The result of their work was the multivolume *Description de l'Egypt,* the first systematic scientific investigation of any area of Africa (Stillman, 1998).

We continue to crave information about faraway places. We want descriptions; we want to go there; and, if we cannot go there, we want to see it anyway. As we enter the twenty-first century, our quest is taking us to places farther away and our search for knowledge and information is expanding daily. A convergence of technologies designed to improve the way we receive, transmit, and process information can provide us with a chariot, tall ship, or lunar module for our quest. This convergence has spawned the Information Age wherein communications, media, and digital computing are becoming one and the same. The Information Age is a direct descendent of all the other ages of discovery and exploration and is enabling us to explore and travel the Earth and beyond. Education at all levels is a critical component of the Information Age, and it is adjusting to the possibilities that this age provides. The technologies that bring us to remote parts of the Earth and universe are now being used as teaching tools in "virtual" classrooms.

During the first half of this century, Edwin Hubble spent endless cold nights on the one-hundred inch telescope at Mt. Wilson searching the heavens for nebulae to prove his theories about the expansion of the universe. Today, astronomers all over the world use the telescope named for him to study the same heavens; however, they never have to leave their laboratories and offices. Computer images of stars and galaxies are downlinked to them in an instant from the Hubble Space Telescope and are clearer than the images from any telescope at any point on Earth. Furthermore, these images are available for study not just by astronomers but by anybody with a computer and modem access to the Internet. Young school children as well as research scientists use these images for simple class projects and for advanced study.

Robert Ballard is a senior scientist affiliated with Woods Hole Oceanographic Institute. Using computers, satellite communications, fiber optics, and robotics, he has developed technology for exploring the ocean depths. Using deep-sea imaging technology aboard a robotic system named ARGO/JASON, scientists in their offices and laboratories see everything they would were they actually on the ocean floor. He and others have used this technology to substantiate theories involving plate tectonics and continental drift, to discover mountains higher than Everest and canyons deeper than the Grand Canyon, and to locate the *RMS Titanic* buried 12,460-feet deep in her North Atlantic grave. One of his major goals today is to share these experiences with others, especially children. Through an initial series of downlink sites across the United States in one of the most ambitious ARGO/JASON undertakings, 600,000 students were able to watch a deep-sea exploration of active volcanoes just off the Galapagos Islands. For Ballard, the highlight of this event occurred when young children at the remote sites took turns steering and manipulating the arms of the deep-sea robots and were actually able to pick up sediment samples from the ocean floor.

In July 1997, NASA sent the Sojourner spacecraft to the planet Mars. While millions of people read about the Sojourner's exploration in newspapers or saw broadcasts on television, NASA reported that more than 200 million people during the week of July 5 viewed and downloaded text, images, and other materials from the Sojourner Web sites. With a few clicks of the mouse, one could read a treatise on Martian geology, check out the weather conditions on the planet, or study the Martian sunset. The materials at these Web sites have become the object of extensive study for students of all ages in major research laboratories, in colleges, and in high schools, but mainly in their homes (Tierney, 1997).

The implications of the newer digital and communications technologies for education are extensive and are being recounted in journals, newspapers, and books every day. Neil Rudenstine (1997), president of Harvard University, while asserting that direct human contact is absolutely essential to serious education, observed that the Internet and other electronic networks allow communications to take place at all hours and across distances, and permit a significant extension of the scope, continuity, and even quality of certain forms of instructional interaction. Indeed, these technologies are having an enormous influence on traditional education while redefining our concept of distance learning.

DISTANCE LEARNING DEFINED

Distance education, distance teaching, distance learning, open learning, distributed learning, asynchronous learning, telelearning, and flexible learning are some of the terms used to describe an educational process in which the teacher and students are physically separated. While it would be tempting to provide a simple definition of the basic distance learning process, a bit more discussion is required.

Distance education is the term that has been used most widely for several decades. As an all-inclusive term, distance education has served well to define the physical separation of teaching and learning. However, in recent years, the term distance learning has become popular particularly in the United States. While used interchangeably with distance education, distance learning puts an emphasis on the "learner." Indeed, the concept of student-centered learning has become popular for all forms of education, distance or otherwise, but is especially appropriate when students need to take on greater responsibility for their learning, as is the case when doing so from a distance. Therefore, distance learning will be the basic term used in this book to encompass all the various forms of learning where teacher and student are physically separated.

The term distance learning conjures up different images to different people in different settings. Distance learning can refer to a wide variety of instructional delivery processes including correspondence courses, broadcast television, and computer-mediated instruction. Desmond Keegan (1996) proposes one of the most thorough definitions of distance learning, which includes the following five basic requirements:

1. The quasi-separation of teacher and learner throughout the period of the learning process.
2. The influence of an educational organization for the planning of courses of study and preparation of materials, and for providing academic and student support services.
3. The use of technology and media—print, video, audio, or computer—to carry the content of the course and to provide mechanisms for interaction.
4. The provision of two-way interaction and communication.
5. The quasi-permanent absence of a learning group so that students are taught more as individuals than as groups (Keegan, 1996, p. 50).

Keegan's definition aptly fits many forms of distance learning in use today. However, excluded from this definition are the use of various materials in print, video, or computer form for private study or for on-campus programs. For example, a video designed to be used at home to learn a skill such as typing or keyboarding is excluded. A computer program designed to simulate a laboratory experiment conducted in a traditional course that is made available in a college library or media center is also excluded.

In response to newer technologies and to questions raised earlier by Garrison and Shale (1987), Keegan also acknowledges that his fifth condition, the "quasi-permanent absence of a learning group," should be reconsidered in light of electronic groupings of students in audio, video, and computer conferencing technologies (Keegan, 1996, pp. 46–47). The proliferation of the various group-conferencing technologies may in fact negate his concept that distance learning requires the quasi-permanent absence of the learning group as an element of the definition.

DISTANCE LEARNING MEANS DIFFERENT THINGS TO DIFFERENT PEOPLE

Distance learning can take on many different forms and characteristics within the framework of Keegan's definition. These will be discussed in more detail in later chapters of this book; however, a brief look at some of these different forms will help to clarify our definition.

Figures 1.1, 1.2, and 1.3 are illustrations of three currently popular forms of distance learning. While all fall within Keegan's definition, they have very different components and characteristics.

EXAMPLE 1   Broadcast Television

An instructor delivering a lecture live over a television network into student homes is a distance learning format that provides for communication by teacher to student via video technology, synchronously (at the same time), from one to many delivery points. This form allows the instructor to conduct the class for hundreds of students. Students do not interact immediately with the instructor but can ask questions using telephone, mail, or e-mail.

FIGURE 1.1   Example 1 - Broadcast Television

EXAMPLE 2   Two-way Videoconferencing

A college professor teaching a course at a main campus that is also being videoconferenced to a class at a local high school is a format that provides for interaction of teacher to student and student to teacher via video technology, synchronously, in a point-to-point, two-way delivery mode. Students can interact immediately and ask questions of the professor and the professor can reply.

FIGURE 1.2 Example 2 - Two-Way Videoconferencing

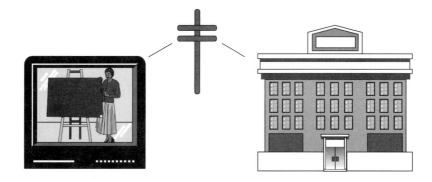

EXAMPLE 3   Asynchronous Learning Network

An instructor using World Wide Web and group e-mail software to teach an Internet-based course is a form that provides for interaction of teacher to learner and learner to teacher via computer technology, asynchronously (at different times), in a multipoint delivery mode. Students and instructor continually interact but rarely at the same time.

FIGURE 1.3 Example 3 - Asynchronous Learning Network

The intent here is not to cover all the various possibilities but to emphasize that distance learning can take on many different forms to meet many different needs. The possibilities are extensive and expanding and will likely continue to expand in the future.

THE EVOLUTION OF DISTANCE LEARNING

Distance learning has an extensive history that can help provide an appreciation of its current state and inform the possibilities of its future evolution. Much of this history relates to the communications technologies available to a society at a particular time. Exactly when distance learning began is difficult to say. In all likelihood, some form of messenger and mail correspondence study existed in all cultures going back hundreds of years or more. Tifflin and Rajasingham (1995) describe the epistles of Paul the Apostle as a form of religious correspondence education. Letters written on papyrus by scribes were delivered by messengers to the early Christian communities to promulgate and explain religious dogma. In the early 1700s, mail and correspondence courses supplemented by public lectures in Lyceum halls existed in colonial America (Willis, 1993).

The first formal distance learning programs appeared in the mid-nineteenth century as postal systems were developed and as more people learned to read and write. Holmberg (1986) traces the development of correspondence courses as far back as the 1830s in Sweden, Germany, and Great Britain. Isaac Pitman is generally credited with establishing a most successful correspondence program in Great Britain in 1840. Using the "Penny Post," which guaranteed delivery of a letter for a penny, Pitman offered shorthand instruction by correspondence. Other successful correspondence programs appeared later at Skerry's College in Edinburg in 1878 and at the University Correspondence College in London in 1887. In Germany, Charles Toussaint and Gustav Langensheidt taught language by correspondence in 1873. H.S. Hermod began offering English language instruction in Sweden in 1886. This eventually evolved into Hermod's in 1898 and in turn went on to become one of the largest distance learning organizations in the world.

In the United States, William Rainey Harpur, who would later become president of the University of Chicago, helped establish one of the first degree programs by correspondence at Chautauqua College of Liberal Arts in New York in 1883. When Harpur moved on to the University of Chicago, he established the University Extension Division in 1892. While the University Extension had mixed success in attracting students, Harpur remained an advocate of correspondence study throughout his career. Other early correspondence programs of note were established at Illinois Wesleyan (1877), the University of Wisconsin (1885), the International Correspondence Schools (1891), and Pennsylvania State University (1892).

During the early part of the twentieth century, correspondence and home study programs were beginning to be established for primary and secondary education as well. The Calvert School, a correspondence-based primary school in Baltimore, enrolled its first students in 1906. This school still exists and continues to enroll thousands of students. In the 1920s, Benton Harbor, Michigan (1923) and the University of Nebraska (1929) began to offer high school students home study courses.

Most of the early pioneering correspondence programs struggled but some, such as Hermods, the International Correspondence Schools, and the Calvert School, went on to become quite successful. By the 1930s, hundreds of correspondence programs were established throughout the world. Adults studying on a part-time basis to improve or develop career skills were the primary target of these programs, which is a trend that continues today. The number and nature of these programs expanded as new communications technologies emerged.

In the 1920s, institutions such as the University of Wisconsin, the State University of Iowa, and Ohio State University transferred and supplemented part of their already established correspondence programs to radio. Buckland and Dye (1991) estimated that at least 176 radio stations were established at educational institutions during this period for the purpose of delivering distance learning. However, most of these were replaced in later years as television and video technologies became popular.

The State University of Iowa, Purdue University, and Kansas State University were among the first schools to use television in distance learning. Most were limited broadcasts of selected courses within communities. In the 1950s, more extensive programs such as *Sunrise Semester* (New York University) and *Continental College* (Johns Hopkins University) were developed and broadcast with the assistance of the two major television broadcast companies—Columbia Broadcasting System (CBS) and the National Broadcasting Company (NBC). However, the commercial television companies supported these efforts only modestly. In the 1970s, the Public Broadcasting Service (PBS) gave a major new thrust to the production and delivery of educational television programs with its affiliates throughout the country. PBS continues to this day to be the major national educational television broadcasting service and is involved with several distance learning projects including the *Adult Learning Satellite Service, Ready to Earn,* and *Going the Distance.*

The 1970s and 1980s saw an investment in newer television delivery technologies, namely cable (CATV), satellite communications, and fiber optics. Because of cost, the first uses of these technologies were state-supported or by consortia of colleges, universities, and state education departments. In 1980, *Learn/Alaska* became the first state educational satellite system operating in the United States. It provided hours of educational television services to more than a hundred of its remote villages. Similar systems also followed in Texas, Hawaii, and Iowa. Among consortia, Oklahoma State University initiated the National University Teleconferencing Network (NUTN) in 1982. Sixty-six colleges and universities agreed to work together to plan and deliver educational programs by satellite. Presently, the Iowa Communications Network (ICN) has established one of the most extensive fiber optic educational networks in the country. The plan is for all school districts, colleges, and public libraries in Iowa to be connected to the ICN. The ICN model is being considered or duplicated in other states because it provides full-motion video, two-way interactive communications, as well as digital (Internet) and voice services. All of this involves a significant financial commitment on the part of the participants and providers of services and, as a result, planning and implementation can take many years.

In the 1990s, digital technology via the Internet and other computer networks was seen as the major new development for distance learning programs. Since 1990, the Alfred P. Sloan Foundation has funded the development of asynchronous learning networks (ALN) at colleges and universities throughout the United States. These programs use relatively inexpensive technology to deliver courses to homes, businesses, and dormitories. Using World Wide Web, text-based e-mail, and group software, ALNs are considered the harbingers of future distance learning delivery systems, especially when digital video can be delivered inexpensively over the Internet. This will be discussed further in Chapter 3.

While many of the twentieth century examples of distance learning refer to developments in the United States, comparable projects were also being undertaken in Europe, Canada, Africa, and other parts of the world. It would be fair to say that distance learning is more advanced in other countries than in the United States. This is a result not of the technology used, but of the nature and scope of the distance learning organizations. In the United States, most distance learning programs are affiliated with or extensions of traditional college and high school programs. In Europe and elsewhere, this is not the case. There, entire schools and colleges have been established as distance learning institutions. In 1962, the University of South Africa was one of the first such dedicated distance learning institutions. In 1969, the Open University of the United Kingdom at Milton Keynes was established and began a new era of distance learning on a scale that had not been seen previously. Using a combination of print, video, and computer technologies, entire degree programs have been designed so that students enroll and complete them entirely at home. The Open University is considered by many to be one of the most successful distance learning institutions in the world, enrolling more than 150,000 students annually in its programs. Following the British Open University model, similar dedicated distance learning schools opened throughout the world.

In France, the Centre National D'Enseignement a Distance (CNED) was established in the 1980s by the French Ministry of Education. The CNED traces its roots to 1939 and the invasion of France by Germany when the French government established the Centre National D'Enseignement par Correspondence (CNEC) to provide an education for displaced French school children. Presently, the CNED enrolls more than 350,000 students annually.

The Central Chinese Radio and Television University Network (DIANDA) is a network of forty-three universities coordinated by Beijing University. It was established in 1979 to meet the demand for skilled workers. DIANDA uses an extensive network of regional television stations, television education centers, and more than 10,000 tutoring groups to deliver its educational programs. Students enrolled in these programs must take and pass national examinations that are given periodically. Almost one million high school and adult students participate in the DIANDA programs annually. As we enter the beginning of the twenty-first century, distance learning has become well established throughout the world.

THE CURRENT STATE OF DISTANCE LEARNING

For most of the twentieth century, distance learning programs and enrollments have continually increased. Today, distance learning is available in most countries of the world and every state in the United States.

Figure 1.4 provides an insight into the extent of distance learning throughout the world. Distance learning is available on all of the continents and in both developed and developing countries. Worldwide, millions of students participate in distance learning every year. In the United States, the U.S. Department of Education (1997) estimates that approximately 750,000 students were enrolled in distance learning programs conducted by colleges and universities in 1995. This number includes primary and secondary education students taking courses offered by colleges but excludes primary and secondary students taking courses offered by non-higher education entities such as state education departments. It also excludes training programs offered by non-higher education entities such as the military. It should also be mentioned that, unlike most other countries, the United States does not have a comprehensive system of national administrative records. Pascal Forgione (1997), U.S. Commissioner of Education Statistics, has commented that reporting even the most basic information on education in the United States is a challenge.

In comparing student enrollments, many countries have distance learning programs that are far more extensive than those in the United States. As noted earlier, many countries have "national" universities, central agencies, or a limited number of colleges dedicated to providing distance learning to an entire country. In some cases, they enroll hundreds of thousands of students yearly. In the United States, most distance learning facilities are administered by colleges, state-supported regional entities, or consortia. Approximately one-third of all the colleges, universities, and post-secondary proprietary schools in the United States provide some form of distance learning. It is estimated that a little more than 58 percent of all post-secondary institutions will be offering distance learning within the near future (U.S. Department of Education, 1997). There are several important

FIGURE 1.4 A Sampling of Distance Learning Programs Worldwide

Country	School	Yearly Enrollment	Founded
Europe			
Finland	Finnish Association for Distance Education	50,000 (1994)	1970
France	Centre National d'Enseignement a Distance	350,000 (1995)	1939
Germany	Fern Universitaet	55,000 (1996)	1974
Norway	Norwegian Association for Distance Education	40,000 (1996)	1968
Russia	University of the Russia's Academy of Education	25,000 (1996)	1990
Spain	Universidad Nacional de Educacion a Distancia	140,000 (1995)	1972
Sweden	Swedish Association for Distance Education	15,000 (1996)	1984
Turkey	Anadolu University	600,000 (1995)	1982
United Kingdom	Edinburgh's Telford College	5,000 (1996)	1980
	Open University	150,000 (1996)	1969
	University of London External Program	25,000 (1997)	1856
Africa			
Botswana	Department of Non-Formal Education	5,500 (1996)	1973
South Africa	UNISA	130,000 (1995)	1949
Tanzania	Open University of Tanzania	2,000 (1996)	1982
Tunisia	Institut Superieur de l'Education et de la Formation Continue	400 (1996)	1983
Zambia	National Correspondence College	5,000 (1996)	1984
Asia			
China	Radio and Television University Network	852,000 (1995)	1979
India	Indira Gandhi Open Univ.	390,000 (1997)	1985
Indonesia	Universitas Terbuka	400,000 (1997)	1984
Korea	National Open University	220,000 (1996)	1972
Pakistan	Allama Iqbal Open University	225,000 (1996)	1987
Philippines	Open University of the Phillipines	1,200 (1997)	1995
Australia			
Australia	Open Training and Education Network	26,000 (1997)	1990
Australia	University of New England	11,500 (1997)	1955
New Zealand	Open Polytechnic of New Zealand	40,000 (1995)	1969
New Zealand	The New Zealand Correspondence School	2,100 (1996)	1922
Papua New Guinea	Institute of Distance and Continuing Education	11,000 (1995)	1976

FIGURE 1.4 *(continued)*

Country	School	Yearly Enrollment	Founded
South America			
Argentina	Circulo de Suboficiales del Ejercito	700 (1997)	1978
Bolivia	Universidad NUR	600 (1997)	1994
Brazil	Universidade Federal do Rio Grande do Sul	15,000 (1997)	1988
Equador	Instituto Radiofonico Fe y Alegria	15,000 (1997)	1974
Venezuela	Instituto Radiofonico Fe y Alegria	5,800 (1997)	1976
North America			
Canada	Alberta Distance Learning Centre	40,000 (1997)	1923
Canada	Athabasca University	19,000 (1997)	1970
Canada	University of Waterloo	5,000 (1996)	1968
Mexico	The Virtual University, Monterrey	26,000 (1997)	1989
Mexico	Universidad Nacional Autonoma de Mexico	4,200 (1995)	1972
United States	University of Alaska, Fairbanks	2,650 (1997)	1970
	University of California Extension Center	3,000 (1997)	1990
	University of Florida	5,000 (1997)	1903
	Pennsylvania State, University Dept. of Dist. Educ.	20,000 (1997)	1892
	University of Wisconsin Extension	12,000 (1997)	1891

differences in the educational organizations, resources, and attributes in the United States as compared to the rest of the world. An examination of these differences can serve to broaden our understanding of the development and current state of distance learning.

First, most countries other than the United States have a strong central department or ministry of education that establishes policies and initiates major educational projects nationwide. In these countries, the vast majority of the funding for all education, including higher education, comes from the central governments. In the United States, the governance of education has been decentralized to the fifty states, and further to the 15,000 plus local school districts and numerous private schools. Funding varies from state to state and from school district to school district, with the federal government generally providing only about 6 to 7 percent of a school's budget. Local school districts typically provide most of the funding, as much as 60 to 70 percent. Distance learning projects historically required substantial funds and resources that many states, school districts, or private institutions either did not possess or that they deemed necessary for other budgetary priorities. Those states or school districts that did decide to fund distance learning projects did so on a regional or local scale.

Second, education has evolved in the United States from a decentralized system wherein villages, towns, and cities built and developed schools for local populations. Universal education at the primary and secondary school level is well established and approximately 65 percent of the population goes on to some form of post-secondary education. The neighborhood school that is within walking distance or a short bus ride is commonplace in most sections of the country. For higher education, every state has established a network of state universities and community colleges to complement a large number of private institutions. A traditional education is more accessible in the United States than in many parts of the world where neither the central government nor the local communities have had the resources to build schools, particularly in the more rural regions. It is not surprising that in the United States, states that have vast expanses of open space or geographical boundaries such as Alaska have been leaders in establishing distance learning facilities.

Third, population density has been a critical factor in the development of distance learning facilities, especially in countries such as China, India, and Pakistan. These countries simply have not been able to afford to build schools fast enough for their growing populations. Distance learning is seen as the only economical alternative for students seeking an education. The United States and most of the developed countries do not have the population densities that have forced them into a similar reliance on distance learning. However, as more and more students and especially adults in the developed countries seek some form of higher education, demand on existing facilities will grow and continue to expand. Distance learning can provide an economical alternative for meeting some of this demand.

Fourth, the prevailing attitude toward distance learning in the United States has been to view it as an alternative or substitute for traditional learning. Students will normally seek out an academic program, enroll, and attend classes in person rather than enroll in a similar program offered in a distance learning mode. In many cases, faculty and students are suspicious of the legitimacy or parity of a distance learning program as opposed to a traditional program (Blumenstyk, 1997). However, this is beginning to change as American colleges and universities are extending their programs both locally and globally. American universities have traditionally recruited students worldwide with the expectation that students would come physically to their campuses. This restricted foreign enrollments to students of means or to those who were extremely capable and could find grants or other sponsorship. However, as the Earth grows smaller with greater economic interdependence, global corporations, and world markets, this is changing. More and more colleges, universities, and private corporations are interested in and considering providing education to students anyplace in the world. This is happening even though the United States lacks a tradition such as that of the University of London (1856) or the Centre National d'Enseignement a Distance (1939) of over the years providing distance learning to hundreds of thousands of students living in more than a hundred different countries.

Lastly, distance learning throughout the world is dependent on the availability of communications technology. Historically, distance learning has changed and advanced as societies have moved to mail services, to radio, to television, and now to computers. Developing countries in Africa, Asia, or South America that do not have modern communications infrastructures have had difficulty in providing distance learning opportunities. On the other hand, countries in Asia, Europe, and North America that do have communications infrastructures in place can more easily support distance learning programs. In 1997, Finland, with sixty-two Internet-connected computers per thousand residents was rated "the most wired country" in the world, at twice the rate of the United States, and was followed by Iceland, with forty-two per thousand residents (Ibrahim, 1997). These and other countries with extensive access to digital communications in homes and in workplaces are especially well-poised to establish and expand distance learning programs in the future.

PLANNING AND THE SYSTEMS APPROACH

Distance learning is emerging as an important planning issue for educational organizations at all levels. Many schools and colleges are considering implementing distance learning programs for the first time. Important decisions will have to be made regarding the goals and objectives of academic programs, equipment, software, facilities, staff development, and finances. For those schools that have already established distance learning programs, decisions regarding newer digital technologies will likewise have to be made and new alternatives considered and evaluated. Planning processes need to be undertaken in order for new programs to be established or for existing programs to be modified or expanded. Planning for distance learning is not an activity to be taken lightly and will test the abilities of faculty and administrators alike.

Planning for any technology-based activity requires concentrating on a total application. By choosing an application and asking what is needed to make it successful, educators will be led to consider subsidiary questions regarding obvious components such as student demand, hardware, and facilities as well as other less obvious components such as staff development and curricular integration. In order to plan for distance learning or any other major activity, a fundamental framework should be established for describing and analyzing the activity within its organizational contexts. Systems theory is a most appropriate framework for studying and planning distance learning in an educational organization. The basic systems concepts of "input, process, output" and their interrelationship are generally accepted as fundamental to all aspects of program development. In addition, the systems approach is particularly appropriate for studying and understanding a technology-intensive activity. The basic configuration of any computer hardware system, for example, consists of one input device, a central processor, and one output device. All other hardware configurations are variations of this, whether with multiple input, processor, or output devices or with multiple hardware systems and subsystems working together in some type of planned unison.

The systems approach is also adopted here, because it is appropriate for studying educational organizations and processes including planning and new program development. Many social scientists and sociologists would describe and analyze schools as social systems. Basic concepts of input, process, and output are regularly applied to communities, students, teaching, curriculum, and outcomes in describing school "systems." Utilizing systems theory to present the technical aspects of distance learning technology as well as the planning and educational aspects of new academic programs provides a consistent, integrated approach for presenting the material in this book. It would be difficult, and perhaps impossible, to identify another framework that would work as well.

PURPOSE

The purpose of this book relates to the purpose of schools and education in general. Most of the views on the purpose of schools and education relate to the intellectual and emotional development of children. Fundamental to these views is a sense that children, as a result of an education, will come away with a desire to learn more about themselves, others, and the world around them. Once a desire to learn has been instilled in them, children will learn a great deal on their own. Seymour Sarason describes this purpose:

> If when a child is motivated to learn more about self and the world, then I would say that schooling has achieved its overarching purpose. . . . [T]he student knows that the more you know, the more you need to know. . . . To want to continue to explore, to find answers to personally meaningful questions, issues, and possibilities is the most important purpose of schooling. (1995, p.135)

Sarason's description is apt for all forms of education and learning. However, when discussing distance learning, the purpose of schools and education needs to be expanded for the adult learner. Malcolm Knowles, generally regarded as the founder of adult learning, posited that adults learn differently than children and that programs directed to them have a different purpose. Adult learners, whether they seek an education they were not able to pursue earlier in their lives, wish to enhance their professional skills, or want to satisfy their curiosity about some subject, are different from children. Programs for adults should be designed for students who have already made decisions regarding careers and occupations, who are spouses and parents, and who must be taught in their own social context. Distance learning programs must take into account their special situations and combine the vision of Sarason with the practical needs of adults.

The purpose of this book is to provide the theoretical framework and present the practical considerations for planning and implementing distance learning programs. Basic concepts of distance learning, planning, and program development, and the basic technologies being used are presented. Emphasis is placed, throughout this book, on the total application of distance learning and program development and not on any one component. Most importantly, this book is meant to provide a foundation from which educators throughout the world will look ahead to the powerful potential of distance learning as an increasingly appropriate approach for meeting the ever-expanding needs of students.

SUMMARY

This chapter introduces the topic of distance learning. While distance learning has an extensive history involving mail, radio, and television, newer technologies such as digital communications and networking have begun to emerge that make it much easier for educators to provide some form of distance learning for their students. However, distance learning means different things to different people and can take on many forms. A comprehensive definition of distance learning developed by Desmond Keegan is presented to begin the process of providing a structure to this topic. Systems theory is established as the basic framework for studying and planning for distance learning. A history and a brief look at the current state of distance learning worldwide are also presented. In addition, comparisons between the United States and other countries are made to expand our understanding of the development of distance learning in different settings and cultures. The chapter concludes with a statement of the purpose of this book, which also includes a statement of the purpose of schools and education.

CASE STUDY

National University Year: 2000

Setting

National University is the primary state-funded public university in the country. It operates a main university center in the country's largest city and five additional colleges in cities in the five largest provinces of the country. Approximately twelve percent of the population attends National University, a percentage that has been growing slowly for the past ten years. Most of the students who attend National University come from urban areas where the primary and secondary education is generally considered better than in the non-urban areas. Eighty percent of the funding for the University comes from the state, which, because of slow economic growth, has not substantially increased the University's budget during the past five years. The faculty have not had a salary increase in two years. Tuition at the university has increased modestly over the past five years; however, poorer students can receive some assistance from the state in the form of grants and loans. The organization structure of National University follows.

National University
|
State Governing Board
|
Chancellor
|

Vice Chancellor for Academic Affairs	Vice Chancellor for Finance and Administration	Vice Chancellor for Student Affairs	Vice Chancellor for Government Relations	Vice Chancellor for Legal Affairs
|	|			
Director of Media Services	Director of Computer Services			

The Issue

In January 2000, the Minister of Education contacted the Chancellor of National University and indicated that the State Governing Board was very much interested in broadening the higher education opportunities for its citizens and would like a feasibility study and proposal for establishing a major distance learning program. The Minister indicated that he thought start-up costs for technological improvements could be provided by the State. At National University, several discussions have been held in the past twenty years or so about distance learning. Two experimental programs were attempted but subsequently discontinued in the late 1970s and early 1980s for lack of enrollment as well as difficulties in establishing the technology infrastructure needed within the university to deliver distance learning instruction. The minister indicated that he would like the proposal by August 2000 in order to present it to the State Governing Board in time for the next budget cycle, which begins in January 2001.

In response to the minister's request, the chancellor appointed a Distance Learning Committee that consisted of the following:

Vice-Chancellor for Academic Affairs and Instruction (Chair)
Vice Chancellor for Finance and Administration
Vice Chancellor for Government Relations
Director of Computer and Information Services
Director of Media Services
Six faculty members
Two executives of successful national businesses

In addition, a consultant familiar with international computer and communications technologies was hired to help assess the technological readiness of the university to deliver distance learning and to estimate costs. The consultant completed an initial report on technological readiness. The data in the report included the following:

> televisions per household
> computers per household
> radios per household
> telephones per household

The above data were cross-tabulated by province.

Among the most important findings were that television access continued to grow, with almost 75 percent of the population having access, and computer access likewise was growing, with approximately 15 percent of the population having access to digital technology and communications. In both of the above statistics, access was somewhat higher in the urban areas than in the non-urban areas, particularly for computer technology.

The faculty indicated that they were supportive of distance learning but had several reservations including the following:

> the need for faculty training and development
> the importance of incorporating interactivity into the instructional delivery
> special compensation for faculty involved with developing and conducting
>   distance learning courses

The committee seemed divided and conflicted as to whether it should recommend a distance learning program based primarily on digital technology (i.e., computer and data communications) or analog technology (i.e., television, radio). The vast majority of the population, especially in the non-urban areas, already had access to television and radio. On the other hand, much of the current thinking favors digital technology as the wave of the future.

Assume you are a member of the committee. What recommendation would you make? What additional information do you think you would need? Would your recommendation change depending on your position in the university?

REFERENCES

Auletta, K. (1997). *The highwaymen: Warriors of the information superhighway.* New York: Random House.

Blumenstyk, G. (1997, June 20). Some elite private universities get serious about distance learning. *The Chronicle of Higher Education,* 3–5.

Buckland, M., & Dye, C. (1991). The development of electronic distance education delivery systems in the United States: Recurring and emerging themes in the history and philosophy of education. Unpublished manuscript (ERIC Document No. ED 345 713).

Forgione, P. (1997). A note from the Commissioner of Education Statistics, U.S.

Department of Education. *Teachers College Record, 99*(1), 10–11.

Garrison, D., & Shale, D., (1987). Mapping the boundaries of distance education: Problems in defining the field. *The American Journal of Distance Education, 1*(1), 4–13.

Holmberg, B. (1986). *The growth and structure of distance education.* London: Croom Helm.

Ibrahim, Y. (1997, January 20). As most wired nation, Finland has jump on 21st century. *The New York Times,* pp. D1, D3.

Keegan, D. (1996). *Foundations of distance education* (3rd ed.). London: Routledge.

Rudenstine, N. (1997, February 21). The Internet and education: A close fit. *The Chronicle of Higher Education,* 37–38.

Sarason, S. (1995). *Parental involvement and the political principle: Why the existing governance structure of schools should be abolished.* San Francisco: Jossey-Bass.

Stillman, L. (1998). Egypt revival. *Natural History, 106*(11), 79.

Tierney, J. (1997, September 28). Our oldest computer upgraded. *The New York Times Magazine,* 46–49.

Tifflin, J., & Rajasingham, L. (1995). *In search of the virtual class: Education in an information society.* London: Routledge.

U.S. Department of Education, National Center for Education Statistics (1997). *Distance education in higher education institutions* (NCES 97-062). Washington, D.C.

Willis, B. (1993). *Distance education: A practical guide.* Englewood Cliffs, NJ: Educational Technology Publications.

CHAPTER TWO

Planning for Distance Learning

In June 1997, the journal *Technological Horizons in Education* celebrated its twenty-fifth anniversary with a special edition that looked back at educational technology milestones from the past twenty-five years. Articles by major contributors to the field of educational technology celebrated achievements and lamented obstacles. All agreed that technology in education had grown since the 1970s from an object of study to an indispensable tool. However, they also agreed that the potential had yet to be realized, and that education was not as advanced as other fields in its use of technology, as the following examples show:

Andrew Molnar–Director for Applications of Advanced Technologies, National Science Foundation
The world of education has changed from an orderly world of disciplines . . . to an infosphere in which communication technologies are increasingly important. While education is changing, it is not changing fast enough (Molnar, 1997, p. 68).

Seymour Papert–Developer of Logo and Professor, The Media Laboratory, Massachusetts Institute of Technology
But with this greater complexity of activities comes greater problems of access to knowledge: the problems and difficulties that come up are increasingly beyond what a teacher can be expected to handle (Papert, 1997, p. 80).

Alfred Bork–Professor Emeritus, Information and Computer Science, University of California, Irvine
Replacing our current educational systems with ones that depend on technology is not a simple and inexpensive process (Bork, 1997, p. 76).

Bernard Luskin, CEO of Luskin International and past president of Polygram, introduced his article with a Chinese proverb that says "the best time to plant a tree was twenty-five years ago and the second best time is now" (Luskin, 1997, p. 81). His point was that if education is truly to harness information technology, a commitment should already have been made but must now be made by educators to develop processes that control its power and use it to "light up our world." As an example, Luskin referred to advances in distance learning. Telecourses that were virtually nonexistent in the early 1970s are now being offered by more than a thousand colleges and universities. Every indication is that distance learning will continue to grow apace, and could very well boom in the next twenty-five years. However, "the rhetoric in this regard is rather high" (Luskin, 1997, p. 82) and much work and planning will have to be done if this is to occur. The major purpose of this chapter is to examine planning as a process that will have to be undertaken in order for educators to actualize the rhetoric.

DISTANCE PLANNING WILL NOT WORK

Planning in organizations has been studied extensively for decades, and no need exists here for a review of the literature base that has been established. Likewise, an extensive body of work including books, articles, and guides exists on the subject of educational planning. For readers wishing to review the educational planning literature, Carlson and Awkerman (1991) provide one of the most comprehensive treatments. However, in preparation for a discussion of planning for distance learning in particular, several basic concepts need to be restated.

First, planning occurs in all educational organizations. In some cases, planning is formal with committees setting goals and objectives and developing plans for achieving them. In other cases, planning is less formal and involves individuals thinking about and preparing their organizations for the future. The essence of educational planning is simply considering how an educational organization will function at a future time and preparing accordingly.

Second, planning activities vary considerably from one organization to another. Top-down, bottom-up, structured, unstructured, participatory, and strategic are some of the descriptors used to define the type of planning that exists in organizations. Clearly, no single type of planning is the most effective, and no single descriptor can be applied. Choosing the most effective type of planning must be left to the judgment of the administrators and educators who are responsible for the future of their organizations.

Third, for plans to be realized, individuals in an organization must be aware of them and must take appropriate actions for achieving them. For major initiatives and endeavors, planning cannot exist solely in an administrator's office but must be shared with the educational community. In short, distance planning will not work. In considering planning for distance learning, an inclusive and participatory approach is recommended. Whether starting a new program or expanding or modifying an existing program, ultimately faculty, support staff, and other administrators must be involved if plans are to be realized.

COMMON ELEMENTS OF EDUCATIONAL PLANNING

In a review of educational planning processes, Sheathelm (1991) identified the following four major elements of successful planning and called them the four Cs:

- Comprehensiveness
- Collaboration
- Commitment
- Continuity

They are very much worth exploring in developing a framework for planning for distance learning.

Comprehensiveness

First, planning needs to be comprehensive. A total view of a college or school and what it is supposed to accomplish for students and the community is an essential element. An important distinction here is between having a total view and necessarily having solutions for everything. Part of planning is examining and understanding both the educational organization and the environment as much as possible with the caveat that they cannot be understood entirely. Likewise, providing solutions for that which is not fully understood becomes imperfect, if not impossible. Nevertheless, administrators need to be aware of the needs of individuals (i.e., students, teachers, other administrators) that may be specific and at times unique. These needs can frequently be converted into goals and objectives on which a plan is formulated. On the other hand, teachers and staff frequently need to have a better understanding of the total enterprise's overall goals and objectives as well as overall resource availability. The essence of a comprehensive plan links individual needs and objectives into overall institutional goals.

Collaboration

A second element of planning is collaboration. Although administrators generally have a good deal of expertise in and knowledge of education, they can never fully know or understand all its aspects. They need to rely on others to provide expertise and to help improve their understanding. Technical staffs responsible for communications, computing, or media generally spend a good deal of their time trying to keep abreast of the latest technological developments. Business managers, librarians, counselors, admissions officers, and other staff have specific expertise that frequently is more complete and more current than that of a general administrator such as a college president, school superintendent, or principal. Faculty and content specialists know their subjects and have developed a myriad of approaches and strategies for teaching and instructing students. This vast pool of knowledge, expertise, and experience needs to be tapped and integrated into the planning process. In addition to the sharing of knowledge, collaboration also allows for greater appreciation of several perspectives of a goal, objective, or need. Deborah Meier (1995), a school principal and nationally recognized school reformer, believes that educators need to develop "the capacity to see the world as others might."

Commitment

Through collaboration, securing the commitment of those who are vital in carrying out a plan becomes easier. Commitment is critical, because the best-laid plan will not be realized if the people who are expected to implement it are not committed to the task. Commitment comes from being involved with formulating overall goals and objectives as well as with developing specific courses of action. Collaboration also allows others to understand a plan, a goal, or a course of action and the purpose behind it. Greater understanding generally fosters higher levels of commitment.

The commitment of administrative leaders to planning is also critical. Commitment from faculty and other administrators will only come if there is a sense on their part that the administrative leadership is committed to a plan or planning process. Administrators must exercise their leadership skills in securing commitment by offering themselves as examples in sharing knowledge, formulating goals, developing objectives, and implementing courses of action.

Continuity

Finally, every planning process is continuous and never-ending. Societies, schools, and people are constantly changing, and plans must change with them. An organization is like a living organism that responds and adjusts to environmental stimuli. As the values of a society change, so must the way schools and colleges prepare students to live and function in that society. This is true whether the students are in primary school learning reading, writing, and arithmetic or are adults attending colleges to improve their professional skills or expand their knowledge. As tools and technologies develop and evolve, so should our methods of training students to use these tools and technologies.

In most circumstances, planning involves developing a written plan as a result of a series of meetings and committee work. However, planning does not begin with these activities and end with the production of the written plan. On the contrary, the written plan is a guideline for everyday activities. Administrators, faculty, and staff follow this guideline and accumulate information on how well the objectives of the plan are being implemented. This new information (including adjustments to the plan) then becomes input for further planning activity.

Jennings and Dirksen (1999) describe a "diffusion of technology" planning process used at the University of Northern Colorado to implement Web-based learning in the entire School of Education. Among their observations was the importance that collaboration, cooperation, and commitment on the part of administrators and faculty played in the success of the process. However, their concluding remark and recommendation was that planning for any technological change must be viewed as a continuous process and "not as one single event" (Jennings & Dirksen, 1999, p. 116).

THE SOCIAL PROCESS MODEL

In developing a model for any organizational process, basic assumptions about the nature of the organization should first be established. A basic assumption recommended here is that educational institutions be viewed as social organizations and that the processes established and undertaken be viewed as social processes. This view is not new and has been posited by organization theorists in education for years. Getzels and Guba (1957) developed a social process model in the 1950s that has formed the basis for describing and analyzing various educational processes. In the social process model, schools function as social systems that in turn operate in larger social systems or societies. The concept of social systems or subsystems operating and interacting with larger systems is a well-recognized and accepted phenomenon in organization theory. Subsystems with inputs, processes, and outputs interact with other systems that have their own inputs, processes, and outputs. The components of one system can interact with and influence the components of another system.

FIGURE 2.1 General Social Process Model

SOURCE: Adapted from the social process model cited in Getzels and Guba (1957).

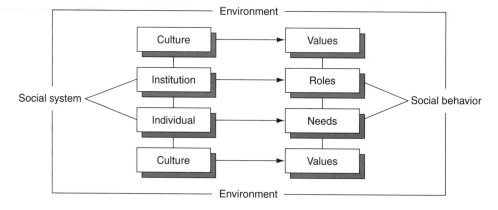

Another fundamental characteristic of the social process model is that educational organizations fundamentally involve people interacting with other people. Teachers, students, and administrators interact and function socially when communicating their values, needs, goals, objectives, etc. The people within the educational organization in turn have social interactions with people in the larger society and so a link is established between the larger social system and the educational system. The assumption here is that the educational organization and the larger society exist to support each other. The society needs the educational organizations to provide an educated citizenry to continue to advance the society, while the schools need the society for support and guidance in terms of societal and cultural needs.

Figure 2.1 provides a simplified version of the social process model developed by Getzels and Guba. In this model, an educational organization functions as a subsystem (institution) that interacts with the larger environmental social system. The needs of individuals as well as the expectations (roles) of the institution operating within and responding to the values of the culture of the larger environment (society) are the essential elements. This model provides the basis for studying various educational processes such as teaching, curriculum development, and planning.

A PLANNING MODEL FOR DISTANCE LEARNING

Figure 2.2 provides a planning model for distance learning. This model incorporates the concepts of the social process model and is derived from a planning model for technology developed by Picciano (1994, 1998). The structure of the model assumes that an educational organization (school/college) operates within

FIGURE 2.2 Model for Planning for Distance Learning

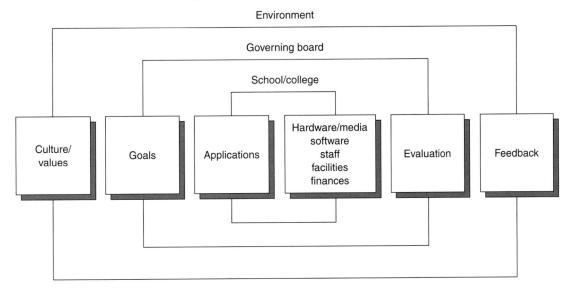

a governing board (board of education, board of trustees, ministry of education) that in turn operates within an environment or society. The governing board generally has the formal responsibility for linking the society with the educational organization and vice versa. The environment provides a culture and values from which goals and objectives are formulated. These goals and objectives, including the need for distance learning, result in applications, the fundamental elements of which include hardware, software, staff, facilities, and finances. Once implemented, these applications are evaluated and reviewed, and feedback is provided, which restarts the entire planning cycle.

The culture and values of societies around the world are different and reflect the history, traditions, religious beliefs, language, etc. of regions and countries. In most countries, education is valued and movements exist throughout the world to provide greater educational opportunities to people. Ever since Gutenberg developed the printing press, societies have continually tried to provide greater access to education for their citizens. This is true whether the educational level involves basic literacy skills, cutting-edge technology skills, or higher education. Distance learning is generally seen as a mechanism through which greater educational opportunity can be provided.

The goals, objectives, and applications that involve distance learning likewise vary considerably. Frequently cited goals involve expanding student learning opportunities and enrollments, providing alternative learning experiences, and maximizing resources. Distance learning is dependent on technology for delivering instruction; hence, the need to *apply* distance learning technology to meet goals and objectives. Each distance learning application involves discussion and decisions about hardware; software, including the development of curricula materials; staffing and staff development; facilities needs; and financing.

As an application is designed and implemented, evaluation is necessary to determine if it meets the intended goals and objectives. If it does, the planning was successful. If it does not, redesign and modifications to the original plan may be necessary. An important aspect of evaluation is that it provides feedback about the entire planning process and serves to establish a basis for another planning cycle. Evaluation is critical to effective planning and requires a positive attitude on the part of all participants.

APPLYING THE PLANNING MODEL

The planning model described above can be applied or can operate in different ways and will meet different needs depending on the nature of the educational organization. Each part of the model has its own considerations, issues, and questions, which can serve as the basis for a better understanding of the intricacies of planning for distance learning.

Goals and Objectives

Goals and objectives are developed in response to the environment, society, or community for which the school organization exists. Goals and objectives for distance learning generally are student-oriented and designed to maximize an organization's resources. Fundamental to establishing these goals and objectives will be the question: Why distance learning? Frequently, the answer involves reaching out to new student populations or providing a convenience for existing student populations. Table 2.1 provides data on the goals of post-secondary institutions in the United States that offer distance learning courses.

In developing goals and objectives for distance learning, knowledge of the environment is necessary. *Environmental scanning* is a term used in planning that essentially means engaging in activities to provide information about the community, society, or the external *environment*. Distance learning goals and objectives that involve increasing educational opportunities for students imply that such a student need exists in the environment. In starting new programs, distance learning or otherwise, it is customary to do market research to determine if the implied need exists. In distance learning, however, students may exist in a local community or throughout the world. A community college whose primary mission is to serve a county or local community generally can determine the need for a new program through mailings to a sample of residents or contacts with high schools or major employers. A large university, on the other hand, that is establishing or expanding a distance learning program for a world-wide student population may have to engage in more extensive market research activities. Representatives/

TABLE 2.1 Percent of higher education institutions currently offering distance education courses indicating that various goals are very important to their distance learning programs, by institutional type.

Goal	Institutional Type			
	All Institutions	Public 2-Year	Public 4-Year	Private 4-Year
Increasing student access by making courses available at convenient locations	82	83	83	78
Increasing institution access to new audiences	64	68	61	54
Increasing student access by reducing time constraints	63	70	58	55
Increasing institution enrollments	54	59	48	53
Making educational opportunities more affordable for students	49	56	44	39
Improving the quality of the course offerings	46	46	47	45
Meeting the needs of local employers	38	43	37	27
Reducing your institution's per-student costs	20	26	17	9

Data for private 2-year institutions not reported as a separate type of institution because too few of them offered distance learning courses in the sample. Data for private 2-year institutions are included in total for all institutions.

SOURCE: U.S. Dept. of Education, National Center for Education Statistics, Post-secondary Education Quick Information System, Survey on Distance Education Courses Offered by Higher Education Institutions, 1995. Sample based on mailing to 1,274 post-secondary institutions in the United States, the District of Columbia, and Puerto Rico with 1,203 returns (94% response rate).

recruiters may need to be sent to cooperating schools and organizations in other countries. Logistical issues such as language and time zones may have to be considered. Regardless of the goal or objective, some market research is required. The amount depends on the extent (new courses, new program, a virtual college) of the goal or objective and the scope (community, nation, or world) of the student population.

Environmental scanning is also important in determining the present and future availability of technology. In developing distance learning goals and objectives, decisions have to be made regarding delivery systems and technology.

Differences exist among students in terms of access to conventional mail, broadcast television, video-cassette recorders (VCRs), and networked computers. The ability to meet goals and objectives will depend on the present and future availability of these or other technologies necessary to deliver or receive instruction.

Developing goals and objectives for distance learning also involves discussions of resources. For some schools, distance learning is seen as a way of expanding resources by increasing enrollments and, consequently, revenue in the form of tuition and fees. The New School for Social Research in New York City established its Distance Instruction for Adult Learners (DIAL) program in 1993 to bolster "flagging enrollments" (Deloughry, 1996). Within two years, the DIAL program had attracted more than 500 students, many of whom lived beyond the school's traditional fifty-mile radius, some as far away as China and Japan. In other situations, distance learning is seen as a way of optimizing or maximizing resources. In many countries, the dramatically increasing demand for education is placing a strain on existing traditional schools and colleges. Distance learning is being considered as a means for broadening educational opportunities without incurring the expense of building new schools or campuses. In Scandinavia, twelve institutions in Denmark and Sweden have formed the Oresund University Network, the purpose of which is to study how the Internet and videoconferencing systems can be used to share classes, collaborate on research, and administer joint degree programs (Bollag, 1996). In the United States, the governors of Colorado, Utah, and several other states agreed to establish a virtual Western Governors University, the purpose of which would be to deliver distance learning to the entire region without duplicating programs and using the resources of existing colleges and universities.

Applications

Once goals and objectives have been established, extensive consideration and discussion of the application(s) of distance learning commences. As defined above, applications are simply the *applying* of distance learning techniques and technologies to meet goals and objectives. Which application(s) will depend significantly on the extent of the proposed distance learning program. Major considerations and issues will evolve concerning teaching, pedagogy, and student populations depending on whether the distance learning program involves offering several courses or entire degree or certificate programs, or establishing entire "virtual" schools and colleges.

In terms of teaching, particularly when extending existing courses or programs, the conversion of these courses into distance learning mode needs to be planned. The idea that a professor who has been teaching a traditional course successfully can simply make a couple of changes for distance learning is naive. The presentation and delivery of material, the use of media, and student assignments may all have to be reconsidered and redeveloped. Certain subject areas or disciplines may lend themselves more readily to distance learning than others. Courses that emphasize critical analysis in the social sciences or humanities for instance, may be more easily converted than courses in the physical sciences that generally involve hands-on laboratory experiences. Teachers who use assignments and tests as a means for students to learn as well as for assessment, may have to make adjustments in distance learning applications. The weekly quiz may be difficult to administer since it is difficult to determine who at a distant location is actually taking a quiz. Oral presentations can be very difficult, if not impossible, in some distance learning applications. Collaborative assignments likewise can be difficult depending on the distance learning technology being used.

Pedagogical approaches in distance learning applications can be far more complex than in traditional instruction. The simple act of a student asking a question, taken for granted in a traditional class, can have significant implications in a distance learning application. For example, if the application uses conventional mail, does the student mail questions to instructors, telephone them, or perhaps use e-mail? And once asked, how, if at all, does this same question reach the eyes or ears of other students? Valued pedagogical techniques, used routinely in traditional courses, can and do take on an added dimension in distance learning mode. Students learning from other student's questions and the spontaneity and energy of a "live" class need to be considered and, if possible, duplicated in a distance learning application.

The nature of the student population must also be considered when designing a distance learning application. Debate and discussion continue regarding the appropriateness of distance learning for all students. Students who are expected to take on responsibility for much of their own learning should have the maturity and self-discipline necessary to allocate their time and energies as needed. Some degree of "match" between the target student population and the nature of the distance learning application must also exist. For example, students who are expected to use the Internet and e-mail extensively in text-mode to participate in a class perhaps should have fairly well-developed reading and writing skills. On another front, distance learning applications designed to make extensive use of technology (television, VCRs, computer networks) require that planners consider student access to this technology. This is an especially important consideration in using computer networks. While some students may have access in their homes, others may not. Are alternate access options available to the target population at work, at public libraries, in dormitories, etc? The purpose here is not to answer these questions but to raise them as important considerations when designing distance learning applications. Good planning processes will generate these questions and, it is hoped, develop answers appropriate to the situations.

Components of an Application

The operational components of a distance learning application include hardware, software, staffing, facilities, and finances. These elements will be discussed in greater detail in later chapters of this book, however, a brief overview here will serve to inform our discussion of planning.

One major planning decision in designing and implementing a distance learning application is hardware selection. The terms *hardware* and *hardware technology* in computer systems are defined as the physical equipment used to transmit, store, and receive information. As used here for distance learning applications, the definition of hardware has been expanded to include any physical element used to transmit, store, and receive information including printed material such as books, newspapers, and magazines. This use of the term *hardware* is important because, when the term is used for computer systems, printed materials traditionally would not have been included. However, print materials are here combined with hardware because of the proliferation of computer-generated and computer-stored text. A printed book can be a physical compilation of pages glued together or a CD-ROM on which the text is stored in an electronic form. The same is true of newspapers or magazines. The *New York Times* as a series of folded pages can be purchased at a sidewalk vendor and read physically on a train or at one's desk. The same *New York Times* can be read at an Internet site as a collection of hyperlinked digital files stored on a magnetic disk. The expanded use of the term *hardware* as used in this planning model will be discussed further in Chapter 3.

We know that distance learning worldwide began with and continues to make extensive use of conventional mail systems for distributing and receiving course materials. However, other hardware technologies using audio, video, and especially computer networks are being used increasingly. In designing a distance learning application, the choice of an appropriate hardware technology is a major decision. Developing or expanding audio and videoconferencing, broadcast television, satellite communications, or computer networks tests the planning abilities of most organizations. These technologies are inherently complex and dynamic. They also can be costly. The basic trend is toward using more computer or digital technology, either alone or in conjunction with other technologies.

Software, including the development of curricula materials, is another important component of a distance learning application. Depending on the hardware selected, video presentations may have to be developed, computer communications software acquired, and course materials written or rewritten for dissemination via conventional mail or e-mail. As mentioned above, even in applications where existing courses are being converted for delivery in a distance learning mode, new curriculum materials will have to developed. This is generally only a matter of time and training for text-based materials, but can be far more complex when considering video or multimedia presentations.

Staffing considerations and issues are numerous, particularly in institutions with very little experience in delivering distance learning applications. Faculty and staff development, incentives, workload, and intellectual property rights are but a few of the issues that can evolve with distance learning. While planning should involve a broad cross-section of an educational organization, in the final analysis the success of a course or program, whether taught in distance learning mode or otherwise, most frequently depends on the abilities and commitment of the instructional staff.

Facilities is an area that receives little attention in most books and articles regarding distance learning. However, depending again on the technology being used, the facilities required can be very complex and costly. Electronic classrooms, video production studios, media libraries, and integrated computer and communications networks must not only be well-designed but flexible in order to grow and advance as the technology evolves. Support staff and management of these facilities likewise must be developed especially for large-scale distance learning applications involving entire programs, schools, or colleges.

Finances constitutes the last operational component of a distance learning application. Among the common goals of a distance learning application is to increase revenue and to maximize resources. But getting started in distance learning may require substantial initial investments. The U.S. Department of Education (1997) in a national survey of post-secondary institutions reported that the major obstacle to the development of distance learning programs was start-up costs. Planning should not only concentrate on the benefits, such as increased enrollments and revenue, but also on the costs. Cost/benefit and cost/effectiveness analyses are fundamental to all effective planning and should be incorporated into any distance learning application. Cost effective approaches such as developing economies of scale, collaborations, and consortia arrangements can produce significant savings in delivering distance learning.

EVALUATION—CRITICAL FOR EFFECTIVE PLANNING

Evaluation is critical to every planning process. Assumptions about the future are *evaluated.* Alternative courses of action are *evaluated* and accepted or discarded. Student performance and progress is *evaluated* by teachers. Educators should accept evaluation as a basic aspect of every planning activity and develop a positive attitude in the organizational culture toward evaluating programs, processes, and plans. Evaluation is also fundamental to planning because it provides an important link between planning cycles. The planning model (Figure 2.2) illustrates how evaluation and feedback from one planning cycle provides input and new information for the next cycle.

Developing a Positive Attitude toward Evaluation

Developing a positive attitude toward evaluation is not difficult if the leaders in the organization convey a positive and supportive posture. If evaluation is used as a vehicle to refine and improve processes, including planning, a positive attitude and organizational culture can develop. On the other hand, if it is used in a punitive fashion or to highlight shortcomings, a wary and cautious attitude toward evaluation will likewise develop. Unfortunately, the latter happens too often and at all organizational levels. Evaluation in planning is not about evaluating people but about evaluating the implementation of the plan.

In developing a positive attitude toward evaluation, a good starting point is the recognition that many educational outcomes are, in fact, not easily evaluated. Unlike the private business sector where profit and loss can be reduced to calculations on a financial statement, educational outcomes are "messy." Universal agreement on measuring student achievement does not exist. While some educators accept standardized testing, others do not. Education is not simply how well one learns a subject but also includes maturation, emotional and attitudinal development, and appreciation for the beauty and benefits of cultures and societies, among other things. These outcomes are not always easy to quantify. They also are not always timely. Educational benefits may not always manifest themselves immediately during or even after a course. In some cases, and especially with younger students, benefits may not be realized until years later.

Another important element in developing a positive attitude toward evaluation is involvement. Those involved with developing and implementing a plan should also come to an agreement on evaluation criteria. Implementation becomes much easier if a planning process is more inclusive. Those involved in planning cannot simply require others to evaluate or be evaluated. Administrators cannot simply require teachers and teaching to be evaluated. By the same token, teachers involved in planning should expect to participate in developing criteria for evaluation and not simply argue that evaluation is too difficult or imprecise. Through involvement and consensus, agreement on evaluation criteria can be achieved. The need for multiple criteria as opposed to a single criterion or measure should be noted at this juncture.

In addition to recognizing the importance of multiple criteria, evaluation should also recognize the importance of both formal and informal measures. Formal measures such as student achievement, grades, costs, and time on task should be considered, as well as less formal measures such as student or teacher attitudes. In distance learning, informal measures relating to student convenience or faculty morale may prove as important as achievement and grades.

Evaluation for Distance Learning

The evaluation of distance learning programs can take many shapes and forms but of course should relate to goals and objectives. If the initial goal was to increase educational opportunities, then a simple summary of enrollments would be a good starting point. Likewise, if the goal was to increase revenue, a summary of tuition and fees would be appropriate. However, evaluation is not always so simple and, as indicated earlier, should always involve multiple criteria. As an example, one college started a distance learning program in 1993 essentially to increase student enrollment and revenue. By 1997, total enrollment in distance learning courses was just over 900 students. On the surface, this simple measure might indicate that the program was a huge success. But a closer look at the students enrolled revealed that all but twelve of them were also enrolled in traditional courses. On further analysis, it was determined that the vast majority of the distance learning students were already enrolled or would have enrolled at the college, so while enrollments and revenue increased in distance learning, they were simply being diverted from the college's traditional program.

In evaluating a distance learning program, formative and summative measures should be used. Formative measures are those that provide information that will help refine, improve, or extend a program. Summative measures are a tallying or summing up of what occurred. Keep in mind that summative measures can also provide insight into program improvement. For this reason, good evaluation will include both.

Commonly used formative measures include student satisfaction surveys, observations of students participating in a distance learning activity such as a video-conference, or monitoring of student on-line activity in an asynchronous learning network. In addition, faculty satisfaction surveys and observations can provide excellent information for refining and improving a distance learning program. Summative evaluation measures include enrollment data, revenue data, student performance and achievement, time-on-task studies, attendance, program completion, and drop-out behavior.

In program evaluation, both quantitative as well as qualitative data should be collected. While quantitative data can provide anonymous, objective, and easily comparable information, qualitative data may be more conducive to program refinement and development. For example, a student satisfaction survey based on a Likert-type scale is useful in developing an overall indication of satisfaction and can be used to compare distance learning courses with other courses. However, open-ended questions asking students to describe experiences, to provide suggestions for improving a course, or to list things they liked or disliked can yield important information that may aid faculty and others in designing and improving course materials and presentations. Figure 2.3 provides a sample student survey instrument for evaluating a distance learning course using e-mail, computer networking, and Internet materials in an asynchronous mode. It contains a combination of Likert-type questions that are easily quantified and several open-ended questions. In conducting surveys and administering questionnaires, good practice recommends doing so more than once during the semester. This will allow for comparison between different periods (i.e., beginning and end, middle and end) of the semester and will neutralize the potential criticism that a survey represented opinions only at one particular point in time.

Accreditation Issues in Distance Learning

In planning and evaluating distance learning programs, accreditation issues will surface especially if entire degree programs are being considered. The accreditation organizations in the United States are adopting distance learning policies that essentially look for parity with traditional programs. Furthermore, during the accreditation process, they are also beginning to accredit distance learning programs separately from traditional programs. The following statement is taken from the

FIGURE 2.3 Sample Student Evaluation Survey

STUDENT EVALUATION OF AN ASYNCHRONOUS LEARNING COURSE

Name (Optional): _____ Date: _____

1. Number of Credits Completed in this Program: _____
2. Age: _____
3. Gender:
   Female ____ Male ____
4. I would rate my level of computer expertise as
   Novice ____ Intermediate ____ Expert ____
5. Where did you most frequently use a computer for this course?
   Home ____ Work ____ Other ____ If other specify: ____
6. How easy/difficult was it for you to use technology to participate in this course?
   Easy ____ Somewhat Easy ____ Somewhat Difficult ____ Difficult ____
7. How would you rate your overall experience in taking this course?
   Poor ____ Satisfactory ____ Good ____ Very Good ____ Excellent ____
8. Would you take another asynchronous learning course if offered?
   No ____ Maybe ____ Definitely ____

For questions 9A through 9H, in comparison to traditional classroom instruction, in this course

	Increased	Somewhat Increased	No Change	Somewhat Decreased	Decreased
9A. The amount of interaction with other students	___	___	___	___	___
9B. The quality of interaction with other students	___	___	___	___	___
9C. The amount of interaction with the instructor	___	___	___	___	___
9D. The quality of interaction with the instructor	___	___	___	___	___
9E. The quantity of your learning experience	___	___	___	___	___
9F. The quality of your learning experience	___	___	___	___	___
9G. The motivation to participate in class activities	___	___	___	___	___
9H. Your familiarity with computer technology	___	___	___	___	___

For questions 10A through 10D, did any of the following pose a problem in this course?

	Not a Problem	Minor Problem	Moderate Problem	Serious Problem	Most Serious Problem
10A. I was not familiar enough with the technology	___	___	___	___	___
10B. I could not get on-line enough to participate because of other time constraints	___	___	___	___	___
10C. I could not get on-line enough to participate because of technical difficulties	___	___	___	___	___
10D. The use of the computer took more time than it was worth	___	___	___	___	___

FIGURE 2.3 *(continued)*

11. Would you rate your experiences to date with this course as
    Successful _____ Not Successful _____
    If successful, what aspect of the course most contributed to its success?

    _____
    _____

    If not successful, what aspect of the course was most problematic?

    _____

12. Should _____ College offer more asynchronous learning courses?
    Yes _____ No _____
    If yes, because

    _____
    _____

    If no, because

    _____   _____
    _____

13. I have the following suggestions for improving this course:

    _____
    _____
    _____

"Guidelines for Distance Learning Programs" published by the Commission on Higher Education, Middle States Association of Colleges and Schools.

> "It is the intention of the Commission on Higher Education to ensure that distance learning programs are subject to the same scrutiny employed in more traditional settings or for conventional campus-based programs . . . One of the major issues facing both providers and recipients of electronically offered distance learning programs is achieving parity with traditional on-campus programs" (Commission on Higher Education, 1997, pp. 1, 6).

Many colleges and schools that experimented with distance learning are beginning to formalize programs and course offerings. And while the accrediting agencies did not specifically evaluate and accredit these programs separately in the past, the proliferation and formalization of distance learning programs has led these agencies likewise to formalize the accrediting process and criteria.

Figure 2.4 provides a list of principles of good practice published by the Western Cooperative for Educational Telecommunications as part of a three-year project funded by the U.S. Department of Education. They were developed by a group

FIGURE 2.4 Principles of Good Practice for Electronically Offered Academic Degree and Certificate Programs. Adopted by the Western Cooperative for Educational Telecommunications/WICHE on June 6, 1995.

The Principles of Good Practice

Curriculum and Instruction

- Each program of study results in learning outcomes appropriate to the rigor and breadth of the degree or certificate awarded.
- An electronically offered degree or certificate program is coherent and complete.
- The program provides for appropriate real-time or delayed interaction between faculty and students among students.
- Qualified faculty provide appropriate oversight of the program electronically offered.

Institutional Context and Commitment

Role and Mission

- The program is consistent with the institution's role and mission.
- Review and approval processes ensure the appropriateness of the technology being used to meet the program's objectives.

Faculty Support

- The program provides faculty support services specifically related to teaching via an electronic system.
- The program provides training for faculty who teach via the use of technology.

Resources for Learning

- The program ensures that appropriate learning resources are available to students.

Students and Student Services

- The program provides students with clear, complete, and timely information on the curriculum; course and degree requirements; nature of the faculty/student interaction; assumptions about technological competence and skills; technical equipment requirements; availability of academic support services and financial aid resources; and costs and payment policies.
- Enrolled students have reasonable and adequate access to the range of student services appropriate to support their learning.
- Accepted students have the background, knowledge, and technical skills needed to undertake the programs.
- Advertising, recruiting, and admissions materials clearly and accurately represent the program and services available.

Commitment to Support

- Policies for faculty evaluation include appropriate consideration of teaching and scholarly activities related to electronically offered programs.
- The institution demonstrates a commitment to ongoing support, both financial and technical, and to continuation of the program for a period sufficient to enable students to complete a degree/certificate.

Evaluation and Assessment

- The institution evaluates the program's educational effectiveness, including assessments of student learning outcomes, student retention, and student and faculty satisfaction.
- Students have access to such program evaluation data.
- The institution provides for assessment and documentation of student achievement in each course and at completion of the program.

of education professionals from state education departments, higher education institutions, and the regional accrediting agencies. These principles are excellent guidelines for planning and evaluating distance learning programs.

SUMMARY

This chapter provides the basic assumptions and concepts underlying planning for distance learning. A great deal of literature exists on educational planning, much of which has roots in organization theory and development. One of the most important concepts is that educational organizations operate as social systems and are part of larger social systems. Individuals (teachers, students), organizations (schools, colleges), and larger environments (communities, cities, societies) interact with one another through social processes. These social processes provide a foundation for their operation.

In applying the social process model, four common elements are identified as important to effective educational planning. Planning needs to be *comprehensive, collaborative,* and *continuous.* In addition, it needs to have the *commitment* of all involved: administrators, teachers, support staffs, and community representatives.

A planning model for distance learning is proposed based on a social process model originally developed by Getzels and Guba (1957) and modified by Picciano (1994, 1998). Environmental scanning is used extensively in the model for gathering data on societal needs and trends.

The planning model posits that goals and objectives are developed in response to environmental factors. From these goals and objectives, distance learning applications develop and become the fundamental building blocks upon which hardware, software, staff development, facilities, and financial components depend.

Critical to effective planning is effective evaluation, and educators should adopt a positive attitude toward its use in planning processes. Evaluation is used not only for determining whether goals and objectives are met but for refining and improving processes and applications. The evaluation of one planning cycle provides feedback and input into the next cycle. The chapter concludes with a consideration of accreditation concerns and guidelines.

CASE STUDY NO. 1

Metropolitan University Year: 1999

Setting

Gwendolyn Davis has been president of Metropolitan University for one year. Metropolitan is a state-funded university founded in 1895. Its current enrollment is 12,000 students, almost all of whom commute to its main campus or to one of five branch campuses that exist within a one-hundred-square-mile area. A state initiative begun in 1995 to connect all public and private colleges, museums, hospitals, and secondary schools on a high-speed fiber optic network is nearing completion.

The Issue

A number of colleges in the state have established distance learning programs. One nearby private college in particular has an extensive program and has seen its enrollments expand over the past four years. Metropolitan's enrollment, which had remained steady throughout the 1980s, has had a small decline for the past three years while college enrollments across the state have increased slightly.

Dr. Davis would like to establish a distance learning program at Metropolitan. She believes that with the fiber-optic network established and more and more students having access to the Internet in their homes, the technology is now available for distance learning. Metropolitan has never had such a program and the faculty are ambivalent and in some cases hostile to the idea. Metropolitan's faculty belong to a collective bargaining agency that represents all the faculty at the state-funded colleges. In discussing the issue with her vice presidents, she has received mixed advice about the feasibility of mounting a successful distance learning program. However, she is fairly well-convinced that Metropolitan should venture into distance learning.

Assume that you are Dr. Davis. How would you pursue the establishment of a distance learning program? What processes would you put in motion? Who would you involve in these processes?

To assist you with this case study, a partial organization chart of Metropolitan University is provided. What are its organizational strengths or weaknesses for supporting a distance learning program? Where on the organization chart might an office for distance learning be established?

Metropolitan University Organization Chart

President

Vice President for Academic Affairs	Vice President for Administration	Vice President for Student Affairs	Vice President for External Affairs
15 Academic Depts.	Comptroller	Admissions	Public Relations
Academic Advisement	Budget Office	Counseling	Annual Giving
Academic Computing	Personnel	Financial Aid	Community Affairs
Media Services	Telecommunications	Recruitment	Continuing Education
Library	Facilities	Student Activities	Gifts & Grants
Institutional Planning	Administrative Computing	Residence Life	College Publications
Registrar			

CASE STUDY NO. 2

Boleyn College Year: 2000

Setting

Boleyn is a private liberal arts college that was established in 1870. It has an excellent reputation for its undergraduate liberal arts program and is considered highly selective. Current enrollment is approximately 3,000 students, most of whom attend full-time and live either on-campus or in close proximity to the college. Boleyn has a modest endowment but also relies on student tuition to support its operations.

The Issue

Since 1980, Boleyn has offered a continuing education program for its local community. This program has been an excellent community relations vehicle for the college and has provided a small but consistent profit from fees and tuition. While most of the program is non-credit bearing, some courses are offered every semester for which students can receive full college credit. In 1997, as part of this program, two credit-bearing, Internet-based courses were offered that students could take in their homes or places of business. Since their inception, these courses have been popular and have been growing in enrollment so that in spring 2000, ten credit-bearing courses were offered with an enrollment of approximately 225 students.

Deborah Eisley, Director of Continuing Education, as part of a new five-year planning process, has just completed a student profile for the entire program. Among those enrolled in the ten Internet-based courses are 105 students who are regular Boleyn College matriculated students who take these courses in their dorm rooms or in their off-campus apartments. While it was known that a few regular students had taken continuing education courses in the past, Ms. Eisley was surprised by the number enrolled in these courses. In discussing this with Robert Nesbitt, Vice President for Student Affairs, she was informed that the college does not have a policy prohibiting regular students from taking these courses, but the intent of the continuing program was not to be a substitute for the regular program.

Assume that you are Dr. Nesbitt. Do you think there is a serious college policy issue here and, if so, what action do you recommend? Should the college limit enrollment in these courses to non-matriculated students? On the other hand, should the College consider offering Internet-based courses as part of the regular program?

REFERENCES

Bollag, B. (1996, September 27). In Western Europe, 12 institutions see the Internet and videoconferences as keys to virtual university. *The Chronicle of Higher Education, 6–7.*

Bork, A. (1997). The future of computers and learning. *Technological Horizons in Education Journal, 24*(11), 69–77.

Carlson, R. V., & Awkerman, M. G. (Eds.). (1991). *Educational planning: Concepts, strategies and practices.* New York: Longman.

Commission on Higher Education/Middle States Association of Colleges and Schools. (1997). *Guidelines for distance learning programs.* Philadelphia: Commission on Higher Education/Middle States Association of Colleges and Schools.

Deloughry, T. J. (1996, September 20). New School for Social Research bolsters flagging student enrollment with 90 on-line courses. *The Chronicle of Higher Education, 8–9.*

Getzels, J. W., & Guba, E. G. (1957). Social behavior and the administrative process. *School Review, 65,* 423–441.

Jennings, M. M., & Dirksen, D. J. (1999). Facilitating change: A process for adoption of Web-Based instruction. In B. H. Khan (Ed.), *Web-based instruction* (pp. 111–116). Englewood Cliffs, NJ: Educational Technology Publications.

Luskin, B. (1997). The best time to plant a tree was twenty-five years ago. *Technological Horizons in Education Journal, 24*(11), 81–83.

Meier, D. (1995). *The power of their ideas: Lessons for America from a small school in Harlem.* Boston: Beacon Press.

Molnar, A. R. (1997). Computers in education: A brief history. *Technological Horizons in Education Journal, 24*(11), 63–68.

Papert, S. (1997). Educational computing: How are we doing? *Technological Horizons in Education Journal, 24*(11), 78–80.

Picciano, A.G. (1994). *Computers in the schools: A guide to planning and administration.* New York: Macmillan Publishing Co.

_____. (1998). *Educational leadership and planning for technology.* Upper Saddle River, NJ: Prentice-Hall.

Sheathelm, H. H. (1991). Common elements in the planning process. In R. V. Carlson & M. G., Awkerman (Eds.), *Educational planning: Concepts, strategies and practices* (pp. 267–278). New York: Longman.

U.S. Department of Education, National Center for Education Statistics. (1997). *Distance education in higher education institutions* (NCES 97-062). Washington, D.C.

CHAPTER THREE

Distance Learning Hardware Technology and Media

Edward Zuckerman (1997), author and television producer, in an article entitled "The Technological Future Behind Us," describes various technological innovations that appeared on the market and quickly disappeared only to resurface again years later when the underlying technology had advanced, improved, or become less expensive. Especially amusing is a story he tells of purchasing one of the first Panasonic Videophone Systems in 1989. The videophone was designed to transmit black and white still photographs while having a conversation over an ordinary telephone line. He actually purchased two units, one for himself and one for his parents "so they could see their grandchildren even though they didn't have any grandchildren at the time and I wasn't even dating, let alone married." He describes how he and his parents used the videophone a few times but soon stopped because the pictures were frequently blurry and the sound seemed muffled. His personal story among others in his article demonstrates that technology makes some of us acquisitive, that is, we purchase or acquire new technology without necessarily knowing how well it will work or whether we have an actual need for it.

The same is certainly true of educators, some of whom have a track record for acquiring technology without knowing how well it will work or how it will be used. Examples include the language laboratories of the 1960s, which were not generally accepted by many language teachers; the television in every classroom craze of the 1970s that, without quality programming or VCRs, lacked educational content; and the microcomputers of the early 1980s that many teachers never learned how to use. This tendency persists; educators purchase or acquire hardware without necessarily having educational applications ready to use it. Reports of computers and other equipment being underutilized, in some cases left in unopened boxes locked away in school closets, still surface a bit too frequently even in the 1990s (Tapscott, 1998, p. 135). The purpose of this chapter is to examine hardware technology appropriate to distance learning applications, emphasizing that distance learning applications should be planned and identified prior to acquiring the hardware.

THE MEDIUM VERSUS THE MESSAGE

In the 1960s, Marshall McLuhan coined the phrase "the medium is the message" in recognition of the importance of the medium that creates the environment in which a message is delivered. New technology can provide not only a new communications environment but also a new human environment. Furthermore, these new environments involve not just passive "wrappings" but active cognitive processes that change fundamentally the way messages are received, interpreted, and understood (McLuhan, 1964). While we can debate McLuhan's thesis, agreement exists that new mass media technologies can create new modes of communication that, in turn, change the way messages are transmitted, received, and interpreted.

McLuhan's thesis, however, was immoderate. The medium is the message implies that the content is not important. McLuhan once described as "idiotic" anybody who thought that the content of a communication was more relevant than its medium (Rothstein, 1997, p. D5). Media is indeed powerful but so are the messages that it contains. Without content, the medium is powerless. This is an important debate that frames the discussion of the merits of various communications technologies as related to teaching and learning.

McLuhan was writing during the ascent of the Age of Television. He did not see the worldwide communications technologies of the 1990s in the form of the Internet. However, others (see Rothstein, 1997), using McLuhan's thesis, are already identifying how digital communications systems consisting of new on-line communities, cyber worlds, and hyperlinked connections are changing the way people transmit, receive, and interpret messages. Don Tapscott (1998) identified the children of the baby boom population born in the 1970s and 1980s as the "Net Generation." As a whole, they are influenced by digital communications via the Internet more than any other demographic group. They are already having a significant impact on education not only through their own use but by expecting others and especially teachers to make greater use of digital technologies. While the implications for education in general are very important, the new technologies are also redefining our concepts and definitions of distance learning (Hanson et al., 1997).

A significant body of research on the uses of various technologies in instruction has been well developed. Hundreds of experimental and descriptive studies have been conducted comparing instruction delivered with technology to traditional instruction without the technology. No need exists here to review this extensive literature. An excellent recent review of the literature with regard to distance learning has been conducted by Hanson et al. (1997) for the Association for Educational Communications and Technology and is highly recommended for additional reading on this subject. However, the issue of the best technology to use in distance learning is important for our discussion.

In the 1970s and 1980s, James Kulik and his associates at the University of Michigan conducted a series of meta-analyses on hundreds of studies dealing with the effects of various computer-based technologies on instruction at different grade levels (elementary, secondary, college, and adult). Their general conclusion was that computer-based technologies were as effective as, and in some cases more effective than, traditional instruction in improving academic achievement (Kulik, Kulik, & Cohen, 1980; Kulik, Bangert, & Williams, 1983; Kulik, 1984; Kulik, Kulik, & Bangert-Downs, 1984; Kulik, Kulik, and Schwab, 1986). However, Richard Clark (1983, 1985, 1989, 1994) refuted these studies and the approach used in comparing the effectiveness of various technologies and media in the delivery of instruction. His conclusion was that most of these studies lacked enough control of other variables, such as student preparedness, instructional organization and design, learning interactions, and socioeconomic factors, that are as important as the delivery mechanisms. He further concluded that in the final analysis when all the various instructional variables were taken into consideration, any one of which can affect outcomes, the content ultimately was the most critical component. The hardware technologies or media were basically vehicles carrying an instructional substance (content) and real improvement in achievement only comes with improving the substance and not the vehicle. In this sense, the content or the message is more important than the medium in education. Clark's conclusions have been accepted in a number of reviews of distance learning research (see Willis, 1993; Moore & Kearsley, 1996; Sherry, 1996; and Hanson et al., 1997).

Equally important to this discussion is the appropriateness of different technologies and media in instruction, since no one technology is the most appropriate for all instructional situations depending on the content, instructional objectives, and student population. In planning for distance learning, hardware technology should not be the central focus of the discussion. To the contrary, the instructional application should determine the hardware. The acquisition of technology in search of applications must be avoided. It is the classic case of the "tail wagging the dog" and indicative of, as Zuckerman stated, our "acquisitive" nature.

DEFINING HARDWARE TECHNOLOGY AND MEDIA

In Chapter 2, hardware technology was defined as the physical equipment used to transmit, store, and receive information. As used here, the definition of hardware has been expanded to include any physical element used to transmit, store, and receive information including printed material such as books, newspapers, and magazines. Media (the plural of medium) is defined as the symbol systems used to communicate and convey messages and information. These symbol systems include text, as in books; sound, as in radio transmission; and images, as in 35mm slides. In many cases, media are used in combination so that newspapers and magazines contain text and images; television contains sound and images; and computers can contain text, sound, and images. While the media refer to the symbol systems themselves (text, sound, images), the delivery systems (books, VCRs, television transmitters/receivers, and microcomputers) are considered to be the hardware technologies. When considering media for instruction, it is assumed that teachers will seek the most appropriate media and frequently will use some combination of media. In addition, the delivery of these media will depend on teachers seeking to use the most appropriate hardware technology available to them and their students. These assumptions form the basis for a discussion of planning, evaluating, and selecting hardware technology for instruction, including distance learning.

THE CURRENT STATE OF DISTANCE LEARNING TECHNOLOGIES

Table 3.1 provides data on the hardware technologies that are being used and that are under consideration for use in distance learning applications in the United States. The first column of percentages indicates that two-way interactive video (57 percent) and one-way prerecorded video (52 percent) are the most commonly used technologies in institutions offering distance learning courses (Fall 1995). In looking at the percentages for the second column, the future plans of these institutions include a substantial investment in computer-based technologies (75 percent and 84 percent) while continuing to provide two-way interactive video (81 percent). In-

TABLE 3.1 Percent of higher education institutions currently offering distance education courses that use various types of technologies to deliver distance learning courses, and the percent of higher education institutions currently offering or planning to offer distance learning courses in the next three years that plan to start or increase their use of various types of technologies in the next three years.

| | | Plan to start or increase use of the technology | |
| | | --- | --- |
Hardware Technology	Currently Use the Technology[1]	Currently offer distance learning courses[1]	Plan to offer distance learning courses[2]
Two-way interactive video	57	81	77
One-way prerecorded video	52	52	44
One-way live video	9	27	31
Two-way audio, one-way video	24	33	38
Audiographics	3	9	7
Two-way audio (e.g. audio/phone conferencing)	11	18	21
One-way audio (e.g. radio, audiotapes)	10	11	11
Two-way on-line (computer-based) interactions during instruction	14	75	64
Other computer-based technology (e.g., Internet)	22	84	74

[1]Percents are based on institutions that offered distance learning courses in Fall 1995.
[2]Percents are based on institutions that did not offer distance learning in Fall 1995, but that planned to offer distance learning courses in the next three years.

SOURCE: U.S. Dept. of Education, National Center for Education Statistics, Post-secondary Education Quick Information System, Survey on Distance Education Courses Offered by Higher Education Institutions. Sample based on mailing to 1,274 post-secondary institutions in the United States, the District of Columbia, and Puerto Rico with 1,203 returns (94% response rate).

stitutions that currently do not offer distance learning courses but plan to do so within three years likewise indicate that they will use computer-based technologies (64 percent and 74 percent) as well as two-way interactive video (77 percent). These data describe the importance that institutions place on the use of video and interactivity in distance learning applications, while indicating that the trend is to use more digital, computer-based technologies for delivering distance learning in the future. The data also accurately present modest but steady uses of audio and audiographic technologies.

Perhaps the most important aspect of the data in Table 3.1 is the indication that within institutions multiple technologies are currently used and are under consideration for future use in distance learning applications. No single technology (see Figures 3.1 & 3.2) as yet is considered the best technology for distance learning. On the contrary, the data suggest that different technologies may be more or less appropriate depending on the application. While the trend to digital, computer-based technologies predominates, it is not all inclusive and many institutions are planning to continue to use other technologies as well. It is likely that in many of these institutions, computer networking for Internet access has been or shortly will be established for reasons other than distance learning. Why not also use it for distance learning applications?

Figure 3.1 compares the advantages and limitations of various distance learning technologies. These data will serve as the basis for discussion in the remainder of this chapter.

PRINT TECHNOLOGIES

By far the most commonly used technology in distance learning, and in all education for that matter, is print. Textbooks, journals, newspapers, syllabi, tutorials, assignments, tests, and papers commonly consist of printed materials. While the demise of the printed word has been predicted as a result of the growth of mass media and the evolution of the electronic age (Birkerts, 1994), in education the printed word continues to be alive and well. It will be a number of years before the standard textbook is replaced completely by another form for educational activities. By the same token, educational planners should also be aware that electronic textbooks on CD-ROM, on-line journals, and Web-based syllabi are also becoming more common and may be particularly suitable for distance learning. Publishing companies such as The Education Management Group, a subsidiary of Simon & Schuster Publishing Company, are delivering live interactive custom curricula to more than 2 million students in 4,000 schools (Fabrikant, 1998). In Texas, the state Board of Education is examining the idea of replacing all textbooks with laptop computers for its 3.7 million students in public schools (*The New York Times*, 1997, p. B11). The Board sees this as a way of keeping up with rapidly changing information and of alleviating the problem of replacing "aging" textbooks, which costs the state approximately $375 million per year. While presently under consideration, it is unlikely that such a plan will be effected before the early years of the twenty-first century. However, the fact that a state governing body is engaged in a serious discussion of this issue is indicative of its importance and possibilities.

Distance learning applications will likely be the educational bellwethers and pioneers in the migration from printed material to electronic forms. In the meantime, printed materials will continue to be used and should be designed with the students as well as the instructional content in mind. Derek Rowntree (1996) has produced an excellent guide for selecting and preparing printed materials for

FIGURE 3.1 Comparison of Distance Learning Technologies

Technology	Advantages	Limitations
Print		
Textbooks	Easy to Use	Non-Interactive
Study Guides	Familiar	Dependent on Learner Reading Skills
Syllabi	Spontaneous	Passive/Self-Directed
Assignments	Inexpensive	
Workbooks	Portable	
	Self-Paced	
Audio		
Audiocassette	Easy to Use	Non-Interactive
	Portable	Passive/Self-Directed
	Inexpensive	Requires Printed Study Guides
	Self-Paced	Non-Graphic
Radio	Mass Distribution	Non-Interactive
	Easy to Use (Student)	Requires Printed Study Guides
		Non-Graphic
Audioconferencing	Interactive	Non-Graphic
	Immediacy	Development Time
		Requires Printed Study Guides
Audiographics	Interactive	Requires Printed Study Guides
	Immediacy	Limited Graphics
Video		
Videocassette	Easy to Use (Student)	Non-Interactive
	Self-Paced	Passive/Self-Directed
	Graphic	Requires Printed Study Guides
Television	Mass Distribution	Non-Interactive
	Graphic	Requires Printed Study Guides
	Easy to Use (Student)	Development Time
		Expensive
Videoconferencing	Interactive	Development Time
	Graphic	Expensive
	Immediacy	Complex Technology
Computer (Digital)		
Packaged Software (CD-ROM, Network)	Interactive (Limited)	Development Time
	Multimedia	Expensive
	Self-Paced	Complex
Synchronous/Network (Videoconferencing)	Interactive	Development Time
	Multimedia	Expensive
	Immediacy	Complex
	Participative	
Asynchronous/Network	Interactive	Development Time
	Graphics (Limited)	Complex
	Self-Paced	Expensive
		Student Access to Technology
		Rapidly Evolving Technology

FIGURE 3.2 Distance Learning Technologies

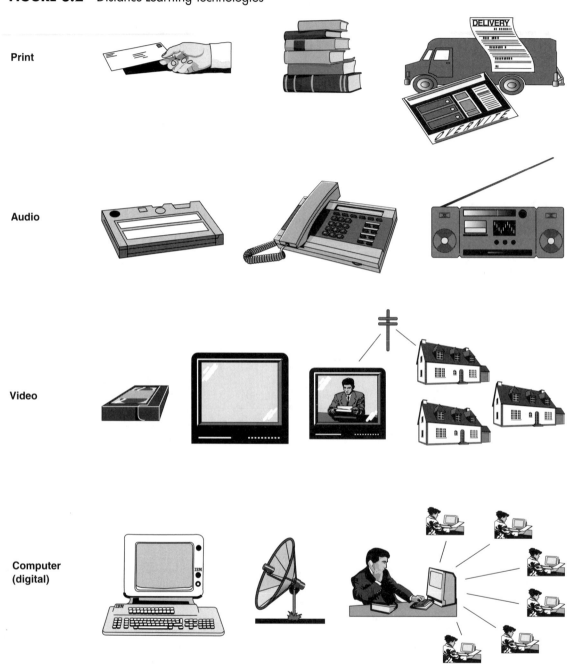

Print

Audio

Video

Computer
(digital)

"open, distance, and flexible learning." His major emphasis is on the importance of profiling the intended student population. While this will be discussed in more detail in Chapters 4 and 5, common sense dictates that the printed materials, whether selected (e.g., textbooks) or developed (e.g., self-study guides), should be useful and readable by students. In distance learning applications, this becomes even more important because the students are more dependent on these materials in the absence of traditional classroom presentations and discussions. This is especially true in correspondence courses where frequently all activities (content, presentation, and interactions) are conducted using mail, fax, and other print-based materials.

The popularity of print stems from its convenience, portability, familiarity, and inexpensiveness. An individual faculty member, with training, can develop print materials for a single distance learning course in little more time than for a traditional course. This is especially true if the faculty member is already familiar with the student population and has been developing and using print material for traditional courses. For large-scale distance learning operations such as open universities serving large, widely dispersed, and international student populations, developing good print materials can be a significant undertaking in terms of both time and money. Teams of content specialists, presentation designers, and text and graphics editors are generally assembled to develop the print material used in such operations. It is not unusual for it to take months and in some cases years to develop good quality printed material for a distance learning course. Rowntree estimates that for each hour of learning time, as many as one hundred hours of design time is needed (Rowntree, 1996, p. 88).

While correspondence courses depend almost exclusively on printed materials, other forms of distance learning using various hardware technologies also require some printed or text-based material. Telecourses using broadcast television or radio generally provide an extensive study guide of materials that include a syllabus, reading assignments, case studies, etc. Two-way interactive video distance learning applications generally use the same printed materials (e.g., syllabus, reading assignments) as a traditional class. Even on-line computer courses using the Internet frequently use a good deal of print material, although increasingly it is provided in the form of Web pages. While Web pages have additional facilities such as easy linkage to other sites and files, many of the design considerations for print materials are applicable to Web page design.

In developing print materials, regardless of whether the final product is in paper or electronic form (CD-ROM, floppy disk, or Web page), consideration should be given to acquiring desktop publishing hardware and software. With relatively inexpensive microcomputer equipment, high-quality print materials combining text, images, maps, graphs, etc. can be produced by anyone with basic word-processing skills. Because they exist in digital form on disk files, desktop published materials can be easily modified and updated, thereby saving significant time. Furthermore, should the distance learning course evolve to newer technologies, the material is readily available in electronic form.

While print material will continue to play a significant role in distance learning, other technologies will evolve as replacements or enhancements. The typical correspondence course of a few years ago that relied entirely on printed materials such as a self-study guide and tutorial is just as likely today to include a videocassette, a floppy disk, a CD-ROM, and/or access to a Web site. This movement and evolution away from printed material will continue and perhaps accelerate as more people in the general population gain access to electronic technologies.

AUDIO TECHNOLOGIES

Audio technologies rely on the spoken word and sound for instruction. Audio was the next logical step in the evolution of distance learning technology. Like print, it is familiar and, depending on the nature of the application, relatively easy to use. The major drawback of all audio technologies is that graphics are either not possible or generally limited. Most audio technologies also require that substantial additional material be provided in the form of study guides to provide additional content.

Audiocassettes

Audiocassettes have been used extensively in distance learning programs throughout the world. From the student perspective, audiocassettes are very convenient, portable, and inexpensive. Students can listen to an audiocassette in any room of a house, in a car, or on vacation. Once an audiotape has been developed (mastered), it can be reproduced for mass distribution at relatively modest cost. The Open University of the United Kingdom has made extensive use of this technology for its large distance learning population. Thousands of students enrolled in the Open University have used this technology successfully. Bates (1990) indicates that the British Open University sends in excess of 750,000 hours of audiocassette materials to students each year. British audiocassette materials are well-designed and are meant to be used in conjunction with printed study guide activities that are integrated into the audio presentation. They are not recorded lectures, which can become very boring. In France, the Centre National D'Enseignement a Distance (CNED) also makes extensive use of audiocassettes for distance learning. Hundreds of thousands of students in almost every country of the world have enrolled in the CNED's programs and used its audiocassettes translated into dozens of different languages. In the United States, audiocassettes have not been used as extensively as in Great Britain or France. A major reason is the availability and popularity of videocassettes.

The main limitation of audiocassette technology is its non-interactive and passive nature. This requires a good deal of student self-direction and discipline to complete courses. Alternative communication methods using mail or telephone are also necessary to enable students to ask questions of instructors, and interactivity among students using this technology is not commonplace. Graphics cannot be delivered via audiocassettes and, therefore, additional and in some cases substantial study guides are necessary as accompaniments to the audio material.

Radio

Radio has been used successfully as mass distribution distance learning technology for decades. While still used in some parts of the United States, most broadcast radio distance learning applications were replaced by television in the 1940s and 1950s, but in developing countries, where access to video technology is limited, broadcast radio continues to be used. As a non-interactive technology, radio also requires other communications technologies to enable students to ask questions. Where telephone and other forms of communications are limited, teaching assistants are sometimes made available. And like audiocassettes, radio requires substantial printed study guides to be used effectively.

Audioconferencing

Audioconferencing overcomes one major limitation of other audio technologies by providing interactive capabilities between instructor and student and between student and student. Of the various teleconferencing technologies, audioconferencing is the least expensive and generally the most reliable. Audioconferencing technology uses some type of telephone message handling equipment, usually referred to as a bridge, that connects the various sites or parties simultaneously. A dedicated audioconferencing network can be established or existing telephone lines can be used to connect sites. The University of Alaska maintains one of the most extensive audioconferencing networks in the world, with the capacity to link more than 330 different sites (Willis, 1993). Sponder (1991), who conducted an extensive study of Native Americans in Alaska using the University of Alaska's network, provides a very descriptive analysis of its use in rural and isolated settings. The University of Wisconsin Mind Extension also has made use of audioconferencing through its Education Telephone Network (ETN), which serves more than 200 sites throughout Wisconsin.

While popular opinion holds that audioconferencing will eventually be replaced by videoconferencing, audioconferencing will continue to be used for many years. Most distance learning programs that presently use this technology have plans for expanding its use in the future. Because of the expense and complexity of videoconferencing technology, audioconferencing is viewed as a cost-effective method of providing interactivity for distance learning. Audioconferencing applications are also generally enhanced through study guides used to help students organize and visualize content. Finally, advocates of this technology have observed that, if the video portion of a videoconference should malfunction and be lost, the conference can continue with just the audio. On the other hand, if the reverse happens and the audio portion malfunctions or is lost, the conference will likely have to be canceled.

Audiographics

The major limitation of a basic audioconferencing network is the lack of graphic capability. However, this has begun to change as graphics capabilities are being added to audioconferencing networks. Audiographics essentially is an audioconference system with some limited graphics capability, usually in the form of an electronic blackboard capable of transmitting and receiving images and illustrations at sending and receiving sites, respectively. Computers, document cameras, and other image-capable technologies have been used successfully in audiographics applications. An instructor uses the electronic blackboard or document camera as he or she would in a traditional classroom. However, the notes, illustrations, or drawings are automatically transmitted via the audio connection to similar equipment at the receiving site so that students can see them as the instructor makes a presentation.

While audiographics significantly improves on the complete lack of graphics found in the basic audioconferencing network, these systems are not as visually stimulating as full video capability. Furthermore, because audiographics requires more substantial transmission capability (bandwidth) to transmit high-quality images in real time, distance learning programs have tended to prefer videoconferencing technology.

VIDEO TECHNOLOGIES

The power of the image has become well-recognized in education at all levels. In distance learning, many successful programs have relied on some form of video to deliver or at least enhance course materials. Videocassettes and educational television have been important vehicles for providing high-quality distance learning materials and activities for decades. In recent years, interactive video technologies delivering high-quality, stimulating class materials have emerged that also allow learners to interact and participate in discussions and activities. The new interactive video technologies are presently complex and expensive but nonetheless have established themselves as major distance learning delivery systems, especially in the United States.

Videocassettes

As the popularity of the videocassette recorder (VCR) grew in the United States and other developed countries in the 1980s, so did its popularity for distance learning. Videocassettes are easy to use, self-paced, and graphically rich. When accompanied by well-designed study guides, videocassettes can be very effective in delivering distance learning. The quality of the instructional video on cassettes is important. It should include stimulating graphics, illustrations, and simulations and not simply a recorded lecture.

The Open University of the United Kingdom has integrated videocassettes into its programs using material produced by the British Broadcasting Company (BBC). In the United States, the Annenberg Foundation, in cooperation with the Corporation for Public Broadcasting (CPB), initiated a grant program in 1981 to fund the development of high-quality video materials that can be used by colleges and high schools to enhance instruction in a traditional classroom. When used in conjunction with study guides, much of this material is also appropriate for distance learning programs. These materials can be purchased or rented for modest fees. As a result, colleges can begin a distance learning program with high-quality videocassette materials relatively quickly. Without the availability of this material, production costs for some schools would probably be prohibitive. Since its inception, more than 400,000 students in seventy different countries have received college credit for courses using video materials produced by the Annenberg Foundation/CPB project.

The major limitation of videocassette technology is its non-interactive and passive nature, which requires a good deal of student self-direction and discipline to complete courses. Alternative communication methods using either mail or telephone are necessary to enable students to ask questions of instructors, and interactivity among students using this technology is rare.

For schools intending to develop their own materials, facilities and equipment for editing and mastering videotape can be expensive and require the assistance of a trained technical support staff. Without such support, even a simple taping of a lecture may result in a poor-quality and instructionally ineffective videotape.

Television

Without question, television has evolved into the most effective mass communication system ever, supplanting newspapers, magazines, and other materials meant to be read. Television has become a fact of daily life. Major news stories such as the Gulf War, the O.J. Simpson trial, and the funeral of Princess Diana were more likely to be seen on television than read about in the newspapers. Hundreds of millions of people view television daily throughout the world. As a result, for education and especially for distance learning, television has emerged as a very important delivery mechanism.

In China, the Central Radio and University Network (DIANDA) provides programs for almost fifty universities serving 850,000 students. DIANDA uses an extensive network of regional television stations, television education centers, and tutoring groups to deliver and support its educational programs. In the United States, the Public Broadcasting System (PBS) through its *Adult Learning System* and *Going the Distance* programs has provided distance learning opportunities for hundreds of thousands of adult students. The *Going the Distance* program is specifically designed to help colleges and universities develop entire distance learning degree programs using the services of PBS. The *Going the Distance* project was launched in 1994 with sixty colleges and twenty-two public television systems and has evolved to include the participation of 175 colleges in thirty-seven states supported by sixty public television systems.

As are videocassettes, television is most effective in distance learning when accompanied by well-designed study guides. As a passive medium, television requires support systems that enable students to ask questions using telephone, mail, or other communications systems. While most distance learning television is broadcast, that is, sent over the airwaves for anyone with an antenna to receive, some colleges also use "narrowcast" transmission for limited distribution to a region or locality of approximately twenty to twenty-five miles. Narrowcast for distance learning, also referred to as Instructional Television Fixed Service (ITFS), requires a microwave transmitter and a transmission studio. Special receiver antennae are required by the students to access the microwave transmission. ITFS is especially effective in rural and less crowded airwave spaces where interference is at a minimum. ITFS can also relay transmissions or "feed" from other sources such as satellite or cable television systems, thereby expanding the programming available.

The use of television for distance learning has a secure future, however the technologies used for transmission are evolving rapidly. In the twentieth century, broadcasting over the airwaves using transmitters and antennae for reception dominated television in most countries. However, satellite and cable television services that can significantly improve and integrate television transmissions with other technologies such as telephone and computer are evolving. Direct satellite services are now available for the modest cost of a small (1.5-foot diameter) satellite dish. Cable television and telephone companies are presently investing millions of dollars in providing fiber-optic, broadband services to people's homes. It is difficult to predict which television technology, if any, will emerge as the dominant technology of the twenty-first century, but it is safe to say that distance learning will benefit significantly from an integrated system capable of delivering video, telephone, and computer services via one transmitting and receiving technology.

Videoconferencing

Videoconferencing or teleconferencing technology provides all the benefits of television and also allows the audience or students to interact in real time with the instructor and other students. While not the same, videoconferencing approximates the traditional classroom more than any other distance learning technology. Instructors conduct classes, students can see the instructor, instructors can see students, and students can ask questions of the instructor or each other. In addition, when accompanied by electronic blackboards and other imaging systems, instructors can use illustrations, write notes, and use images or video to enhance their class presentations. While most frequently being used in a two-way interactive mode, videoconferencing technology is evolving so that multiple sites can participate. Using digital technology, videoconferencing is also now available on desktop computers so that a session may include individuals in many different locations. The delivery technologies being used for videoconferencing include high-speed telephone systems, satellite, cable, and dedicated fiber-optic networks.

In the United States, according to the data provided by the National Center for Educational Statistics (see Table 3.1), interactive videoconferencing has emerged as one of the most popular forms of distance learning technology as we enter the twenty-first century. Many statewide systems such as those in Oklahoma, Iowa, Wisconsin, Maryland, and Florida support videoconferencing links for a variety of educational, medical, and other nonprofit agencies. The Georgia Statewide Academic and Medical System (GSAMS) is a videoconferencing system that connects most of the state's colleges, high schools, and hospitals. GSAMS is especially effective in bringing distance learning programs to health-care and medical professionals who need to update regularly their skills and knowledge of current medical practices and techniques. The Public Broadcasting Corporation's *Adult Satellite Service System* operates one of the largest satellite-based videoconferencing networks for higher education. Videoconferencing is also being provided by private corporations such as the Distance Learning Network in Pennsylvania. Many of these networks specialize in professional training for adult and continuing education as well as degree-credit programs in conjunction with educational institutions.

Compared to other distance learning technologies, videoconferencing is an expensive, complex, and evolving technology that will test the administrative and technical expertise of most educational institutions. The institutions that have been developing this technology for years and have grown with it, are in a much better position to upgrade, expand, and move ahead as videoconferencing technologies evolve. The institutions just beginning to use this technology will probably find it daunting and may rely on others (consultants, private providers, and consortia) for services. States and other regional entities that have established and provide technical support for videoconferencing networks have been most helpful in assisting schools to start cost-effective distance learning programs. Unfortunately, videoconferencing systems have experienced growing pains and have not always been as reliable as one would hope in an educational activity. In traditional face-to-face learning, sessions are rarely canceled due to technical difficulties. In real-time videoconferencing sessions, prudent planning requires that backup and alternative activities be provided in the event the system fails or technical difficulties are encountered. For large or widely dispersed student audiences, the instructor will likely need the assistance of facilitators to help in answering questions or assisting with technical difficulties.

COMPUTER TECHNOLOGIES

Computer or digital technologies incorporate most of the capabilities of print, audio, and video and, in addition, allow for a certain degree of user control. Computer technologies have made significant progress during the second half of the twentieth century. In the United States and some of the developed countries, an increasing number of students of all ages have access to computer technology in their homes as well as in their schools. A computer that as late as the 1970s consisted of a large, room-size gray electronic box now fits in an attaché case or book bag. While complexity still exists, the mystique of computer technology is evaporating as more people use computers in everyday activities. In distance learning applications, this has had and will continue to have important ramifications.

Computer technology is also referred to as digital technology because all instructions, symbols, and information are stored as a series of electronic binary digits. Letters of the alphabet, numbers, sounds, and images are converted into a series of binary digit codes that are interpreted and executed by various types of computing or digital-based equipment. Printing, audio, and video have in the past used mostly analog technologies that require some continuous physical property such as voltage, airwaves, or frame processing. However, for media distribution, many formerly analog-based technologies are converting to digital technology. In the not-too-distant future, digital technology as presently used in computers, compact discs, and television will likely dominate all media distribution systems including those used for distance learning.

Packaged Software

Packaged computer software used in distance learning is similar in content to material provided in audio and video technologies. Learning modules, specific skills instructions, and entire courses are offered or packaged on floppy disk and CD-ROM, and increasingly at an Internet or World Wide Web site. In addition to text, sound, and images, these packaged programs provide for a good deal of student control and interaction. Study guides may be provided but frequently are built into the content. Many of the techniques used for packaged software include programmed instruction, self-paced learning, and student testing and prescription. Most of these techniques were developed during the past thirty years via technology referred to as computer-assisted instruction (CAI) and computer-based education (CBE). In the early years of CAI and CBE, some of these programs were viewed as impersonal, "big brother is watching you" software and were centered on drill and practice exercises. This has changed significantly and many of these programs are now visually stimulating, provocative, and in some cases, fun.

Many of the video materials developed by the Annenberg Foundation/CPB project mentioned earlier have been converted into CD-ROM format. A reader might ask why not simply convert everything. The answer is that the conversion from videotape material into a packaged CD-ROM or other computer medium is not simply the conversion of the video portion but also the development of control programs that guide and assist the student in using the video material. These are labor-intensive activities usually requiring the expertise of high-salaried software specialists and instructional designers. Frequently, the investment of money and time for the conversion is only worthwhile for the more popular titles.

Designing and developing original packaged software for distance learning programs requires a team of specialists (content, software, graphics). Such an investment is typically only considered by large, comprehensive distance learning programs and institutions.

Synchronous Networks/Videoconferencing

In addition to packaged software, distance learning is also available in several different forms on computer networks including the Internet. These activities can be synchronous, that is, instruction happening at a specific time; or asynchronous, instruction happening at any time.

Increasingly, synchronous distance learning via computer networks involves digital videoconferencing. The benefits and limitations of this approach are similar to those discussed earlier in the section on video technologies. One major difference is that students participate while sitting at a computer workstation rather than as part of a class viewing a large monitor of an instructor presenting material at a distant site. Rather than pushing a button on a microphone to ask a question, a student might key in the question in text mode and receive a prompt text reply. Videoconferencing using standard video technologies almost always assumes an "instructor" is leading the presentation while with computer technology, the presentation may be "led" by a packaged software program with the instructor acting more as a facilitator available to answer a question or help a student having some other difficulty.

The technology for this approach has been evolving for many years. Computer-managed instruction (CMI) is a term used to describe systems that organize and track student records and progress. Student databases are developed containing enough information to customize on-line sessions so that learners are able to progress and master material at their own pace. More recently, the term computer-mediated communications (CMC) has been used to describe systems that incorporate more extensive e-mail and other communications facilities to enhance CMI for individuals and for groups of students. The most extensive use of computer technology using CAI, CMI, and CMC has evolved into what are commonly referred to as integrated learning systems (ILS). Integrated learning systems are integrated computer systems of hardware, software, curriculum, and management components that are generally marketed by a single vendor. Many of these programs were originally developed for primary and secondary school instruction but are now also being used in adult, continuing, and higher education. Companies that have had success with this technology include Computer Curriculum Corporation; Jostens Learning Systems; Wicat Systems, Incorporated; and Sylvan Learning Systems. As with any packaged computer software, development costs and time are significant and generally only attempted by larger organizations employing a number of specialists.

Using synchronous computer conferencing without packaged software but depending on an instructor to present, control, and interact with the students is also similar to other audio or videoconferencing techniques. However, with large and widely dispersed student audiences, the instructor will likely have to have the assistance of facilitators to help in answering questions or assisting with technical difficulties, which again can become costly. As a result, schools and other organizations using computer networks for distance learning are beginning to consider asynchronous approaches that may be less costly.

Asynchronous Computer Networks

Among the most recent developments in distance learning is the use of asynchronous learning networks (ALN). An asynchronous learning network generally is defined as using computer networking technology to provide instruction at any place and any time. An instructor provides a file of instructional materials that students can access remotely from any computer work station that has a modem or other communications capability. Interaction, discussion, and questions are handled through group software systems (i.e., *LISTSERV, First-Class, Lotus Notes*) and course management software (i.e., *LearningSpace, TopClass, WEBCT*) that provide e-mail, electronic bulletin board, and other communications facilities. With the emergence of the Internet, ALNs increasingly are relying on the World Wide Web for part or all of their networking features.

In an example of an asynchronous learning session, an instructor provides a file of materials or introduces a topic that students can read or otherwise use for some activity at a Web site on a Sunday evening. The instructor might supplement the materials by posing key questions on an electronic bulletin board or other group e-mail system that all students in the class are able to access. Students access this material at any time during the week and can post comments to the electronic bulletin board for the entire class to see, and ask questions directly of the instructor or of other students through regular e-mail. An assessment or review of the material and the week's instructional activity (discussions, questions, etc.) is conducted on Saturday. The cycle begins again on Sunday evening with a new topic. In this example of asynchronous learning, at no time did the instructor and students communicate synchronously, that is, at the same time. The instructor and students accessed all materials and asked questions from computer work stations in their homes, at a school, or in their places of business.

Many schools in the United States and developed countries have begun to use ALN for distance learning activities. Course modules, entire courses, entire programs, and entire "virtual" colleges are beginning to use ALN techniques. The Alfred P. Sloan Foundation has a major grant program that has funded more than one-hundred ALN projects in colleges and universities in the United States. The major benefit of ALNs is that they are very convenient for students, especially adults who may work full-time, have family responsibilities, and are attempting to improve their professional skills or complete an academic program. They are able to participate at any time—early morning, at lunch time, or late at night—and any place—at home or where they work. The major limitations of ALNs are that instructors and faculty must have access to networking technology in their schools and beyond. Schools that have already invested in a computer networking infrastructure that provides ready access to the Internet can more easily support this approach. Schools that are just considering developing this infrastructure will have to plan for some major budgetary and technological changes. Likewise students wishing to enroll in ALN courses generally must have access to the Internet either in their homes or work places or in both in order to participate effectively.

BLENDING TECHNOLOGIES

At this juncture, readers should have come to understand that a wide variety of technologies are available for distance learning. Furthermore, each of these technologies has certain benefits and certain limitations and, as indicated earlier, a best technology does not yet exist for distance learning. Educators should attempt to use the technology that will best meet their goals and objectives, that is most readily available, and that will be educationally sound as well as cost effective. The data in Table 3.1 indicates that the trend is for video and computer technologies to be used more extensively in the future for distance learning. But even within these technologies, various options are available.

In selecting a technology for distance learning, educators should assume that they may pick and choose or blend technologies to provide the best approach. While one technology may be the primary technology used for delivering instruction, other technologies may be more appropriate for some aspect of a distance learning course or program. For example, interaction and communication between student and instructor is a major consideration in selecting a particular technology. Where available, e-mail is increasingly viewed as an excellent and cost-effective method of improving interaction and communication among distance learning participants. Even in traditional classrooms, e-mail is being used to improve communications and interaction between instructors and students. If access to e-mail or the Internet is not available, standard telephones and fax machines provide an easy-to-use technology by which faculty and students can communicate. Students who encounter problems might be encouraged to telephone an instructor, tutor, or advisor to speak with someone who can help them. Students might be able to fax written assignments rather than mail them. The point here is that educators do not have to take a purist attitude and commit to the idea that all distance learning must be conducted via one technology. On the contrary, common sense and good planning dictate that the most effective and available technologies be used and in combination if need be. Naturally, other factors such as costs need to be considered that may limit the number of technologies that are available in any given school or organization.

Finally, many of the technologies discussed above are evolving. In planning distance learning programs, educators should remain flexible in their selection of a technology. Using several technologies may seem costly but in the long run may protect against major shifts or advances in technological approaches. Change, and in some cases rapid change, is becoming a dominating characteristic of many of the newer video and digital technologies. As late as the mid-1990s, the Internet was only being used by a few thousand scientists, academicians, and engineers. As we enter the twenty-first century, the Internet is being used by hundreds of millions of people from every walk of life on every continent. Internets II and III are already evolving. Flexibility with cognizance of major trends will best serve planning activities for distance learning.

SUMMARY

This chapter examines the major technologies used in distance learning. Marshall McLuhan's thesis that the "medium is the message" was examined. While McLuhan's position is well respected, researchers such as Richard E. Clark posit that in education the content or message may be more important than the medium. This discussion also requires that a careful definition of and distinction between terms such as hardware technology and media be established.

Data provided by the U.S. Department of Education was used to establish the current state and future direction of distance learning technologies. The data suggest that video and computer technologies are beginning to dominate in the United States as the primary delivery systems for distance learning. This is not as true in other countries, especially those still developing their technological capabilities.

A review of the major print, audio, video, and computer technologies used in distance learning is provided. Benefits and limitations indicate that no single technology is best for distance learning yet. On the contrary, educators should attempt to select the technology that will best meet their goals and objectives, that is available, and that will be educationally sound as well as cost effective. The chapter concludes with the suggestion that educators consider combining or blending technologies to best meet their goals and objectives for distance learning.

CASE STUDY

State Agency for Social Services Year: 2001

Setting

The State Agency for Social Services (SASS) is responsible for monitoring the delivery of social services in one of the states in the Eastern United States. Among its programs is a comprehensive training program designed to maintain the skills of professionals and other staff members of social services providers throughout the state. SASS has four staff developers who perform much of this training at its centers located in the state's two major metropolitan areas. SASS also awards approximately $25 million dollars a year in training grants to colleges and universities in the state to provide specialized training and to reach populations distant from the two training centers. All of the training is conducted in face-to-face classroom formats.

The Issue

Much of the funding for the training program has been subsidized by the federal government. Unfortunately, this funding has been reduced by approximately 20 percent over the past three years. While the state has increased its funding for training, much of the budget reduction has been absorbed by reducing the grants to colleges and universities while maintaining the program at the two SASS centers. However, the demand for social services is rising, especially for the aged and for nursing home care, and hence the demand for training is growing. Furthermore, several state legislators have written to Rose DeBroff, the Commissioner at SASS, expressing concern about the reduction of the training programs in their districts.

Bob Stroper, head of the training program, who reports to Commissioner De-Broff, has just returned from a national conference. One of the presentations featured the use of a combination of point-to-point video conferencing and Web-based distance learning to provide professional career training in hospitals. Of particular note were comments indicating that some savings were realized because the hospital employees did not have to travel to medical schools and universities for their training. SASS, as part of the training grant awards to colleges and universities, has always allowed funding (approximately 10 to 15 percent of the award) for travel and accommodations for participants in the training programs. In discussing this with Commissioner DeBroff, Mr. Stroper suggested that distance learning might provide a way to save on training expenses without reducing the number of participants. Commissioner DeBroff asked him to develop a position paper on the use of distance learning for SASS's training program.

Assume you are Mr. Stroper. What additional information would you need in order to develop this position paper? Also what alternatives or strategies for delivering distance learning are available? For example, should SASS develop its own distance learning program for the entire state? Should SASS centralize or decentralize its training operations? Should SASS require the colleges and universities receiving grant awards to consider using distance learning by eliminating any future funding for travel in their grant proposals?

REFERENCES

Bates, A. W. (1990). *Media and technology in European distance education.* Milton Keynes, UK: Open University.

Birkerts, S. (1994). *The Gutenberg elegies.* Boston: Faber and Faber.

Clark, R. (1983). Reconsidering research on learning from media. *Review of Educational Research, 53*(4), 445–459.

_____. (1985). Evidence for confounding in computer-based instruction studies. *Educational Communications and Technology Journal, 33*(4), 249–262.

_____. (1989). *Evaluating distance learning technology.* Washington, D.C.: U.S. Congress, Office of Technology Assessment.

_____. (1994). Media will never influence learning. *Educational Technology Research and Development, 42*(2), 21–29.

Fabrikant, G. (1998, January 14). Viacom seems set to sell most of publisher. *The New York Times,* p. D1.

Hanson, D., Maushak, N. J., Schlosser, C. A., Anderson, M. L., Sorenson, C., & Simonson, M. (1997). *Distance education: Review of the literature* (2nd ed.). Washington, D.C.: Association for Educational Communications and Technology.

Kulik, J. A. (1984). Evaluating the effects of teaching with computers. In G. Campbell & G. Fein (Eds.), *Microcomputers in early education.* Reston, VA: Reston.

Kulik, J. A., Bangert, R., & Williams, G. (1983). Effects of computer-based teaching on secondary students. *Journal of Educational Psychology, 75*(1), 19–26.

Kulik, J. A., Kulik, C., & Bangert-Downs, R. (1984). Effectiveness of computer-based education in elementary schools. *Computers in Human Behavior, 1*(1), 59–74.

Kulik, J. A., Kulik, C., & Cohen, P. (1980). Effectiveness of computer-based college teaching: A meta-analysis of findings. *Review of Educational Research, 2*(2), 525–544.

Kulik, J. A., Kulik, C., & Schwab, B. (1986). The effectiveness of computer-based adult education: A meta-analysis. *Journal of Educational Computing, 2*(2), 235–252.

McLuhan, M. (1964). *Understanding media: The extensions of man.* New York: McGraw-Hill.

Moore, M., & Kearsley, G. (1996). *Distance education: A systems view.* Belmont, CA: Wadsworth Publishing Co.

Rothstein, E. (1997, June 9). McLuhan preferred form to content. So does the Internet—to its sorrow. *The New York Times,* p. D5.

Rowntree, D. (1996). *Preparing materials for open, distance and flexible learning.* London: Kogan Page Limited.

Sherry, L. (1996). Issues in distance learning. *International Journal of Distance Education, 1*(4), 337–365.

Sponder, B. (1991). *Distance education in rural Alaska: An overview of teaching and learning practices in audioconference courses* (2nd ed.). Fairbanks, AK: University of Alaska, Fairbanks, Center for Cross Cultural Studies.

Tapscott, D. (1998). *Growing up digital.* New York: McGraw-Hill.

Texas may drop texts for laptops (1997, November 19).*The New York Times.* p. B11.

Willis, B. (1993). *Distance education: A practical guide.* Englewood Cliffs, NJ: Educational Technology Publications.

Zuckerman, E. (1997, September 28). The great technological future behind us. *The New York Times Magazine,* Section 6, pp. 98–99.

CHAPTER FOUR

Instructional Design for Distance Learning

Stephen Hawking, British theoretical physicist and Lucasian Professor of Mathematics at the University of Cambridge, while writing his best-selling book, *A Brief History of Time*, was most concerned about being able to communicate his thoughts and ideas to a general reader population. Modern science had become too technical, and only a handful of specialists were able to master the mathematics used to describe it. His readers, on the other hand, would be everyday people who knew little about quantum mechanics, general relativity, or points of infinite distortion of space and time. He believed that each mathematical equation he included would "halve" his audience. Dr. Hawking, who has battled an incurable motor neuron disease all his life, developed pneumonia while in the middle of writing his first draft. As a result, he had a tracheotomy, which completely removed his ability to speak and made it almost impossible for him to communicate. However, with the help of one of his students and the use of a synthesizer and computer mounted on his wheelchair, he developed a new way to communicate that he described as "better now than before I lost my voice" (Hawking, 1988, pp. vii–viii).

Dr. Hawking's lesson is twofold. First, to convey complex content effectively, one must know the audience and tailor the message accordingly. And secondly, the most common acts of communication, such as speaking a phrase or writing a sentence, are not taken for granted. These are important lessons for developing and designing instructional materials, especially for distance learning where common methods of communication may not be available. Instructional materials must be designed for the audience. Teachers who have come to rely extensively on basic oral communications for instruction—teacher talks–students listen—will find that in distance learning, other communications tools will have to be considered and used.

PEDAGOGY AND DISTANCE LEARNING THEORY

A general pedagogical theory for distance learning does not exist now and will likely not exist in the near future. This is not surprising, because generally accepted theories for complex social phenomenon such as learning, distance or otherwise, are difficult to come by. During the past few decades, discussions and debates of proposals for distance learning theories, distinct and separate from traditional learning, have been developed. Keegan (1993) conducted an excellent review and analysis of these theories. They relate to certain aspects of distance learning such as independent study (Wedemeyer, 1977), learner autonomy (Moore, 1972, 1994), industrialization (Peters, 1988), and interaction and communication (Holmberg, 1989). In the end, Keegan concluded that while these theories were important for describing and understanding distance learning, none could be considered all-inclusive. In addition, new technologies such as asynchronous "virtual systems" have significantly changed the concept of distance learning and have made many of these theories less applicable. Keegan later recommended further research, "theoretical or otherwise, to determine if 'virtual systems' were a subset of distance learning or a new field of study in their own right" (Keegan, 1996, p. 214–215).

In searching for or developing a pedagogical theory for distance learning, a major question to be addressed is whether or not it is a distinct form of education. Shale (1988) suggests that it is not and that the process of education and learning is the same, whether teacher and student are face-to-face or at a distance.

Major societal forces such as the demand for greater educational opportunity and lifelong learning, and rapidly evolving technological advances are changing the nature of distance learning. As a result, distance learning is becoming more decentralized and more student-centered, and is routinely being offered in conjunction with traditional academic programs. In the United States, the majority of post-secondary schools will be offering some form of distance learning by the early part of the twenty-first century. The segmenting or separation of traditional education, distance education, and perhaps virtual education, as Keegan suggests, does not reflect the reality of the emerging situation. It is quite possible that distance learning is, in fact, becoming more traditional while traditional learning is using techniques formally associated with distance. Virtual systems may be the vehicles whereby traditional learning and distance learning begin to merge and form a new paradigm for education. As an example, a faculty member who teaches several courses a semester may teach one section of a course in a traditional face-to-face form and another section in distance learning mode using the Internet and World Wide Web software. The content is the same, but the instructor makes adjustments depending on the delivery mechanisms. Students in both sections may access the same Web pages for the syllabus, readings, and other assignments. Students in both sections may contact the faculty member via e-mail to seek advice or to clarify some aspect of a lesson. With the exception of delivery, these students are learning the same content and are using many of the same tools. In Chapter 3, references were made to Richard Clark's position that the medium is not the message and that the substance or content is most important in learning. Separate theories of distance learning will continue to evolve and may be appropriate for the highly centralized, dedicated distance learning institutions. However, the emerging model based on new virtual technologies supports Clark's premise and suggests that a separate theory for distance learning is not needed but that a new common theory that merges distance and traditional education should be considered and pursued.

THE INSTRUCTIONAL DEVELOPMENT MODEL

Instructional development occurs at many levels and in many shapes and variations. When teachers design a simple lesson plan with goals, objectives, activities, materials, and student assessments, they are engaging in instructional development. Instructional development for large distance learning projects, such as entire programs, is frequently a formal process involving specialists for content, media, and technology. For individual distance learning courses, a single faculty member may comprise the entire development team. Regardless of the scope of the project, some form of instructional development is required. However, a good rule of thumb is that the larger the project, the more formal the instructional development process should be.

FIGURE 4.1A
4D Model for Instructional
Development

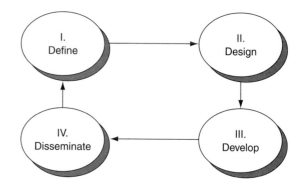

The literature on instructional development, especially when integrated with learning theory and cognitive development, is extensive. It is not the intent here to cover this literature. Some of this material will be presented in Chapter 5 in a section on adult learners and learning theory. Readers may also wish to review the work of Bloom (1956), Krathwohl, Bloom, and Masia (1964), Gagne (1977), Briggs (1977), or Kemp (1985) for in-depth presentations of this topic. Bloom, Krathwohl et al., and Gagne are well-known theorists who have developed taxonomies to classify and define the types of learning that frame discussions of the learning goals and objectives that result from instructional development. Gagne, Briggs, and Kemp have examined and developed *process* models for defining the necessary steps in instructional development. Generic to most of these process models is the 4D instructional development model (see Figure 4.1A) of Thiagarajan, Semmel, and Semmel (1974). The four major components or phases of the 4D model are define, design, develop, and disseminate. Several derivatives of the 4D model have evolved including the ADDIE (*a*nalysis, *d*esign, *d*evelopment, *i*mplementation, *e*valuation) model, which expands on the original four steps (see Figure 4.1B). All of these models essentially involve definition, design, development, and dissemination.

The definition phase is the preliminary analytical step in the process. Goals and objectives for the course or program are identified. Student characteristics such as academic preparedness are considered. A search for and evaluation of available materials is made. This last item is important to distance learning projects that involve media, especially graphics, audio, and video. Developing high-quality media can be an expensive proposition and if acceptable audio-visual materials already exist, they should be considered for adoption.

The design phase involves prototyping initial ideas and approaches. A prototype is a smaller or limited version of a full-blown product and is commonly used in many technology and media-based undertakings. An individual faculty member might start with one or two prototype lessons before instituting an entire course. For a larger distance learning project, a prototype for a single course may be developed before attempting the development of an entire academic program.

FIGURE 4.1B   ADDIE
Model for Instructional
Development

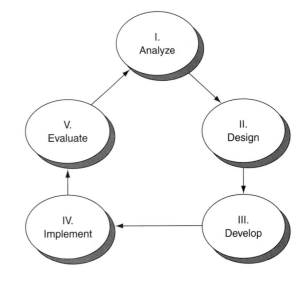

In the development phase, the prototype is tested or implemented in a limited or controlled environment. Feedback is actively sought from experts in content and instructional delivery, as well as from students. Adjustments and refinements to the prototype are made as needed. The testing of the prototype can be repeated several times until the designers believe they have collected enough feedback and information to proceed to the next phase.

Dissemination requires evaluating all previous phases, especially the information gathered during the development phase. Adjustments and refinements again can be made to the prototype before final packaging and full adoption and implementation. Once the prototype is adopted, it is no longer considered a prototype but a fully implemented instructional product, such as a learning module, course, or academic program. Instructional development is a continuous process. Information will continue to be collected, and adjustments and refinements to the adopted instructional product made as needed. Information gathered and decisions made during this phase serve as input into the design phase for a new instructional development cycle.

COMMUNICATIONS AND INTERACTIVITY IN DISTANCE LEARNING

Fundamental to all instruction is the ability to communicate and interact. In preparing a lesson, a teacher attempts to provide mechanisms and activities through which he or she communicates with students and shares ideas about a topic. If students do not understand some aspect of a lesson, they ask questions of the teacher and receive appropriate responses. In a traditional classroom, this model of instruction is well established and familiar to both teacher and students. Even in laboratory or studio classes where students are engaged in experiential activities designed to help them learn by handling and manipulating materials, the ability to ask a teacher a question and to receive feedback is critical to their success. In distance learning, communication and interaction are likewise fundamental to the design and development of appropriate instructional lessons and materials. Because a distance exists between teacher and student, though, the simple act of communicating cannot be taken for granted. Alternative forms for interaction must be considered and are critical to the successful design of instruction.

Synchronous versus Asynchronous Communication

In traditional classroom activities, communication between teacher and student, and student and student are generally synchronous, that is, they occur at the same time and place. The typical classroom discussion, lecture, laboratory experiment, or studio art class are all examples of synchronous activities. From pre-kindergarten through graduate school, teachers and students have traditionally engaged in this type of communication. A teacher leads the lesson by orally presenting some information or asking a question that students hear within the space of a classroom or lecture hall. Students generally assume that if they do not understand a comment made by the teacher or another student, they can raise a hand and ask a question close to the moment in which the comment was made. In short, the instructional activity is synchronized to take place in a specific place during a specific period of time. In distance learning, this same synchronization does not always exist. By definition, teachers and students are physically separated by distance. They do not occupy a common classroom or laboratory. A teacher may be five, ten, a hundred or a thousand miles away from students. Furthermore, depending on the technology being used, teacher and students may or may not be communicating with each other at the same time. A teacher may post a lesson or question to an electronic bulletin board on Sunday evening, and the students may not access that bulletin board until Monday, Tuesday, or later. Furthermore, students may access the bulletin board from work, from home, or from a library's media facility. In this situation, learning is asynchronous, that is, occurring in different places at different times.

In designing instructional material for distance learning, a fundamental consideration is determining which aspects of the communication and interaction are synchronous and which are asynchronous. A point-to-point distance learning class using interactive video allows for a great deal of synchronous activity. A teacher can ask a question and students at a local or distant site can respond within seconds. One major benefit of interactive video technology is that it enables teacher and student to interact synchronously and comparably to a traditional classroom environment.

On the other hand, a distance learning class using the Internet or other data communications network where instruction is conducted via e-mail, electronic bulletin board, and World Wide Web materials is generally asynchronous. Students may respond to questions days after they were originally posed by a teacher, and it may be hours or days before the teacher responds to a student's question or comment. This may lead to situations in which several students ask the same question because of a time delay in receiving or transmitting messages. This would rarely happen in a traditional classroom or in an interactive video environment. Generally, the more synchronous the communications, the more familiar both teacher and students are with the format of a class and, hence, the easier it is to design instruction based on traditional learning approaches. The converse is also true. The more communications are asynchronous, the less familiar teacher and students are with the class format and the more difficult it is to design instruction based on traditional learning approaches. The differences in synchronous versus asynchronous communication may also have important ramifications in terms of the quality and quantity of interaction, faculty time for course development, and student access to and knowledge of technology.

Types of Instructional Interaction

Instructional interactivity exists between and among the instructor, the learner, and the content (see Figure 4.2). Each of the possible interactions among these three entities is important for instructional design. In distance learning, each must be considered to achieve success in a course or program.

Most distance learning development begins with the instructor-to-student interaction. How does the instructor communicate with the student and vice versa? The interaction and communications technologies used by instructor and student may be the same or may be different. As an example, an asynchronous learning network using the Internet or other data communications network provides a common e-mail, electronic bulletin board, or World Wide Web software facility for both

FIGURE 4.2 Instructional Interaction

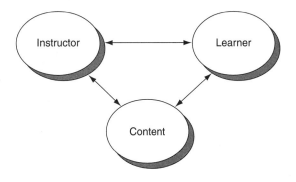

instructor and students in a distance learning course. The instructor sits at a microcomputer and most likely uses the same or similar software to communicate with students as the students use to communicate with the instructor. Here the communications comfort level curve is comparable for both instructor and student. On the other hand, in some delivery mechanisms the method of the interaction may be different for instructor and student. For example, distance learning using broadcast television or one-way video communication requires the instructor to become comfortable with camera angles, to look into the camera, and to use materials that can be clearly visible on a standard television monitor. Students, on the other hand, while comfortable in receiving or watching the broadcast, may be concerned about using telephone, e-mail, fax, or on-site tutors to ask their questions. Interaction between instructor and student must be designed from both perspectives when necessary.

In designing instruction for distance learning delivery, familiarity or comfort level on the part of instructors and students is important. Training activities and practice to increase comfort level may be beneficial. Instructional designers should not assume that instructors and students will learn best as they work and go along. Herbert Simon, computer scientist and Noble laureate in economics, tells a pertinent story. Simon visited China in 1972. It seems that his Chinese hosts, before engaging in any formal work or study activities, preferred social activities to acquaint themselves with their American colleagues. The Americans were anxious to get started on their collaborative activities. Simon explained to his hosts, "Americans are queer, hasty folk and . . . people become friends in America by working together" (Simon, 1991, p. 337). In distance learning, following the Chinese prescription of patience and familiarity is the more prudent and recommended approach.

Student to student interaction is another element of distance learning that is important and that depends on the technology used. In a traditional school environment, students interact pedagogically and socially. A comment or question from an individual student and the response provided by an instructor is an important component of the learning dynamic. Not only does the student learn who asked the question but so do all the other students who heard the question and response. While some designs for distance learning such as group e-mail and interactive video automatically allow all students to read or hear questions and responses from their peers, other designs such as one-to-one e-mail, telephone, or fax do not allow automatically for this. In these situations, a good design might require an instructor to summarize the most substantive student comments and questions and provide them to all students.

Students also learn from each other in social situations. Most instructors are not aware of the extent to which students exchange course-related information with each other in social situations outside the classroom. In a traditional environment, two students in the same class may meet by accident in the library, go to the cafeteria to have a snack, and talk about things they have in common, including the class. They share perspectives, opinions, and insights about what was discussed, and the learning process is continued and naturally extended beyond the class. In distance learning, this is less likely to happen, particularly when the technologies are designed to be delivered to individual homes such as broadcast television, asynchronous learning using Internet technology, or home-study guide material. The likelihood that students in the same distance learning class using these technologies will meet by chance is not very high. Again, good design might include activities or projects that allow or encourage students to interact with one another, since research has shown benefits of collaborative learning in both traditional and distance learning environments. With newer technologies such as e-mail, collaborative projects are possible even for students who live miles away from each other. A single, extended collaborative project might provide the incentive for students to not only interact about the project but also to share other interests, ideas, or information with one another.

Instructor and student interaction with content is another critical element of learning. In traditional environments, textbooks, notes written on chalk boards, diagrams shown by overhead projectors, works of art displayed through a slide projector, video clips, etc. comprise the instructional content for a class. The art of teaching requires an instructor to spend a good deal of time organizing, developing, and delivering this content. In distance learning, the instructor must do the same. However, the common delivery mechanisms used in traditional classrooms may not be available in distance learning. Instructor notes may have to be copied and distributed in advance to distance learning sites. Transparencies used with overhead projectors may have to be scanned into a computer. Slides may have to be converted into image files and made available at a World Wide Web site. Moreover, the instructor should not simply convert the existing materials used in traditional environments without considering how distance learning technologies can allow the materials to be used more effectively and efficiently. Depending on the technology used, distance learning content may be easier for students to use or to interact with than traditional classroom content. Instructor notes made available in advance reduces the drudgery of copying notes from a chalkboard. Images available on a computer network can be viewed over and over again by a student without necessarily having to go to a library, museum, or media center. Digital animation simulating experiments allow students to control variables or factors that might be difficult in a traditional laboratory. In fact, if the simulation involves materials that are inherently dangerous, it may be a more effective and safer way for students to interact with these materials.

For many years now, various types of programmed instruction have been used, particularly in large-scale distance learning institutions. Whether printed learning guides with "proceed to next page" markers or sophisticated computerized integrated learning systems (ILS) that combine hardware, software, and curriculum are used, design considerations from both the instructor and student perspectives are paramount to their success. An instructor should be easily able to customize the content, monitor student progress, or provide guidance for further study. Likewise, students should be able to understand instructions for proceeding without difficulty. Technology used in these situations should not be intrusive but should be as seamless as possible. With some training, the technology should provide an instructional process that flows effortlessly for both instructor and student. When too many questions are being asked by students or instructors about the technology and not the content, distance learning designers should review and perhaps revise the interactive components of the process.

APPLYING INSTRUCTIONAL DEVELOPMENT TO DISTANCE LEARNING

In this section, some of the instructional development suggestions made earlier in this chapter are applied to distance learning materials. Figures 4.3A, 4.3B, and 4.3C are examples of distance learning materials appropriate for three different delivery systems: the printed study guide, the interactive video conference, and asynchronous learning using the Internet and World Wide Web. All three use the same general content that encompasses the U.S. Supreme Court's landmark decision, Brown v. Board of Education of Topeka, Kansas (1954), its aftermath, and its relevance to modern American society. This content is commonly used in American history, sociology, political science, cultural studies, education, and constitutional law courses at the secondary and post-secondary education levels. Each example concludes with the same written assignment. However, while the content and student assignment are the same, the materials and presentations have been customized to suit the benefits and limitations of the technology used.

The Printed Study Guide

Figure 4.3A provides a sample lesson from a printed study guide that could be used for a learning module on the Brown decision. In the interests of space, the material presented here is abridged but should serve to give the reader a sense of the nature of printed study guides. Assume that this printed study guide is used by students individually and not as part of a group learning activity. The design of printed study guides is a skill that develops through experience and repetition. Derek Rowntree (1996), a professor of educational development at the Open University in Great Britain, has an excellent guide for preparing such materials that is highly recommended for further study. He covers extensively the organization of such guides, their writing style, graphics, fonts, etc. His fundamental precept is that the guide should meet the needs of the intended student body. Student reading levels and comprehension are critical factors in the development of a good study guide.

By its nature, the printed study guide relies on text to communicate the content to the student. These guides are organized in paragraph form but make extensive use of enumerations, bullets, or different font sizes and styles to highlight important comments. The writing style is succinct and to the point. Paragraphs tend to be shorter than in textbooks and other text-based instructional material.

FIGURE 4.3A Excerpt of a Sample Lesson from a Printed Study Guide

This excerpt is part of a larger instructional unit on the United States Supreme Court's Brown v. Board of Education Decision in 1954.

Lesson Objectives:

1. To study the checks and balances system in the American governmental system.
2. To analyze how a democracy responds to crisis.
3. To explain events before and after the Brown v. Board of Education Decision.

Key Questions:

1. Why is the Brown v. Board of Education Decision regarded as one of the most significant decisions of the U.S. Supreme Court in the 20th century?
2. What was the reaction to the Brown decision on the part of various segments of American society?
3. What has been the effect of the Brown decision on American society in general?

Synopsis of the Case:

In the early 1950s, de jure (by law) segregation in public schools was well-established in seventeen states and Washington, D.C.

In Topeka, Kansas, a black third-grader named Linda Brown had to walk one mile through a railroad switch yard to get to her black elementary school, even though a white elementary school was only seven blocks away. Linda's father, Oliver Brown, tried to enroll her in the white elementary school, but the principal of the school refused. Brown went to McKinley Burnett, the head of Topeka's branch of the National Association for the Advancement of Colored People (NAACP) and asked for help. Other black parents joined Brown, and, in 1951, the NAACP requested an injunction that would forbid the segregation of Topeka's public schools. The U.S. District Court for the District of Kansas heard Brown's case from June 25-26, 1951. At the trial, the NAACP argued that segregated schools sent the message to black children that they were inferior to whites; therefore, the schools were inherently unequal. . . .

The Board of Education's defense was that, because segregation in Topeka and elsewhere pervaded many other aspects of life, segregated schools simply prepared black children for the segregation they would face during adulthood. The board also argued that segregated schools were not necessarily harmful to black children; great African Americans such as Frederick Douglass, Booker T. Washington, and George Washington Carver had overcome segregated schools to achieve what they achieved.

The request for an injunction put the court in a difficult decision. On the one hand, the judges agreed with the expert witnesses; in their decision, they wrote: "Segregation of white and colored children in public schools has a detrimental effect upon the colored children. . . . A sense of inferiority affects the motivation of a child to learn."

On the other hand, the precedent of Plessy v. Ferguson (1896) allowed for "separate but equal" public facilities including school systems for blacks and whites, and no Supreme Court ruling had overturned Plessy yet. Because of the precedent of Plessy, the court felt "compelled" to rule in favor of the Board of Education.

Brown and the NAACP appealed to the Supreme Court on October 1, 1951 and their case was combined with other cases that challenged school segregation in South Carolina, Virginia, Delaware, and the District of Columbia. The Supreme Court first heard the case on December 9, 1952, but failed to reach a decision. In the reargument, heard from December 7-8, 1953, the Court requested that both sides discuss "the circumstances surrounding the adoption of the Fourteenth Amendment in 1868."

(continued)

On May 17, 1954, Chief Justice Earl Warren read the decision of the unanimous Court: (Brown I) "We come then to the question presented: Does segregation of children in public schools solely on the basis of race, even though the physical facilities and other "tangible" factors may be equal, deprive the children of the minority group of equal educational opportunities? We believe that it does. . . . We conclude that in the field of public education the doctrine of 'separate but equal' has no place. Separate educational facilities are inherently unequal. Therefore, we hold that the plaintiffs and others similarly situated for whom the actions have been brought are, by reason of the segregation complained of, deprived of the equal protection of the laws guaranteed by the Fourteenth Amendment."

With this decision, the Supreme Court struck down the "separate but equal" doctrine of Plessy and ruled in favor of the plaintiffs. One year later, the Supreme Court issued its implementation decree ordering all segregated school systems to desegregate (Brown II).

Major Personalities:

Oliver Brown - father of Linda Brown. . . .
Thurgood Marshall - lead attorney for the case for the NAACP Legal Defense Fund. . . .
John W. Davis - lead attorney for the defense. . . .
Kenneth Clark - social scientist and expert witness in the case. . . .
Charles Houston - dean of Howard University's Law School. . . .
Earl Warren - Chief Justice of the U.S. Supreme Court. . . .

Aftermath of the Brown Decision:

Integration of Central High School in Little Rock, Arkansas (1950s). . . .
School Decentralization and Community Power in New York City (1960s). . . .
Busing as a Remedy for Segregated Schools in Boston (1970s). . . .

Legacy of the Brown Decision:

Provided the Legal Foundation for the American Civil Rights Movement. . . .
Catalyst for Federal Legislative Initiatives and Entitlement Programs. . . .
Established the Legal Precedence for other Groups on Constitutional Issues of Equality. . . .

Reading Assignments:

Carter, R.L. (1995). The unending struggle for equal educational opportunity. *Teachers College Record, 96*(4), pp. 619–626.
Kluger, Richard (1976). *Simple Justice: The History of Brown v. Board of Education and Black America's Struggle for Equality.* New York: Alfred A. Knopf (Selected Chapters).
Miller, L.P. (1995). Tracking the progress of Brown. *Teachers College Record, 96*(4), pp. 609–613.

Writing Assignment:

In 1994, writers for *The Nation* conducted interviews with a number of activists and scholars on the relevance of the decision to America in the 1990s. Ben Chavis, civil rights activist and former head of the NAACP, and Jack Greenberg, an attorney who assisted Thurgood Marshall in preparing the case in 1954, and presently a professor at Columbia University's School of Law, gave the following responses to the question, "Does Brown Still Matter?"

FIGURE 4.3A *(concluded)*

"In many cases access to schools has been achieved while access to knowledge has not. African-Americans and Latinos are disproportionately isolated in underfunded school systems and substandard schools. Wealthier school systems provide their mostly white students with experienced teachers, modern technology, better facilities and lower student/teacher ratios."—Ben Chavis, May 23, 1994

"There is now a large black middle class and substantial black political power (forty members of Congress, many mayors) as a result of a civil rights revolution, of which Brown was one of the main progenitors. This political and economic power is a direct consequence of Brown's perceptions and requirements."—Jack Greenberg, May 23, 1994

After studying the Brown v. Board of Education Decision, do you tend to agree more with Chavis or Greenberg? Prepare a brief (1200 words) paper explaining your position and cite examples either from your personal experiences or publicized current events to support it.

If you have any questions, do not hesitate to contact your instructor.

Each guide, lesson, or lesson component has a beginning, middle, and end. The beginning usually identifies the learning objectives and key questions to be explored. The middle presents the material in text form but, where appropriate, illustrations and pictures are added to provide visual clues for the learner. Increasingly, video materials are being developed and provided along with the printed guide. The end of the lesson directs the student to further study or formal assignments. Self evaluation, if being used, should be both formative and summative, and should provide the learner with enough feedback to determine if he or she can proceed to the next section or should review the current lesson again.

In the sample in Figure 4.3A, objectives and key questions are clearly stated at the beginning of the lesson. A synopsis of the case (in abridged form here) along with other pertinent elements (Major Personalities, Aftermath, Legacy) of the lesson follow. The example concludes with both reading and writing assignments and encouragement to contact "your instructor" should you have any questions.

The Interactive Video Conference

Figure 4.3B provides an excerpt of a script for a three-hour interactive video conference in which an instructor will teach to both a local and distant student audience. Scripting is highly recommended in developing any type of conference, whether audio, video, one-way, two-way, or multipoint. The conference should be carefully organized, to the extent possible, according to a time schedule, so that the parties at all sites have a clear understanding of the sequence of a lesson's activities. In addition to helping an instructor organize his or her lesson, the script is used extensively by site facilitators to prepare for and assist in the delivery of

FIGURE 4.3B Excerpt of a Script for a Two-way Interactive Video Conference

This excerpt is part of a script of a lesson on the United States Supreme Court's Brown v. Board of Education Decision in 1954.

1:00 p.m. - Prepare audio-visual setup for today's session.
Test interactive video connection for audio and video quality.
Test instructor and student microphones.
Discuss with teaching assistants at the remote and local sites that they have received back-up material and understand lesson and procedures for today.

1:30 p.m. - Interactive video session starts.
Welcome the students at both sites and verify that they can see and hear you.
Take attendance.

1:40 p.m. - Begin the lesson.
Orally present the synopsis of the U.S. Supreme Court's Brown v. Board of Education Decision from prepared notes.*

2:00 p.m. - Ask for questions from each of the sites.

2:10 p.m. - Orally present background of major personalities involved with the Decision from prepared notes.*

2:30 p.m. - Ask for questions from each of the sites.

2:40 p.m. - Break

2:50 p.m. - Welcome the students back.
Provide a brief summary of the material/discussion during the first half of this session.

3:00 p.m. - Show a series of video clips from the award-winning documentary *Eyes on the Prize* from videodisc player. These clips will include the following:
Additional background on the Brown Decision;
Footage of the integration of Central High School in Little Rock, Arkansas in the 1950s;
Footage of the school decentralization movement in New York City in the 1960s;
Footage of the school busing issue in Boston in the 1970s.

3:40 p.m. - Highlight pertinent comments/scenes made in the video clips.

4:00 p.m. - Ask for questions from each of the sites.

4:15 p.m. - Distribute/announce/refer students to the reading and writing assignments.*

4:20 p.m. - Ask if there are any questions with the assignment.

4:30 p.m. - Interactive video session ends.

*Note: Prepared notes, reading and writing assignments are the same as those used in Figure 4.3A

the conference. For the oral delivery in an interactive video conference, an instructor can adapt much of his or her own traditional teaching style into the lesson. However, encouraging questions from students, particularly at the remote site(s), is critical. A major advantage of interactive videoconferencing is its inherent interactivity, and instructors should plan their lessons accordingly. Study and observation of video conferences indicate that students at the local sites frequently are able to read the body language and energy of an instructor better than those at the remote sites, especially at the beginning of a course. It is not unusual to see students at a local site asking more questions than the students at a remote site. A good script will identify specific periods for questions from all sites. Instructors should also be comfortable with camera angles and positioning and, to the extent possible, be looking into the camera. Some of this depends on the layout of the transmitting facility, which will be discussed in more detail in Chapter 7. Another advantage of interactive video conferencing facilities is the ability to use media such as videotape, videodisc, slides, document cameras, etc. in instruction. Where appropriate, instructors are encouraged to use media to enhance their basic oral delivery.

The script excerpted in Figure 4.3B starts with a testing of all technology, especially audio and video connections. Site facilitators or teaching assistants should be familiar with the session's activities. A back-up plan is highly recommended in case a connection is lost or some other technical difficulty occurs. The session starts promptly at 1:30 P.M. with a welcome, another brief test of audio and video quality, and taking attendance. The instructor proceeds to introduce the topic orally, much as he or she would in a traditional class. The script allocates frequent and specific times for questions to ensure that the students at the remote site(s) are encouraged and have the opportunity to ask questions. In a video conference of two or more hours, at least one break is recommended. The example script also makes use of videodisc material to illustrate and support the oral presentation. PBS markets the highly acclaimed *Eyes on the Prize* documentary series of the Civil Rights Movement in the United States in both videotape and videodisc formats. In this situation, where several video clips are being used, videodisc with its rapid direct accessing capability is the recommended choice. Distributing prepared notes on the topic is generally the prerogative of the instructor. Some instructors in traditional classes make their notes available, others do not. The same is true in distance learning lessons. Minimally, it is assumed that teaching assistants and site facilitators have received a copy of the instructor's notes. For this script, assume that the notes are similar to those in the printed study guide, which are presented in abridged form in Figure 4.3A. The lesson also concludes with the same reading and writing assignments that were required in the printed study guide. The reading assignments are generally provided as part of the entire schedule of assignments in the course syllabus. While it may be helpful to students to have writing assignments scheduled in advance, some instructors prefer to distribute writing assignments as needed.

Asynchronous Learning Using the Internet and World Wide Web

Figure 4.3C provides the outline for an asynchronous learning class using the Internet and World Wide Web. Instructional activities described in this outline rely on Internet-based facilities such as e-mail, Web pages, and electronic bulletin boards. Students participate from their homes, places of business, or wherever they have access to the Internet and at times, within given parameters, that are convenient for them.

In this example, the course is organized according to weekly discussion topics. The discussion commences on Sunday evening on an electronic bulletin board and formally concludes on Saturday morning. Additional material is also provided at a class Web site. Several students are selected each week to serve as facilitators of instruction and are reminded on Friday of this assignment via e-mail. Student facilitators are expected to be especially active in making comments, in responding to questions, and in moving the discussion along for the week. In asynchronous learning, open-ended questions are very effective in allowing students to express themselves and are highly recommended. In the example outline, each scheduled posting by the instructor concludes with an open-ended question. In addition to the bulletin board, students are encouraged to contact the instructor directly via individual e-mail if need be throughout the session. In the absence of face-to-face contact, positive feedback and reinforcement techniques such as frequent compliments or references to students are desirable. In this particular outline, the discussion continues for a week and ends with the instructor providing a summary of the week's discussion and posting his or her notes on the class's Web site. At the Web site, students can also find the reading and writing assignments for the class. In this example, the reading assignment includes material provided on the Web at another site from a symposium that was held on the Brown v. Board of Education decision. Where possible, using information resources of the Web is highly recommended for asynchronous, Internet-based learning. Students in these classes are familiar with the Web and generally can access Web-based materials. Unfortunately, depending upon the topic and content, quality reading and other instructional materials are not always available on-line. While the book and journal publishers are moving toward providing access to some of their materials on the Web, too frequently user fees are required that may be prohibitive for students. An instructor might be tempted to scan in an excerpt from a particularly useful article and post it at a Web site. However, this might involve serious copyright issues, which will be discussed in more detail in Chapter 6. The writing assignment is the same as in the previous examples and can be submitted by fax, e-mail, or regular mail depending on the preferences of the instructor.

In reviewing the three examples, readers should compare the benefits and limitations of each of the distance learning methods used. While all three examples provide for routine communication and interaction between the instructor and student, the same cannot be said for student-to-student interaction. In the printed

FIGURE 4.3C Excerpt of an Outline for an Asynchronous Learning Class

This excerpt is part of an outline for an asynchronous learning session on the United States Supreme Court's Brown v. Board of Education Decision in 1954.

(This class is conducted entirely in asynchronous mode over the Internet. Students access all material remotely via e-mail and the World Wide Web from their homes or in their places of business. Each session lasts one week beginning on Sunday evening and ending on Saturday morning.)

Friday - Remind student facilitators via e-mail for the coming week's discussion that they should have read all the material and are familiar with key questions.*

Sunday - Initiate week's discussion on the class electronic bulletin board by introducing the topic and concluding with the following open-ended question:
"Why is the Brown v. Board of Education Decision regarded as one of the most significant decisions of the U.S. Supreme Court in the 20th century?"
Refer students to a synopsis and major personalities of the case that is available at the class Website.
Remind students that if they have any questions, feel free to e-mail the instructor at any time.

Monday - Monitor student comments and questions on the electronic bulletin board and individual e-mail.

Tuesday - Compliment students who made exceptionally good postings to the electronic bulletin board over the past forty-eight hours.
Review the wording of the Brown Decision (Brown I) and the implementation decree (Brown II).
Conclude with open-ended question:
"What did the Brown Decision mean to those states that had established de jure segregated school systems? How did these states attempt to implement the Brown Decision?"
Remind students that if they have any questions, feel free to e-mail the instructor at any time.

Wednesday - Monitor student comments and questions on the electronic bulletin board and individual e-mail.

Thursday - Compliment and refer to students who made exceptionally good postings to the electronic bulletin board over the past forty-eight hours.
Briefly review the discussion for the week.
Emphasize that the Brown Decision did not just affect the states that had established de jure segregated school systems but that it ended up affecting the entire country. Provide examples in New York City in the 1960s and Boston in the 1970s.
Conclude with an open-ended question:
"What has been the effect of the Brown Decision on American society in general?"
Remind students that if they have any questions, feel free to e-mail the instructor at any time.

Friday - Monitor student comments and questions on the electronic bulletin board and individual e-mail.

Saturday - Compliment and refer to students who made exceptionally good postings to the electronic bulletin board during the past week.
Indicate that a summary of this week's discussion and further information from the instructor's notes** will be available at the class's Website by 4:00 p.m. this (Saturday) evening.
Refer students to class Website to a written assignment.**
Thank student facilitators for their contribution to this week's discussion.
Wish everybody a Happy Weekend!

*Note: Reading assignment includes material available at a Website maintained by Woodstock Technological Center at Georgetown University that held a symposium in 1994 commemorating the 40th Anniversary of the Brown Decision.

**Note: Instructor notes and written assignment are the same as in Figure 4.3A.

study guide example, student to student interaction would be rare. The use of high-quality media, such as a video documentary, is highly desirable in all learning, distance or otherwise, but may not be possible or cost-effective depending on the technology used. In the three examples, video was only provided in the interactive video conference. In terms of student convenience in taking classes, the printed study guide and asynchronous learning are better suited for students who want to learn at their own pace or according to their daily schedules. Other comparisons such as cost for facilities; need for student preparedness, especially in terms of reading and writing ability; and student access to technology are also important and will be discussed in later chapters.

APPROPRIATENESS OF DISTANCE LEARNING FOR ALL SUBJECT AREAS/DISCIPLINES

Distance learning has been used to deliver instruction in just about all subject areas and disciplines. The open university or virtual college model are testaments to the fact that almost any subject area can be delivered via distance learning. However, in terms of instructional development and design, some subject areas pose specific practical or pedagogical problems that need to be considered.

Sener (1997) describes the development of mathematics, science, and engineering programs for home-based learners using asynchronous learning techniques at North Virginia Community College (NVCC). The distance learning program at NVCC was established in 1975 and has served the needs of more than 130,000 students since its inception. NVCC offers approximately ninety college courses per year in a wide variety of subject areas. In designing courses for distance learning in chemistry and physics, the decision was made to require students to come to the campus to do their laboratory work under supervision and in collaboration with fellow students (Sener, 1997, p. 30). The reasons for this decision were varied but included the lack of access to laboratory equipment outside of the college; the issue of safety, particularly in using chemicals; and the desirability of working collaboratively with other students on laboratory projects. These considerations are valid for both practical and pedagogical reasons.

The NVCC example is provided because, while distance learning has expanded into almost every subject area, experienced designers are finding that not necessarily every course can easily be adapted to a distance learning mode. Laboratory courses requiring expensive equipment or chemicals; studio courses in art, music, dance, and drama; or mathematics and statistics courses requiring access to expensive software or simulation packages are examples of subject areas that can pose specific problems when delivered over a distance. While creative distance learning designers provide alternative distance learning activities, others have decided that the compromise of the pedagogical experience is too great and have required students to return to the campus for on-site work. In a place such as NVCC, where the distance learning students live in close proximity to the campus, requiring them to return to campus for selective on-site activity is desirable and a good instructional design. This would not be possible if students lived hundreds or thousands of miles away. Where students are geographically dispersed, distance learning designers are using videos or computer simulations especially for laboratory activities, or making arrangements with local facilities as substitutes to provide appropriate instructional experiences. Good instructional design requires that the best possible pedagogical experiences be provided for students. Distance learning, particularly when delivered over a wide geographical area, can pose serious practical and pedagogical problems in some subject areas that test the creativity and abilities of instructional designers.

TESTS, STUDENT ASSIGNMENTS, AND GRADES

Tests, student assignments, and grades are important aspects of instructional design. Instructors use a wide variety of student evaluation methods including-multiple-choice tests, written essays, take-home examinations, term papers, and oral reports. In distance learning, any of these methods can be used. However, depending on the technology and instructional delivery systems, some forms of student evaluation are easier to administer than others. Students using a printed study guide at home can easily take a short-answer examination, but the instructor cannot know for sure who actually answered the questions. Students in an Internet-based asynchronous course likewise can take an on-line examination that is short answer or essay, but again the instructor cannot be sure who completed the questions.

In distance learning, student evaluation should be addressed as part of the instructional development process. The following broad principles should be considered. First, since students frequently do not have the same contact with an instructor as they do in traditional class environments, special attention should be given to developing formative as well summative evaluation activities. Formative evaluation is defined simply as enabling or assisting students to learn from the evaluation activity, while summative evaluation basically assesses whether students have mastered the content or skill. The essence of self-paced instruction, which is a fundamental aspect of many distance learning programs, requires students to know that they have mastered the content before moving on to the next module or lesson. However, if they are having difficulty, they need to know what material to review or reread in order to master the content. Good distance learning design will provide for self-administered tests that can direct the student to additional targeted material.

Second, students should know what is expected of them in terms of evaluation and grades. A summary of the evaluation activities and grading criteria should be provided early on as part of a course outline or syllabus. This allows distance learners to plan their schedules accordingly. Adult learners, in particular, appreciate knowing in advance what the evaluation criteria will be and when the evaluation will be administered.

Third, instructors should not compromise their methods of evaluation if they truly believe that they are an important aspect of the pedagogical experience. However, certain evaluation activities may be more difficult to administer or conduct in a distance learning environment, so instructors need to be flexible and creative enough to adjust accordingly. If the technology is not adaptable enough, then evaluation may need to be conducted in more traditional settings.

The U.S. Department of Education's National Center for Education Statistics (1997) conducted a survey of post-secondary institutions offering distance learning programs. In response to a question about how tests were administered, two-thirds of the respondents indicated that tests were almost always administered in a traditional group setting either at a remote or local site. Only 15 percent indicated that they used individual testing mailed or faxed to students. Eight percent indicated that tests were administered interactively via computer, video, or telephone. This suggests that while distance learning providers use various innovative technologies to deliver instruction, when it comes to testing and evaluation, these same providers tend to rely on traditional evaluation methods. Regardless, instructional designers are still encouraged to be creative in designing student assessment activities. This is especially true for distance learning programs enrolling large numbers of adult students.

Beyond standard testing, a wide variety of alternative assessment strategies should be considered. Student projects including writing essays and reports, creating media projects, developing portfolios of activities, or solving mathematical and engineering problems can be completed over time and with open access to reference materials. These are appreciated by older students and generally work well in a self-paced distance learning environment. Distance learning programs directed to employed adults and professionals can easily incorporate alternative assessment activities geared to workplace skill development or analytical problem solving. Open-ended questions, case study analyses, and problem-solving exercises are very popular in the workplace and can likewise be effective in a distance learning environment. The development of semester or year-long portfolios of accomplishments, papers written, participation in relevant activities, etc. are also gaining in popularity, especially in programs designed to upgrade skills or to help advance students professionally.

Collaborative assessment projects and activities may also be appropriate for distance learning programs in which students easily maintain contact with other students, such as those based on Internet and World Wide Web technologies (i.e., e-mail, electronic bulletin boards). Pairs or groups of students can work together on writing assignments, media projects, or problem-solving tasks. A major benefit of collaborative activities is that a good deal of informal learning can occur as students share and explore ideas. The Internet and World Wide Web also allows students to share more easily their finished projects with other students in a class. For example, by having students develop Web pages of their finished projects (i.e., papers, media projects, solutions to problems), all students can learn from each others' work thus adding instructional value to the entire assessment activity. Lipham (1991) and Anderson (1996) described these types of Internet-based collaborative activities as electronic "communities of inquiry" that enhance individual learning as a result of participation and interaction with others. Anderson further concluded that these communities are ideally suited for working professionals separated by geographic and temporal distance.

DESIGNING INSTRUCTION FOR STUDENTS

Distance learning has evolved and will continue to grow in response to student needs and requirements. As discussed in Chapter 2, the original goals and objectives of the vast majority of distance learning providers were student oriented. Likewise, in the continued development and instructional design for distance learning, student goals and objectives should be of primary concern. In the next chapter, the student perspective will be examined in depth.

SUMMARY

This chapter examines issues related to instructional development underlying the delivery of distance learning courses and programs. While a good deal has been written on pedagogical theories of distance learning, an all-encompassing theory is elusive. Furthermore, given the rapid advances in digital technologies and computer networking, many existing theories may no longer be appropriate.

The 4D instructional development model (see Thiagarajan, Semmel, and Semmel (1974)) is recommended for developing distance learning courses. The four major components or phases of the 4D model are define, design, develop, and disseminate. Throughout the instructional development process, student needs and characteristics are emphasized as essential.

Communication and interaction are vital to learning, distance or otherwise. The chapter presents several important issues related to communication and interaction in a distance learning environment. Synchronous versus asynchronous communications as well as interaction among teacher, student, and content are discussed. This discussion includes an analysis and comparison of the development of distance learning materials for three different delivery systems: the print study guide, the interactive video conference, and Internet-based asynchronous learning.

The chapter concludes with a discussion of other issues related to instructional development, including the appropriateness of distance learning for all subject areas, testing and student evaluation, and student needs.

CASE STUDY

Lowen State College Year: 1999

Setting

Lowen State College was established in 1931 as an agricultural and technical college. In 1965, Lowen's mission expanded and it now enrolls approximately 8,000 students in a variety of undergraduate and graduate programs. Lowen has established a good reputation in its community and region and prides itself on having established a number of outreach programs designed to bring the college to the people. In 1996, a Center for Distance Learning was established at Lowen. The center makes extensive use of a statewide fiber optic network that is capable of delivering broadband analog and digital signals to a number of institutions throughout the state. The center has been especially successful in providing interactive video courses to four rural high schools that are situated approximately seventy-five miles from the college. These courses are regular college courses taught by college faculty for which students in the high schools can receive advanced placement. In addition, the state reimburses the college for offering these courses, which helps support the center.

The Issue

A new Director, John Ward, was recently hired for the Center for Distance Learning. Among his initial objectives is the expansion of the center's programs and course offerings. Since the center opened in 1996, the same courses have been offered by the same cadre of "pioneering" faculty. While history, foreign language, literature, and social science courses are regularly offered, the high school principals have made repeated requests for more courses in sciences and mathematics. Discussions have taken place with the chairpersons from the science and mathematics departments. While many of the faculty in these departments are very positive about using distance learning technology, they do not feel that laboratory-based courses are conducive to delivery via interactive video. They also mentioned that the high schools do not have properly equipped laboratories, and it would be impossible to offer these courses without the high school students coming to the college.

Assume you are Mr. Ward. Do you have any suggestions for the chairpersons of the science and mathematics departments to resolve these issues? What additional information do you need from the high schools, from within the College, or from other sources?

REFERENCES

Anderson, T.D. (1996). The virtual conference: Extending professional education in cyberspace. *International Journal of Educational Telecommunications, 2*(2/3), 121–135.

Bloom, B.S. (1956). *Taxonomy of educational objectives handbook: Cognitive domains.* New York: David McKay.

Briggs, L. (1977). *Instructional design principles and practice.* Englewood Cliffs, NJ: Educational Technology Publications.

Gagne, R.M. (1977). *Conditions of learning.* New York: Holt, Rinehart, & Winston.

Hawking, S. (1988). *A brief history of time.* Toronto: Bantam Books.

Holmberg, B. (1989). *Theory and practice of distance education.* London: Routledge.

Keegan, D. (1993). *Theoretical principles of distance education.* London: Routledge.

Keegan, D. (1996). *Foundations of distance education* (3rd ed.). London: Routledge.

Kemp, J. (1985). *The instructional design process.* New York: Harper & Row.

Krathwohl, D.R., Bloom, B.S., & Masia, B.B. (1964). *Taxonomy of educational objectives: Handbook II: Affective domain.* New York: David McKay Company.

Lipham, M. (1991). *Thinking in education.* Cambridge: Cambridge University Press.

Moore, M. (1972). Learner autonomy: The second dimension of independent learning. *Convergence, 5*(2), 76–78.

Moore, M. (1994). Autonomy and interdependence. *The American Journal of Distance Education, 8*(2), 1–5.

Peters, O. (1988). Distance teaching and industrial production: A comparative interpretation in outline. In D. Sewart, D. Keegan, & B. Holmberg (Eds.). *Distance education: International perspectives* (pp. 95–113). New York: Routledge.

Rowntree, D. (1996). *Preparing materials for open, distance, and flexible learning.* London: Kogan Page Limited.

Sener, J. (1997). Creating asynchronous learning networks in mathematics, science, and engineering courses for home-based learners. *International Journal of Educational Telecommunications, 3*(1) 23–40.

Shale, D. (1988). Toward a reconceptualization of distance education. *The American Journal of Distance Education, 2*(3), 25–35.

Simon, H. (1991). *Models of my life.* New York: Basic Books, Inc.

Thiagarajan, S., Semmel, D., & Semmel, M. (1974). *Instructional development for training teachers of exceptional children: A sourcebook.* Reston, VA: Council for Exceptional Children.

U.S. Department of Education, National Center for Education Statistics (1997). *Distance education in higher education institutions.* Washington, D.C. (NCES 97-062).

Wedemeyer, C. (1977). Independent study. In A.S. Knowles (Ed.), *The international encyclopedia of higher education* (pp. 2114–2132). Boston: CIHED.

CHAPTER FIVE

The Student Perspective

Vivian Gornick (1998), an essayist, in a piece for *The New York Times*, described the genesis of her love for books and reading. As an eight year old growing up in the 1940s, her mother took her to the local library. There, she developed a relationship with a librarian that at "a solemn moment" translated into an understanding between them that "the book is everything" and the gateway to knowledge. She then proceeded "to read my way" around the children's section. As she grew older, went to college, and developed her career as a writer, reading and books continued to be everything for her. Ms. Gornick still goes to the library and, while many changes have occurred, she continues to observe children being introduced to the world and its informational treasures through books and reading.

Don Tapscott (1998), in observing young people in the 1980s and 1990s, sees a different picture. Without de-emphasizing the importance of reading, Tapscott observes children not only using books but increasingly using media such as the Internet and CD-ROMs to access information. These media require the user to read but also to inquire, to navigate, and to interact. Indeed, a young person today is quite likely to experience his or her "solemn moment" in front of a computer monitor.

For centuries, the book and printed page were without a doubt the most important media for sharing knowledge and for learning. Not until the twentieth century, as computer databases and on-line services became the major depositories of information, did this begin to change. Today, as we enter the twenty-first century, students are not only comfortable with the new media but are influencing educators to incorporate it into teaching and learning. The implications are significant for education in general but especially for the future development and advancement of distance learning.

The purpose of this chapter is to examine the student perspective in planning and developing distance learning applications. As discussed in Chapter 2, the goals and objectives of the vast majority of distance learning providers were student oriented. Likewise, in the design and development of distance learning, a student perspective should be of primary concern.

LEARNERS AT A DISTANCE—WHO ARE THEY?

A fundamental step in designing any academic program is determining who the students will be. When academic programs are designed, the basic characteristics of students, including their age, interests, skill levels, academic preparedness, and career goals are considered. With respect to distance learning, these same characteristics must be considered.

Much of the literature suggests that older students and adults are the primary targets and enrollees in distance learning programs. As an example, distance learning institutions around the world that have adopted the British Open University model were established essentially for adult populations. Keegan (1996) reports that the average distance learning student in the Open University of the United Kingdom is thirty to fifty-five years of age with a "diverse accumulation of experiences."

In the United States, typical adult distance learning students are between the ages of twenty-five and fifty. Two-thirds of them are female, and most are married and work full-time. Data collected by the National Center for Education Statistics (1997) shows that more than 90 percent of the distance learning programs are directed to adults in undergraduate, graduate, and continuing education programs. The Center further reports that most distance learning programs are targeted to

TABLE 5.1 Percent of higher education institutions currently offering distance learning courses targeted toward certain types of individuals.

Type of Individual	Percentage
Workers seeking skill updating or retraining	49%
Professionals seeking recertification	39%
Individuals with disabilities	16%
Military personnel	12%
Native Americans/Alaskan Natives	7%
Non-English speaking individuals	3%
Other types of individuals	17%

SOURCE: U.S. Department of Education, National Center for Education Statistics, Postsecondary Education Quick Information System, Survey on Distance Education Courses Offered by Higher Education Institutions, 1995. Sample based on mailing to 1,274 postsecondary institutions in the United States, the District of Columbia, and Puerto Rico with 1,203 returns (94% response rate).

certain types of individuals (see Table 5.1) and specifically to professionals seeking recertification and workers seeking skill updating or retraining.

In recent years, however, a growing number of distance learning programs are being directed to primary and secondary school students. Large-scale literacy programs in developing countries with geographically remote or dispersed populations have been established for younger students as well as for adults. In the United States, rural school districts unable to offer courses to fulfill graduation requirements to small student populations are relying on distance learning programs offered by other districts, colleges, or statewide consortia. In addition, major distance learning programs, such as the United States Department of Education's *Star Schools* created in 1988, have been established for primary and secondary school populations. More than 1.6 million students (see Figure 5.1) annually enroll in Star Schools, although it should be mentioned that in many cases, Star School programs enhance and do not necessarily replace existing traditional classroom instruction.

While working adults interested in developing or improving their professional and work skills continue to represent the major student population enrolled in distance learning programs, the number of other individuals including primary and secondary students is growing.

ADULT LEARNERS AND LEARNING THEORY

In Chapter 1, Malcolm Knowles' work on adult education was mentioned. Malcolm Knowles (1978), in referring to adult learning or andragogy, posited that adults learned differently than children and that programs directed to them have

FIGURE 5.1 Star Schools

SOURCE: U.S. Department of Education (http://star.ucc.nau.edu/starschools/StarSchl.html)

Star Schools

What is the Star Schools Program?

The Star Schools Program provides quality, cost-effective instruction through distance learning to more than 1.6 million learners annually in 50 states and U.S. territories. Although the program began with small rural schools in 1988, it is now equally valuable to schools in large urban areas.

Projects offer instructional modules, video field trips, enrichment activities, and semester-long and year-long courses. Through Star Schools, students can question astronauts about the principles of physics. Japanese- and German-language students can talk with native speakers and visit Japan and Germany through live and interactive teleconferences. For most students served, distance learning is their only access to science, math, foreign language, and advanced placement courses.

How do Star Schools projects work?

To deliver services, projects use many distance education technologies including the Internet, satellite delivery systems, open broadcasts, cable, fiber optics, microcomputers, digital compression, interactive videodiscs, facsimile machines, and the ordinary telephone.

What services are available from Star Schools projects?

Through Star Schools projects, schools have access to instructional programming, including hands-on science and mathematics, general mathematics, algebra, calculus, physics, advanced placement courses, and workplace skills. Foreign language offerings include Russian, Japanese, Swahili, Arabic, Spanish, and Mandarin Chinese. Instructional programs serve K–12 students, including limited English-proficient students and disabled students.

Who operates Star School projects?

The U.S. Department of Education awards grants to telecommunications partnerships to operate Star Schools projects. Partnerships include local school districts, state departments of education, public broadcasting entities, and other public and private organizations.

---

a different purpose. Adult learners, whether they seek an education they were not able to pursue earlier in their lives, wish to enhance their professional skills, or want to satisfy their curiosity about some subject, are different than children. Programs for adults should be designed for students who have already made decisions regarding careers and occupations, who are spouses and parents, and who live within an adult social context.

While adults do come to school for different reasons than children and have greater responsibilities, Knowles' theory should be considered in conjunction with other basic theories of learning that were formulated with a younger population in mind. Piaget, Bloom, Gagne, and Vygotsky are well-recognized theorists in the area of cognitive development. Piaget (1952), in addition to his contributions in the area of cognitive development in children, makes an important case for experiential learning. Experiential learning is defined here simply as learning by doing. Bloom (1956) and later Gagne (1977) established taxonomies of learning that related to the development of intellectual skills and that stressed the importance of problem-solving as a higher-order skill critical to the learning process. Vygotsky (1978) also posited that problem-solving and the construction of knowledge were the essence of the learning process. Vygotsky defined the learning process as the establishment of a "Zone of Proximal Development" in which exists the teacher, the learner, and a problem to be solved. The teacher provides an environment in which the learner can assemble or construct the knowledge necessary to solve the problem.

Evolving from Piaget, Bloom, Gagne, and Vygotsky is a constructivist theory of learning that stresses the importance of experiences, experimentation, problem-solving, and the construction of knowledge. While initially directed to children, constructivism can also be applied to adult learning by drawing on the vast experiences of an older population. In distance learning, this translates into presenting problems and learning situations to which the adult learner can relate, as well as providing the materials, media, and informational resources needed to solve the problems. Case study methodology, as used in many traditional professional programs in business administration, public administration, or law, for instance, works well in distance learning when learners can relate a case study to their own environments. Seymour Papert (1980), in describing a popular programming language for children called *Logo*, talks about creating a computer-based microworld in which children solve problems by drawing on the resources of a computer. With guidance from a teacher, the learner can access databases, test mathematical equations, or manipulate a geometric figure by using a computer. This concept can be broadened and applied to the design of distance learning applications for adults as well. The designer could consider the distance learning environment as a microworld in which problems (mathematical, scientific, social issues, case studies, etc.) are presented. Available to the learner are a teacher or tutor who acts as a guide in the process, and informational tools and resources, such as computer databases, media, and written materials, that enable learners to solve the problems. The learner learns by interacting with the available resources—teacher, tutor, information, media, etc.—and drawing on his or her own experiences to construct the knowledge to solve the problem. In this scenario, the ability to interact with teachers or tutors as well as to access other materials becomes very important. Designers must ensure that the ability to do both is available in the distance learning environment.

Many of the ideas and concepts just described locate themselves under the rubric of learner-centered education. A number of individuals have related Knowles' pioneering work in adult education to learner-centeredness in distance learning. Burge and Howard (1988) evolved a set of criteria that summarize this relationship. Included in these criteria are the following:

1. The learner has responsibility for his or her own learning.
2. The subject matter has relevance and meaning to the learner.
3. Involvement and participation are necessary for learning.

4. The teacher is a facilitator and resource person.
5. The learner sees himself or herself differently as a result of the learning experience.

These criteria provide an appropriate extension of the work of Knowles and others and are useful as a framework for considering the student perspective in developing a distance learning program.

SUCCESSFUL DISTANCE LEARNERS

Academic planners are rightfully concerned about the success of distance learning programs (Phipps & Merisotis, 1999). Success here is defined as students completing a course or program of study. Distance learning in many different situations has been extensively studied with varying degrees of student success or attrition reported. Keegan (1996) comments that measuring success is a "preoccupation" in distance learning, especially where adults rather than primary or secondary school students are concerned. In some cases, student attrition has been reported to be as high as 50 percent (Moore and Kearsley, 1996.) Naturally, whether students complete a program is a valid concern and will depend on many factors.

Adult education in general has a higher attrition rate than other types including primary, secondary, and traditional college (ages eighteen to twenty-two) education. Continuing education programs and post-secondary institutions with large adult populations, such as community colleges, have frequently observed that adults enter a program; drop out, in many cases for a semester or two; and then re-enter a program. This cycle of coming and going is common, and students who engage in this behavior are frequently referred to as "stop-outs" as opposed to the more final "drop-outs." A multivariable analysis indicates that, in many cases, changes in educational or career goals, finances, time constraints, or family obligations all contribute to decisions to defer one's education.

Hanson et al. (1997) provide an excellent review of the literature on learner attributes that contribute to success or attrition among distance learning adult students. There is little difference based on gender or age, other than the fact that attrition occurs more frequently for all students over the age of twenty-five. Academic preparation was determined to be an important factor. Students who have achieved higher levels of education, who have higher grade point averages, or who have already successfully completed a distance learning course are more likely to succeed. Successful distance learners also tend to be abstract learners who possess an internal locus of control, and who are self-directed and persistent in achieving their goals. Motivational factors such as having higher educational or career goals and objectives were also mentioned as important determinants of success. Academic integration, that is, the ability to integrate distance learning activities such as studying with other daily activities, is an important determinant of success. Typically the greater the academic integration, the greater the chances of success. Social integration and the ability to interact with others, including teachers, tutors, and other students, likewise is a very important determinant of success.

Educational planners have a responsibility to provide distance learning environments that will maximize factors that contribute to success and minimize factors that contribute to attrition. Naturally, situations such as family obligations or job-related time constraints cannot be controlled by the distance learning providers. On the other hand, factors such as well-planned and clearly presented instructional materials can help distance learners to integrate their learning into their daily lives. The availability of a teacher or tutor to students, especially those at a distance, is very important. Students in all learning situations, distance or otherwise, need to ask questions and to receive advice and assistance. As mentioned in Chapter 4, one of the most important aspects of planning is establishing the interactive and communications components (teacher to student, student to student, student to course materials) of the distance learning environment. In addition, students, particularly those who might be "at risk," need advisors and counselors with whom to share and discuss issues and concerns that might affect their academic performance.

PROFILING A STUDENT POPULATION

A recommended activity in designing a distance learning program is to undertake a profile of the students to be served. A variety of characteristics are important, including demographic, motivational, academic preparedness, and access to resources. Figure 5.2 provides a list of student characteristics that planners should consider in developing a distance learning program. These characteristics are not all-inclusive but provide a general framework for profiling a distance learning student population.

In addition to doing an initial profile at the time an institution is contemplating establishing a new program, planners should also collect this data after the distance learning program has been implemented. This is easily accomplished if the program is directed to a target student population within a given industry, a company, or a limited geographic location. Such a survey can provide valuable information on the readiness of students and the appropriateness of distance learning as a modality for meeting their needs. Administrators might consider adopting or developing a questionnaire that students would complete along with the application to a program. The questionnaire could address many of the factors identified in Figure 5.2 as well as any other items that might be of particular concern to the institution. Sharing the results of this information with instructors, advisors, or counselors might help to contribute to student success.

FIGURE 5.2 Student Profile List

Demographic Characteristics

What are the age, sex, ethnicity, race, primary language spoken, family responsibilities, disabilities, and occupation of potential students?

Motivational Characteristics

What are student educational goals and objectives?
What are student career goals and objectives?
Why might students be interested in a (your) distance learning program?

Academic Preparedness

What is the student educational achievement level (primary, secondary, community college, four-year college, graduate school)?
What are student skill levels (reading, writing, basic mathematics, technical where appropriate)?
What formal background do the students have with the subject matter of the program?
What are their personal interests and experiences that relate to the subject matter?
What experience(s) do students have with distance learning?

Resources

How will students pay for tuition and fees?
How much time will students be able to devote to distance learning?
What access do students have to media and technology (radio, television, computer, Internet, etc.)?
Where do students have access to media and technology (home, work, school, community center)?
What access do students have to academic support facilities (library, media center)?
What access do students have to people resources (tutors, mentors, colleagues, other learners)?

STUDENT FEEDBACK AND EVALUATION

In Chapter 2, the need for ongoing evaluation of a distance learning program was emphasized as an aspect of planning. Critical to this evaluation is data collected about student performance and participation, and satisfaction with their distance learning courses or programs.

In traditional programs, faculty are easily aware of student performance and participation. They give assignments, grade tests and papers, take attendance, and note students who answer questions or make important contributions to class discussions. In most distance learning environments, gathering data on student performance should be straightforward since some form of student assessment will likely be integrated into all courses. Performance data also include data on students who do not complete requirements or who withdraw from a course.

Gathering data on student participation, on the other hand, may require special consideration depending on the nature of the distance learning delivery systems. Point-to-point video conferencing applications allow students to participate in a fashion that is similar to traditional classes. Attendance is taken; students can ask questions and make comments. Despite the absence of a face-to-face classroom setting, instructors over the period of a semester or year will come to know students who actively participate in class activities. Internet-based distance learning applications that require students to participate via electronic bulletin boards or group e-mail systems also have built-in mechanisms for monitoring student participation. However, if the distance learning delivery system does not provide for ongoing group activity, such as broadcast television or videocassette instruction, teachers or tutors need to be more active in encouraging and monitoring participation from students. Shorter, more frequent assignments will likely yield more information on student participation and progress than long-term assignments. Frequent assignments will also serve to alert faculty to potential problems and provide the rationale for student contact. In most instructional activities, the more a learner participates, the greater the chances that he or she will succeed. In traditional classes, this is taken for granted. In distance learning, especially where direct contact or instructor- to student-interaction is limited, additional effort may be required to encourage and evaluate student participation.

Student evaluations of courses and faculty are becoming commonplace, especially at the post-secondary level. Seldin (1993) reports that the number of American colleges using formal student evaluations increased from 27 percent to 85 percent between 1970 and 1990. Furthermore, these evaluations are frequently used in faculty personnel decisions where promotion or tenure is being considered. Likewise in distance learning, data on student satisfaction can be helpful in improving a course or program and planning for future programs. While data gathered from student satisfaction surveys tend to be quantitative (see Figure 2.3 in Chapter 2) and are most important for comparison to other courses or programs, qualitative data can also provide insight into which aspects of a course work well and which are problematic.

Figure 5.3 provides a sample of comments made by students completing a satisfaction survey after taking an Internet-based, asynchronous distance learning course for the first time. Their responses provide helpful insight into their satisfaction with the course and also into the nature of this type of distance learning.

The students who completed the responses in Figure 5.3 were enrolled in a graduate course in education administration. All of these students were working full-time as teachers or other professionals in primary or secondary schools. The average age was thirty-six years. Their comments are organized by theme.

It is interesting to note that even this experienced group of teachers is concerned about speaking up in class. The Internet-based, asynchronous learning approach does not remove this concern, but reshapes it from speaking up for a moment in a traditional class to opening oneself up to "more scrutiny" by having to write more extensive comments that become available for continual review on an electronic bulletin board. The students' evaluation comments indicate that while some students prefer speaking up in class, others do not. On the other hand, some students preferred having the time to develop their thoughts before

FIGURE 5.3 Selected Student Comments from an Evaluation of an Internet Course

---

Posting to an Electronic Bulletin Board versus Speaking Up in a Traditional Class

"I was very hesitant to write my first comment. I guess I felt exposed. Writing a comment allows for more scrutiny. Participating in [a traditional] class is easier. You say a brief comment and it is considered briefly."——Rochelle

"It was interesting to see how everyone interpreted the question, and then responded to each other. In a regular class, many people would not have contributed because they either felt uncomfortable speaking or feared repeating another person's comments."——Todd

"In a [traditional] classroom setting, not everyone is comfortable speaking. In a fast-paced class, individuals who need more time to process information before speaking may not get the opportunity to be involved in the discussion."——Sonya

Time Commitment to an Internet Course

"I will never fall behind on discussions again. It was awful trying to catch up on everyone's comments. . . . I find the discussion more in-depth than a traditional course."——Bonnie

"I am enjoying reading the comments of my peers, but it is sometimes overwhelming to read all of the replies."——Lori

"They [asynchronous classes] are good learning opportunities if one is committed to the time it takes."——Joanna

Student/Instructor Roles

"Seems like we're all becoming more comfortable—much more interchange. . . . Dr. P's comments help center the discussion and move it forward."——Shelley

"Learning is very much alive! I can't wait to see where the discussion is going. There is always time for that extra comment or question. The bell never rings and the class is never over. . . . E-mates are always prepared."——Sonya

"I found it intriguing that I felt like I was in a classroom even though I was in front of a computer."——Paulette

"The system is relatively easy to use. Advice and assistance from the instructor were frequent and effective."——Dan

"It seems we [students] have more of a voice in the discussion."——Rochelle

"It is a totally different way of learning and sharing."——Judy

"This course requires students to read and prepare in order to participate and respond. It provides a good opportunity for learning."——Lori

"Increased reflection and intelligent discussion on my part and others in class."——Shelley

Convenience of Taking an Asynchronous Course

"As graduate students, most of us work. It is hard to travel from point A to point B. . . . Asynchronous classes are a solution to our high-paced, hectic lives."——Rick

"It is a more flexible form of class and allows one to participate around one's personal life."——Devorah

"The fact that I can log on at my convenience and as often as I want. . . . I can work at my own pace."——Mirza

"[While] it reduces travel time, saves money, and people can work in the privacy of their homes, as a full-time working mother and student, it has been difficult to find the time every night to participate. In [a traditional] class, there are not disturbances from members of the family."——Teresa

---

SOURCE: Picciano, A. (1998). Developing an asynchronous course model at a large, urban university. *Journal of Asynchronous Learning Networks, 2*(1). (http://www.jaln.org)

expressing them. This is not always possible in a traditional class because of the pace of the discussion.

The students' comments also indicate that the Internet-based, asynchronous learning in this class required a more substantial time commitment than a traditional class. Reading and writing electronic bulletin board postings took more time than the normal verbal exchanges in a traditional class.

Student and instructor roles changed in this course, with students having more of a voice in the discussions. Students were able to establish new threads that became the foci of substantial parts of the discussions. Some of them came to view the instructor as a facilitator of their learning.

A major reason for providing Internet-based learning was to provide a convenience for students. While most students agreed that this was indeed the case, ironically some cited distractions and disturbances at home that they would not have had in class at the college. While at home or work, the students remained available to their family or others. In a traditional class, the students are primarily available to the instructor and fellow students. This supports observations that for many students, the demands of profession, family, and community provide little extra time at any hour, and that the physical relocation that normally occurs during face-to-face classes provides a spatial separation from day-to-day pressures and commitments. "This separation can provide the face-to-face participant with increased amounts of available time" (Anderson, 1996, p. 133). It is a provocative caveat with which to conclude this section.

STUDENT SUPPORT SERVICES

When students seek admission to a traditional school or program, they receive a good deal of information regarding the nature of the academic program, a listing of the services that a college or school provides, and telephone numbers or addresses of key people who might assist and advise them. Once admitted, traditional students attend an orientation session that commences or continues the advisement process. Academic advisors, financial aid counselors, and others are available to help the student register for courses. The same is not always true for students in a distance learning program.

By definition, many distance learning students are geographically separated from their colleges or schools. A simple act such as purchasing a textbook, taken for granted at a campus where a bookstore customizes its inventory for the courses offered, may prove problematic for a student who lives many miles away. Obtaining more complex campus services, such as accessing the reserve section of a library or receiving assistance in completing a financial aid application, can prove insurmountable if not planned or specifically provided for with the distance learner in mind.

In planning a distance learning program, all of the services that support instruction in a traditional program also need to be considered. Some distance learning programs have been initiated with only the instructional components such as training faculty, acquiring equipment, or designing learning materials being considered. Colleges and universities take a good deal of pride in the collections in their libraries or the number of computer work stations that are available on campus for students to use. The availability of these and other student services to distance learners surely contributes to a program's success.

Basic Student Services

Basic student services such as admissions advisement, financial aid counseling, registration, and paying tuition and fees are complex activities in most institutions. Long lines of students desperately seeking advice from a program advisor are common even in this day of advanced computer on-line information systems, telephone registration, and payment of fees by credit cards. While distance learning providers are not expected to duplicate services in every locale in which a student resides, they are responsible for providing or assisting students to obtain these services. The telephone and fax machine become indispensable. Most successful distance learning providers have a help line that is dedicated to distance learners and staffed many hours during the day. If distances between the students and providers are extensive, toll-free "800" numbers are made available.

Distance learning providers, especially those who use Internet-based technologies for instruction, are also providing a full array of college services via on-line networks. Students can seek application to a program, register for their courses, and pay fees from a computer work station. While progress is steadily being made in on-line support services, inherently complex activities such as completing financial aid applications still frequently require human interaction. If one or more services are not provided specifically for distance learners, schools, colleges, or programs must advise students how they will be accommodated. If obtaining a particular service requires going physically to a campus, so be it; but students need to be aware of this requirement in advance.

Library, Media Services, and Technology

Services that directly support instructional activities, such as libraries, media centers, or computer laboratories, need to be considered when delivering distance learning. Reserve readings, video clips, recordings of classical music, or simulation software needed to solve science problems are examples of instructional materials generally available on campus to students. How these same materials are provided at a distance can become a major issue.

For students enrolling in their courses at a distance but at another educational facility as is done in point-to-point video conferencing applications, copies of any necessary instructional materials can be provided at the receiving site. For students who are participating in their courses at home via broadcast television, videocassettes, or the Internet, providing these materials becomes more complicated. Copyrighted print, film, video, or music materials cannot be duplicated without permission, and this is not likely to be received for a substantial number of students. Arrangements can be made with local educational institutions or libraries, but this too becomes complicated and costly for a widely dispersed learner population. Academic planners must reduce the need for additional materials in distance learning courses, bear the cost of copying needed materials, and pass these costs along to students, or they must rely on material that is readily available in most libraries or on the Internet. Again, students need to be made aware of what is expected of them in participating in a course. If they need to make arrangements at local libraries or other schools to participate effectively, then they should be advised accordingly and in advance.

Advisement and Counseling

Earlier in this chapter, mention was made that the attrition rate for distance learning students is high and can be as great as 50 percent. While many academic programs that attract adult learners are vulnerable to high attrition, distance learning poses its own unique problems because of the physical separation of students from a school. While high attrition for distance learners might relate to pressures of time, employment, or family, institutions should not accept this as a natural outcome of this type of learning. On the contrary, distance learning providers must consider support services such as advisement and counseling that might help stem attrition. A responsible administration will provide capable and readily available advisement and counseling services to help students through a problem, crisis, or difficulty in completing a course or program. Again, a capably staffed telephone help line may provide the lifeline for students who are at risk of dropping out of a course or program. Neither should the distance learning student be forgotten when school-initiated interventions are planned for the traditional student.

As colleges, universities, and other distance learning providers gain more experience in this area, they are finding that integrated teams that include instructors, counselors, and administrative personnel are needed to support distance learning students beyond basic instruction (Commission on Higher Education/Middle States Association of Colleges and Schools, 1997). Whether these services can be integrated into the support services provided for traditional students or established as separate entities must be decided by the institution. In any case, if a program is to be successful, the need for these services is apparent and academic planners must provide for them accordingly.

ACCESS TO TECHNOLOGY AND EQUITY ISSUES

As discussed in Chapter 2, a major goal of distance learning programs is to increase the opportunity for students to pursue an education. The choice of a distance learning technology is an important factor in determining which students will be able to participate and enroll in the program. This is particularly critical in developing countries where access to television or computer-based Internet technologies is limited or nonexistent. Even in developed countries, access to newer computer technologies may be limited to segments of the population.

Equity issues in technology and informational resources is becoming well-documented especially with regard to access to computer technology, which is distinguished by whether the location of the technology is in the home, at work, or in a school. For distance learners, the most flexible and desirable access is in the home. Around the world, access to technology varies considerably. Countries such as Iceland and Finland have developed the extensive infrastructure needed to provide most of their citizens access to the digital networks in their homes, while many developing countries are still struggling to provide basic television and telephone access.

Even in developed countries, the issue of access to technology can be complicated. In the United States, for instance, while access to television and telephone is widely available in the home, access to digital technology differs depending on demographic factors. According to the Department of Commerce, while standard telephone lines are readily available and can be a pathway to the riches of the Information Age, a personal computer and modem are rapidly becoming "the keys to the vault" (NTIA, 1995). President Bill Clinton and Vice President Al Gore have both expressed concerns about information "haves" and "have nots" among the population in the United States. Demographic factors such as gender, income, race, and educational background have been found to be important factors in determining access to the Internet.

Gender issues in technology have a long history in the United States. A concern exists that females are less likely to engage in technology-based, and especially computer-based, activities than males (Ory, Bullock, and Burnaska, 1997). However, with regard to distance learning technology and especially Internet access, any gap that existed between the sexes seems to have narrowed (Novak & Hoffman, 1998). Furthermore, recent research (Ory et al.) indicates that females are enrolling in Internet-based distance learning programs and succeeding comparably to males. Both males and females made similar use of Internet-based distance learning, had similar attitudes about their experiences, and shared a common desire to take more courses using the technology (Ory et al. p. 49).

Minority access to technology is yet another issue. The U.S. Congress's Office of Technology Assessment (1988) reported that in primary and secondary schools, predominantly African-American schools were significantly less likely than predominantly white schools to have computer equipment. In terms of access to Internet technology in the home, 44.2 percent of the white households in the United States have access to the Internet as compared to 29.4 percent for African-Americans (Novak and Hoffman, 1998). Novak and Hoffman also indicated that the gap or "digital divide" between the two races was narrowing and that a more significant factor in Internet access was family income. While all households in the lower income brackets were less likely to have Internet access, black families in the higher brackets had comparable access to that of white households. Bier et al. (1997) found that low-income families who were most disadvantaged in terms of computer and modem access were the most enthusiastic users of on-line services when provided with the necessary equipment in their homes.

Educational background is also an important determinant of Internet access in a home. To a degree, this relates to family income since a high correlation exists between educational level and income. However, where a primary, secondary, or post-secondary student was present, home access to the Internet increased significantly (Novak & Hoffman, 1998).

Distance learning technology also can become the educational vehicle for homebound or disabled persons. The data presented earlier in Table 5.1 shows that 16 percent of the distance learning providers target their programs for disabled persons. Every indication is that these programs are popular and provide a valuable service to this population. Computer-based technologies have evolved to become important communications tools for the disabled. Regardless of the impairment (hearing, vision, or mobility), computer-based assistive technologies have been developed that can greatly aid the learning process in both distance learning and traditional settings. An extensive, separate literature (see Flippo and Inge, 1997) on assistive technologies for the disabled exists for those interested in pursuing this area further.

In conclusion, educational planners should assess early on whether or not all segments of their intended student audience have equal access to the available technologies. Conducting a potential student profile as suggested earlier in this chapter should provide the necessary information.

CORPORATE CLIENTS

Before concluding this section on students and their perspective, a brief mention should be made of corporate clients in distance learning. Corporate training and learning centers are one of the fastest growing segments of post-secondary education in the United States (Commission on Higher Education, 1998). Traditionally, corporate clients contracted with a college or university to provide training to meet specific needs. Generally these contracts were for staff development and technical training in company-related job skill areas. This market is growing considerably as companies come to accept the fact that their employees need to be provided with opportunities for ongoing training. Lifelong learning is already a reality in several technology, engineering, and other professional fields, and distance learning is increasingly being seen as an important component of this type of training for a variety of reasons. In addition to the need to fit training into their employees' work schedules, many of yesterday's regional companies have grown into global enterprises with employees dispersed all over the world. The cost of training these individuals becomes far more acceptable if the courses can be delivered to their workplaces rather than arranging for them to travel to college campuses.

Students in these ventures tend to be mature, goal-oriented, and appreciative of the opportunity to upgrade their skills. They see promotion and the attainment of career goals as dependent on maintaining one's skills. The fact that their companies pay for their tuition or fees insures their active participation. By the same token, distance learning programs for these students need to be well organized and customized to achieve specific instructional goals and objectives. In most cases, a coordinator or liaison from the corporate entity will work with college personnel to customize the program. The selection of students, registration, payment of fees, support services, and other administrative matters frequently are handled by the corporation. If colleges or universities wish to work with corporate clients, an administrative coordinator (see Figure 5.4) who understands the nature of corporate training as well as the concepts involved with distance learning may be required. More importantly, colleges will also have to have faculty and instructors who understand the needs of corporate clients.

FIGURE 5.4   Excerpt of an Advertisement for a Director of Corporate Training and Continuing Education (*The New York Times,* 1999)

Director of Corporate Training and Continuing Education

The College of Aeronautics is a private, independent college offering education in technology and engineering leading to appropriate bachelor and associate degrees. The resources of the College are devoted to the education of men and women for careers in aviation, aerospace, and related industries. The educational experiences are designed to develop a high degree of technical competence and a sense of responsibility. The College serves a culturally diverse population of approximately 1,200 students. The College is in the process of substantially upgrading its campus facilities and classroom technology.

The College seeks an educational leader and administrator whose responsibilities will include:

• Responsibility for distance, on-line, and extension site programs
• Establishing extended and lifelong learning initiatives both for credit and non-credit
• Establishing new opportunities for education and training
• Seeking out opportunities which will result in increased enrollment and revenue.

Clients: Domestic and international airlines, aviation and related industry manufacturers, and United States and foreign government agencies.

Organizational Relationship: Reports to the vice president for academic affairs, works closely with academic departments and the admissions office.

Special Qualifications: Highly motivated, self-starter, contact experiences with potential clients a strong plus; aero-industry and/or education background desired; position requires extensive travel; proposal preparation; bachelor's degree.

The Director is full-time, 12-month position...............

Some large, multi-national companies such as IBM, Disney, Motorola, and Hewlett-Packard are having difficulty locating colleges and universities capable of delivering this type of distance training and are developing many of their own programs or universities. While these large companies can afford to invest in their own professional development and training programs, small to mid-size companies will want to continue to contract a good deal of their work to colleges. However, if colleges are not able to meet their needs, corporate clients will likely begin to look to other companies and the growing for-profit education providers.

SUMMARY

This chapter considers distance learning from the student perspective. Fundamental to every academic program is the determination of who is to be served. While most programs in distance learning are designed for adults over the age of twenty-five, in recent years major programs such as the U.S. Department of Education's *Star Schools Program* have also been developed for primary and secondary school students.

Traditional learning theories developed for children can be applied with some modification to adults. The work of Malcolm Knowles, who many consider to be the father of adult education, can be studied and integrated with that of cognitive development theorists such as Piaget, Bloom, Gagne, and Vygotsky. An emphasis on problem-solving and experiential learning integrates these theories under the rubric of "constructivism" or the construction of knowledge. Both children and adults can benefit from this approach.

Student attrition in distance learning programs is a concern for educators and academic planners. Attrition rates as high as 50 percent are not uncommon. A good deal of research has been undertaken that concludes there is little difference based on gender or age other than the fact that attrition occurs more frequently for all students over the age of twenty-five. Academic preparation was determined to be an important factor. Students who had achieved higher levels of education, who had higher grade point averages, or who had already successfully completed a distance learning course were more likely to succeed. Other factors such as motivation, academic integration, locus of control, and social integration contribute to student success.

In designing a distance learning program, a profile of the students to be served should be developed. A variety of characteristics including demographic, motivational, academic preparedness, and access to resources are important. Also important is the need for ongoing student evaluation. Critical to this evaluation should be data collected on student performance, participation, and satisfaction with their distance learning courses or programs.

Distance learning programs need to provide for support and student services comparable to those provided in traditional programs. Basic services such as admissions, registration, financial aid, counseling, and advisement are just as important as direct support services such as library, media, and access to technology. Providing these services for home-based distance learning programs can be a challenge.

Equity issues related to access to technology are critical in providing distance learning opportunities to students. Around the world, access to television, telephone, and computer technologies varies considerably. Academic planners need to understand these issues in relation to the student populations to be served. The chapter concludes with a brief look at the corporate client market. This market is growing considerably as companies come to accept the need to provide their employees with opportunities for ongoing training and skill development.

CASE STUDY

Baxter Community College Year: 1999

Setting

Baxter Community College exists just outside a major metropolitan area in the southeast United States. Baxter has an enrollment of 8,000 students, many of whom are part-time adult students taking courses to improve job and career skills. The college offers a variety of liberal arts and professional two-year programs. Business, technology, and nursing are among the most popular programs in terms of enrollment. The college also administers an extensive outreach program for the community that allows students to take courses in local high schools, business centers, and local hospitals. This program enrolls approximately 800 students and generates substantial additional revenue for the college.

The Issue

Recently, Baxter has been noticing a decline in enrollment in its outreach programs, especially in business courses. Two years ago, Stevenson University, a four-year private college located approximately 300 miles west of Baxter, began offering distance learning courses and set up a learning center at the site of a major industrial park located eight miles from Baxter. Many students who were previously enrolled in Baxter's program are now taking distance learning courses with Stevenson.

Jerome Tilden, the president of Baxter, has established a task force to look into the feasibility of starting a distance learning program to compete with Stevenson and lure back the students that Baxter has lost. The task force has met for the past six months and has recommended that Baxter establish a blended distance learning program that would use the Internet combined with broadcast television provided through the local cable TV provider. The present Director of Outreach Programs, Cheryl Grave, has expressed several reservations about the recommendation. Her major concern is that most of the students in the area who are taking courses at Stevenson, are doing so mainly because of its four-year programs and not necessarily because of the convenience of its distance learning facilities. She further recommends that Baxter establish a joint two-year/four year program in business with one of the state university colleges.

Assume you are President Tilden. How do you evaluate the recommendations you have received. What additional information do you need?

REFERENCES

Anderson, T.D. (1996). The virtual conference: Extending professional education in cyberspace. *International Journal of Educational Telecommunications, 2*(2/3), 121–135.

Bier, M., Gallo, M., Nucklos, E., Sherblom, S., & Pennick, M. (1997). Personal empowerment in the study of home Internet use by low-income families. *Journal of Research on Computing in Education, 30*(2), 107–121.

Bloom, B.S. (1956). *Taxonomy of educational objectives handbook: Cognitive domains.* New York: David McKay.

Burge, E., & Howard, J. (1988). *Learner centredness: Views of Canadian distance education educators.* Unpublished manuscript, Ontario Institute for Studies in Education.

Commission on Higher Education. (1998, Winter). Corporate universities bridge school, workplace gap. *CHE Letter,* 1,6.

Commission on Higher Education/Middle States Association of Colleges and Schools. (1997). *Guidelines for distance learning programs.* Philadelphia: Commission on Higher Education/Middle States Association of Colleges and Schools.

Flippo, K.F., & Inge, K.J. (1997). *Assistive technology: A resource book for school, work, and community.* Baltimore: Brookes Publishing Co.

Gagne, R.M. (1977). *Conditions of learning.* New York: Holt, Rinehart, & Winston.

Gornick, V. (1998, February 20). Apostles of the faith that books matter. *The New York Times,* p. E43.

Hanson, D., Maushak, N.J., Schlosser, C.A., Anderson, M.L., Sorenson, C., & Simonson, M. (1997). *Distance education: Review of the literature* (2nd ed.). Washington, D.C.: Association for Educational Communications and Technology.

Keegan, D. (1996). *Foundations of distance education* (3rd ed.). London: Routledge.

Knowles, M. (1978). *The adult learner.* Houston, TX: Gulf Publishing.

Moore, M., & Kearsley, G. (1996). *Distance education: A systems view.* Belmont, CA: Wadsworth Publishing Co. (1999, July 25). *The New York Times,* Section 4, p. 7.

Novak, T.P., & Hoffman, D.L. (1998). Bridging the digital divide: The impact of race on computer access and Internet use. *Project 2000, Vanderbilt University.* [On-line]. Available: http://www.2000.ogsm.vanderbilt.edu/papers/race/science.html. This paper is a longer version of the article, Bridging the racial divide on the Internet, published in *Science,* April 17, 1998.

Ory, J.C. , Bullock, C., & Burnaska, K. (1997). Gender similarity in the use of and attitudes about ALN in a university setting. *Journal of Asynchronous Learning Networks, 1*(1), 39–51.

Papert, S. (1980). *Mindstorms: Children, computers and powerful ideas.* New York: Basic Books.

Phipps, R., & Merisotis, J. (1999). *What's the difference: A review of contemporary research on the effectiveness of distance learning in higher education.* Washington, D.C.: The Institute for Higher Education Policy.

Piaget, J. (1952). *The origins of intelligence in children.* New York: Norton.

Seldin, P. (1993). The use and abuse of student ratings of professors. *The Chronicle of Higher Education, 32*(46), 8.

Tapscott, D. (1997). *Growing up digital.* New York: McGraw-Hill.

U.S. Congress, Office of Technology Assessment. (1988). *Power on! New tools for teaching learning* (Report No. OTA-SET-379). Washington, D.C.: U.S. Government Printing Office.

U.S. Department of Education, National Center for Education Statistics (1997). *Distance education in higher education institutions,* NCES 97-062. Washington, D.C.

U.S. Department of Commerce, National Telecommunications and Information Administration (1995). *Falling through the cracks: A survey of the "Haves Nots" in rural and urban America.* Washington, D.C.
http://www.ntia.doc.gov/ntiahome/fallingthru.html

Vygotsky, L. (1978). *Mind in society: The development of higher psychological processes.* Cambridge, MA: Harvard University Press.

CHAPTER SIX

The Faculty Perspective

Peter Drucker, economist and futurist, caused a major stir in academic circles when, in an interview for *Forbes* magazine, he stated that universities thirty years from now would be "relics . . . [and] won't survive" (Lenzer & Johnson, 1997, p. 127). Two years earlier, Eli Noam (1995), Professor and Director of Columbia University's Institute for Tele-Information, presented a paper titled "Electronics and the Dim Future of the University." In it, he forecasted the demise of universities as we know them or, minimally, their relegation to a "diminished role." He traced their beginnings back 2500 years to Assyria, Greece, and Egypt, but he sees their role diminishing in the not-too-distant future because of the emergence of communications and information technologies. He predicts that the major activities of scholarly life, namely to create knowledge, to preserve it, and to pass it on to others, no longer will require campus-like buildings and facilities such as academic departments, research laboratories, and dormitories. Instead, he sees electronic communities, using high-speed communications and computing technologies, evolving and replacing these twentieth-century features. He is not alone in his prediction (see Davis & Botkin, 1994; Tapscott, 1996; and Lenzer & Johnson, 1997).

Both Drucker and Noam have made their careers in academia and some credence should be given to their predictions. However, while playing an important role in alerting the academic community to the need for change, they do not give this same community credit for adjusting and evolving as society and its technologies evolve. Universities may have existed as many as 2500 years ago, but the modern university has changed drastically during this time. In many ways, it has been a pioneer in the use of communications technologies. The Internet is the result of academicians and scientists working together with government and, to some degree, with private industry to develop and evolve this technology. The precursors to the Internet, namely ARPANET, BITNET, and NSFNET had their genesis in academia and nonprofit government sectors. There is no doubt that universities and their faculties will be able to evolve. Communications and computing technologies will have an important role in fostering this and may, in fact, be preconditions for this evolution.

The purpose of this chapter is to examine faculty issues in relation to distance learning applications. These applications need to be planned, and part of this planning requires faculty involvement. Issues such as faculty development, workload, compensation, and intellectual property rights are important distance learning issues that should be discussed as part of planning.

THE SOCRATIC METHOD IS ALIVE AND WELL

Good teachers take pride in their teaching. A stimulating lecture, a student responding enthusiastically to a question, or an audio-visual aid that hits the mark are all clues that a lesson is going well. A good teacher in a traditional classroom can feel the energy and vibrancy of the learning process as a lesson develops and proceeds. While teachers would like to think that learning is occurring in every lesson, realistically this does not happen. A student looking at his watch and perhaps tapping it to make sure it is working, heads bowed when a question is asked, or that look of confusion on the faces of students all tell a tale.

Teachers in primary and secondary schools are trained to teach and to be alert to clues from their students. Teachers in colleges and universities, on the other hand, generally are not trained to teach. They have developed an expertise in their disciplines and subject matter, which they attempt to share with their students. Some are good teachers and some are not. What is not learned in the class-room is expected to be learned by students on their own through reading pertinent material, consulting with other students, or seeking out a tutor. College teachers generally employ methods that they learned as students by observing their own teachers, especially those they thought were stimulating and effective. A crucial question here is what makes for effective teaching. The answer is not simple. The style or technique of one teacher is not that of another, although both may be effective.

Numerous teaching techniques and theories have been developed by the likes of Johann Pestalozzi, Maria Montessori, Jean Piaget, John Dewey, and Howard Gardner. The art of teaching has been debated extensively and the conclusion is that there are many ways to teach effectively. However, in most classrooms at any level, the importance of asking a question and receiving an answer is fundamental to the teaching/learning process. The *Socratic Method* survives as an important key to this process. While facts and information must be presented, student minds are not simple vessels needing to be filled with knowledge, but rather channels that analyze and explore knowledge and that serve as the conduits to build on what already has been learned and is known (Viau, 1994). Critical inquiry and inductive processes rely on raising the right questions, the answers to which eventually lead to a firmer grasp of some universal law or meaning. Good teachers, regardless of the discipline or subject matter, will seek to create the environment in which the right questions are raised and explored. Teachers possess lifework experiences and should therefore be involved in the decisions to create learning environments, whether they exist at a distance or in close proximity.

ADAPTING TO NEW TEACHING TECHNIQUES AND THE NEED FOR FACULTY DEVELOPMENT

Those with experience in developing distance learning courses have come to realize that existing materials meant for delivery in traditional classrooms cannot simply be transferred to distance mode. As was discussed in Chapter 4, depending on the distance learning delivery method chosen and the technologies used, existing course materials will have to be converted. The reasons for this vary but essentially center on adaptability, taking advantage of available technology, and student learning needs. For example, using an overhead projector to diagram an industrial process or to write a mathematical equation is routine in a traditional classroom, where the instructor is present to explain symbols and to answer a student inquiry. Take the instructor away and this routine act can become an insurmountable hurdle. In the traditional classroom, students accept the handwriting or illustration limitations of the instructor because she or he is there to enhance the illustration or blackboard notation by answering any questions they may have. This is not necessarily so in a distance learning mode. Therefore, the illustration and notation must be converted and presented in a manner that insures clarity. If the illustration is one, no matter how clear, that naturally generates questions on the part of students—how are these questions to be handled? Are explanations provided in an accompanying narrative? If so, then student questions have to be anticipated based on experience, and relevant answers or explanations must be provided. Indeed, this one overhead illustration may be part of a lesson that contains dozens of illustrations. Courses, in turn, are made up of dozens of lessons, so adapting existing traditional classroom materials for distance learning can become a major undertaking. Consider the complexity of other situations, such as a teacher using video clips, conducting a live biological experiment, or requiring students to engage in a collaborative group activity. Faculty who are successful teachers in a traditional classroom will need time and training to be successful in a distance learning environment. Furthermore, a realization may be reached that some traditional classroom techniques might not be easily duplicated in or adapted to a distance mode.

The need for faculty and staff development programs should be apparent. Their lack has been referred to as the "Achille's heel" of distance learning (Cyrs, 1997, p. 391). In cases where distance learning is heavily technology-based, such as with on-line computer networks, faculty will need to be trained not only in distance learning techniques but also in using technology. This may be a formidable undertaking depending upon the knowledge and experience of the faculty. While many faculty, particularly those who were educated after 1980, have developed expertise in technology, the same may not be true for older faculty or faculty in disciplines where technology is less important.

Beyond the substantive issues of conversion of content and distance learning technology, a major concern in faculty development is attitude. While some faculty enthusiastically participate in distance learning development activities, others are less than enthusiastic and perhaps even antagonistic. Faculty doubt exists about the quality of distance learning programs, the effort involved in developing materials, and the perceived lack of social interaction on which teaching has traditionally been based. In planning development activities, administrators should be prepared to deal with these attitudinal issues. With this in mind, perhaps the most important decision in planning a faculty development activity is identifying the faculty who would benefit most from it. In *Diffusion of Innovation,* Rogers (1995) provides excellent insight into dealing with attitudinal issues when organizations attempt to expand or implement new techniques, including technology. A major observation is that in most organizations a small percentage of innovators and early adopters provide the base for training of and diffusing an innovation to the remaining (majority and laggards) personnel.

THE STAFF DEVELOPMENT PLANNING MODEL

Figure 6.1 provides a schematic for a staff development planning model that can be integrated with the planning model for distance learning discussed in Chapter 2. A basic assumption is that *staff development* is a product of the larger distance

FIGURE 6.1 Staff Development Planning Model

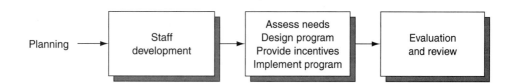

learning planning model. The major components of the staff development planning model are as follows:

Assess needs
Design program
Provide incentives
Implement program
Evaluate and review

This model forms the framework for much of the discussion in the remainder of this chapter.

DESIGNING AND IMPLEMENTING EFFECTIVE STAFF DEVELOPMENT PROGRAMS

Designing a staff development program should be done so that the proposed program relates closely to the overall distance learning plan. Simply offering several workshops each year that may or may not be relevant to goals and objectives will not be effective. The first requirement in planning a staff development program is identifying what needs to be done through a needs analysis. If an educational organization has not provided a great deal of staff development in the past, an in-depth or comprehensive analysis may be in order. On the other hand, if the organization has been active in providing staff development and is experienced in using distance learning, then the analysis can be targeted to specific applications and objectives.

A comprehensive needs analysis for the purpose of designing a staff development program for distance learning requires an in-depth examination of the proposed applications, followed by an evaluation of the staff and their abilities to develop and implement these applications. The needs that are identified become the targets of the staff development plan.

While some educational organizations are able to do comprehensive needs analyses, most limit them to specific faculty or specific applications. For example, a college might start a distance learning program for a particular subject area, such as business administration. The initial staff development program should then be targeted to the business administration faculty who teach in the program.

In designing staff development activities, the input of the target groups is most important, as the group members will provide many suggestions regarding the nature of the development activities. Optimally, programs should provide some variety of activities (i.e., lectures, demonstrations, discussions, hands-on workshops, etc.) and should take place over an extended period of time to allow participants to practice and experiment. Staff development programs also require resources, and budgets must be allocated as part of the design and implementation.

The types of staff development activities that organizations utilize are wide-ranging and include workshops, both on-site and off-site; large group conferences; small group seminars; and user group activities to name a few. It is not the intent here to review all the modes and characteristics of a good staff development program but to identify common elements (see Figure 6.2) that are considered especially effective for distance learning. They include the following:

One-on-one coaching
Training the trainer
Hands-on activities
Access to equipment and facilities

One-on-One Coaching

Individualized training or coaching is a common element of many staff development programs. If the organization has support staff who can function as individualized trainers or coaches, they should be utilized. If not, coaching should be provided by outside experts or consultants. Regardless of who provides the individualized training, short (one or two hours), one-on-one coaching sessions are

FIGURE 6.2 Elements of a Staff Development Program

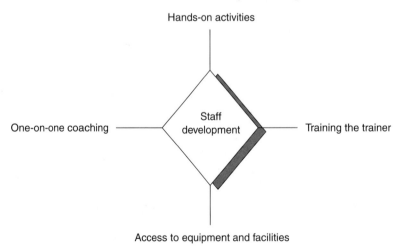

more effective than longer, large-group activities. A common format is a large-group information delivery session followed by much smaller coaching sessions in which participants can practice or experiment with the assistance of a coach who customizes the training to individual needs. This approach is popular for distance learning because the creation of a course or the conversion of an existing course to distance format will take place over time. The availability of a coach to assist and to guide as the course evolves is valuable and assuring to faculty using distance learning techniques for the first time.

Training the Trainer

While a certain amount of outside expertise and consulting is required for many staff development activities, relying on external trainers can become costly over the long term. A popular approach is to have outside consultants train a small cadre of staff, who in turn train more of the staff. This "train the trainer" approach develops a core group of mentors or in-house experts who become actively engaged in sharing their knowledge with others. Such a group can begin with technology faculty and support staff, media specialists, and representatives from every department who have shown a particular interest in distance learning. Eventually, this group can become the critical component that drives the entire staff development activity for a whole organization.

Deciding whether to convert numbers of present employees into full-time trainers depends on the size of the organization and the number of people to be trained. Large educational organizations with thousands of faculty and employees would probably find that a cadre of full-time trainers would, in fact, be less expensive than large-scale use of outside consultants. On the other hand, very small schools might make training a part-time or add-on responsibility (for extra compensation or reassigned time) for existing full-time staff who have had success in distance learning.

Utilizing existing staff for training also can provide many attitudinal benefits. Faculty might relate better to colleagues who are a few steps ahead of them in using distance learning. A sense of "If they can do it, so can I" frequently can develop. This approach also can be very effective in developing an esprit de corps among the faculty. Given the many issues and problems associated with developing a distance learning program, training a cadre of faculty trainers may be one of the most effective ways of resolving them.

Hands-On Activities

Fundamental to staff development for distance learning is the concept that one learns by doing. This is especially true when newer technologies such as point-to-point video or computer networking are the chosen delivery mechanisms. Therefore, a portion of any training program should include hands-on activities. While participants can listen to and read about distance learning technology, not until they use it will they develop an understanding that will lead to expertise. Consider how one learns typing or keyboarding. A teacher may lecture on how to type or a student can read about typing, but until the student actually types, he or she cannot develop the skill of typing. The same is true with distance learning technology. To understand it, one needs to use the hardware, stand in front of a television camera, or experiment with software. The more one practices, the greater will be one's proficiency and knowledge development. This holds true regardless of the background of the target population—whether they are engineers and computer scientists or other faculty who have used technology for little more than word processing or e-mail applications.

The design of a staff development program that includes hands-on activities implies that equipment, software, and other facilities are available for the participants to use. While administrators readily understand the need to acquire equipment and develop facilities for instruction, making separate provisions for the purpose of teacher training, practice, and development is also a necessity.

Incentives

The topic, *Is Teaching with Asynchronous Learning Networks so Tough?*, was explored extensively in a recent on-line discussion (URL: http://www.aln.org/alntalk) sponsored by Vanderbilt University. Lanny Arvan of the University of Illinois, the forum moderator, commented that "to teach with ALN the instructor has to be a hero. It takes a lot of time—a badge for the dedicated instructor—and is perhaps an insurmountable barrier for those less dedicated." Participants' comments indicated that converting/developing a first ALN course may take as much as 50–100 percent more time than developing a traditional course.

In light of the time required to develop a first distance learning course, special incentives must be provided for faculty and others in order to ensure active participation. Both intrinsic and extrinsic rewards need to be considered for faculty involved with developing staff and implementing distance learning in their schools. Professional growth, service to students, stimulating involvement with instructional innovations, experimentation with different teaching styles, and other intrinsic rewards may be among the most important reasons teachers become involved with distance learning. However, because of the time and effort involved, more extrinsic incentives such as extra compensation, release time, awards of equipment, or special recognition are also needed.

Staff should be compensated for attending workshops, seminars, and other activities conducted in the summer or on weekends. Tuition reimbursements or sabbatical leaves should be considered for teachers who upgrade their skills by taking courses. Teachers who agree to be mentors or trainers should receive extra compensation for assuming additional responsibilities. Those involved with developing a major new distance learning program or courses should be provided with release time to plan and to evaluate their materials carefully. Recognizing faculty who make a major contribution to staff development, perhaps in the form of a cash award or a gift of a personal computer, can be a very strong inducement for others to participate.

While the possibilities for providing incentives are extensive, administrators should make sure they are appropriate for the staff involved and the nature of the contribution, and conform to existing employee compensation policies. Schools that have advanced in distance learning eventually develop a culture in which incentives involve recognition and professional acknowledgment. Schools that are planning major leaps forward should consider more direct rewards such as extra compensation and release time. Regardless, administrators should be able to identify incentives to which a school staff will respond, and provisions for them should be made accordingly.

Evaluation and Review

Like any other technology planning activity, staff development should be evaluated and reviewed. Participants in workshops or demonstrations should evaluate the effectiveness of these activities and make suggestions for improvements if needed. Simple evaluation questionnaires that are distributed and collected at the end of a staff development activity is common practice. Depending on financial resources, external evaluators might also be considered. Evaluation should also provide for follow-up to determine whether participants have, in fact, been able to transfer their training to actual distance learning applications.

Evaluation and review activities should not be considered the end of staff development. On the contrary, evaluation should naturally restart the process of assessing needs and designing new staff development programs.

A Continuous Process

Staff development programs should be planned as a continuous process, primarily because distance learning technologies are constantly changing and new equipment and software are regularly being introduced. Mechanisms should be permanently in place for evaluating and sorting out new technology to determine its appropriateness for a program. Some individuals must be provided with the resources to visit other schools or attend vendor meetings and specialized workshops that enable them to keep up with the technology. Determining who these individuals are is also part of an overall planning activity. Obviously, distance learning coordinators and trainers are the most likely candidates; however, teachers who show an interest in or who have been successful in developing distance learning courses should also be included.

The need for continual staff development will become apparent as planners review and evaluate their activities. Whether it is an evaluation of a single workshop or an entire year's program, the most common suggestions and requests from participants are for additional staff development opportunities and activities. Besides the enjoyment they experience when attending such activities, staff quickly recognize their need to learn and advance, advance and learn. As planners look at the broader staff development picture, they will see individuals functioning at different levels within the process. The goal of their staff development planning will be to keep all these individuals moving through this process. Increasingly colleges and schools are establishing development centers for faculty and staff to assist in planning and implementing technology-related projects. Personnel in these centers are dedicated to working with faculty and helping them achieve their instructional objectives. Columbia University's Center for New Media in Teaching and Learning is an example of such a center. Readers may wish to visit its home page where a variety of on-line resources are provided (see URL: http://www.ccnmtl.columbia.edu/). On a broader scale, the American Association for Higher Education also provides services to help colleges and schools establish TLT (Teaching, Learning, and Technology) Groups, which are also referred to as ITG (Instructional Technology Groups). The purpose of a TLT or ITG is to establish an internal advisory group that brings together the diverse individuals, including faculty, academic leaders, administrators, and technical staff, who must work together to make effective use of technology including that used for distance learning. These groups provide excellent forums for discussions about faculty and staff development needs and programs.

A Sample Distance Learning Workshop

Figure 6.3 is an excerpt of the schedule for a nine-day workshop titled *Distance Learning: A Cutting Edge Resource for EFL (English as a Foreign Language) Programs*. This workshop was first offered in 1997 and was attended by faculty and educational administrators from twenty-two countries. The faculty who developed the workshop came from Great Britain and the United States.

Several elements of the workshop are worth mentioning and should serve as examples of good workshop design. First, the program has a subject or discipline focus, namely English as a Foreign Language. Second, the workshop blends basic information on distance learning concepts, content information on EFL, and hands-on training in the appropriate technology. Plenary sessions are designed to integrate distance learning techniques with the subject area or content. Third, the workshop design goes beyond "talking at" participants. Group projects and hands-on activities are important aspects of the workshop. Every afternoon, time is allowed for participants to develop projects with their group partners and to practice, explore, and tinker with distance learning technology. Facilities are available to the participants throughout the day and into the evening. Each group is expected to complete a substantial, Internet-based distance learning activity by the end of the workshop. Lastly, the workshop concludes with an evaluation and summary of what was accomplished.

A Sample Faculty Development Course

Figure 6.4 is an outline for a course titled, *Interactive Distributed Learning for Technology Mediated Course Delivery (IDL)*, which is offered at the University of Central Florida (UCF) as part of a faculty development program. UCF has a successful

FIGURE 6.3   Excerpt of an Outline for a Nine-Day Faculty Development Workshop

Workshop: Distance Learning:

A Cutting Edge Resource for EFL (English as a Foreign Language) Programs

Day 1

Morning: Welcome/Introduction to the Workshop
                Plenary Session: Distance Learning: What Is It and What Is Cutting Edge?
                Participant Discussion of Plenary Session

Afternoon: Introduction to the Internet, E-mail, and Electronic Bulletin Boards (Laboratory)
                Introduction to the World Wide Web and Search Engines (Laboratory)
                Assignments and Discussion of Group Projects

Day 2

Morning: Plenary Session: The Internet for Teaching English
                Participant Discussion of the Plenary Session

Afternoon: Introduction to HTML and Microsoft *Frontpage* to Develop Web Pages (Laboratory)
                Group Project Work

●

●

Day 5

Morning: Plenary Session: Planning Effective Distance Learning Projects
                Plenary Session: Distance Learning: The Student Perspective
                Participant Discussion of the Plenary Sessions

Afternoon: Practice Using Microsoft *Frontpage* (Laboratory)
                Group Project Work

Day 6

Morning: Plenary Session: The Future of English: Implications for the EFL Profession
                Plenary Session: The Internet and ELT: The British Open University Experience
                Participant Discussion of the Plenary Sessions

Afternoon: Group Project Work
                Status Reports on Group Projects/Participant Discussion

●

●

Day 9

Morning: Plenary Session: Status of Distance Learning: Problems, Solutions, and the Future
                Presentations of Student Group Projects

Afternoon: Presentations of Student Group Projects
                Evaluation/Summary

Web-based distance learning program that enrolls more than 6,000 students. Academic administrators consider faculty training and development an important part of its success (Hartman, J. L., Dzubian, C., & Moskal, P., 1999).

The IDL course was revised from what was essentially a one-week workshop to an eight-week format to provide additional activities and to allow faculty more

FIGURE 6.4 Outline of a Faculty Development Course
Designed to Introduce Instructors to Web-Based Teaching

Title: Interactive Distributed Learning (IDL) for Technology Mediated Course Delivery

Description: IDL is an eight-week simulation course that models the use of interactive discussion facilitation, time, media, and the on-line environment. It is offered twice a year at the University of Central Florida for the faculty who apply or are invited to participate in the program.

Components: IDL includes three major components: in-class sessions, asynchronous on-line modules, and hands-on laboratories.

The in-class sessions cover the following topics:

1. Orientation to Web-based, asynchronous learning
2. Sharing of experiences and expertise by faculty or "Web Vets" who are already teaching on the World Wide Web
3. Instructional design
4. Interaction and Student Assessment
5. Course administration
6. Group-based projects

The asynchronous on-line modules are designed to extend the in-class sessions for a longer period and to give participants a chance to reflect on the material and to engage in asynchronous discussions with colleagues.

1. Introduction to asynchronous learning
2. Best practices
3. The design process
4. The course development process
5. Interaction
6. Assessment
7. Course administration
8. Group work
9. Copyright issues

The laboratories sessions are hands-on activities that require the faculty participants to learn and practice with the software (WebCT) used for asynchronous learning at the University of Central Florida and includes the following:

1. Beginning WebCT
2. WebCT Administration
3. Advanced WebCt
4. Library Web Searching
5. Advanced Group Work

SOURCE: Hartman, J.L., Dzubian, C., & Moskal, P. (1999, August). *Faculty satisfaction in ALNs.* Paper delivered at the Sloan ALN Summer Workshop, Urbana, Illinois.

time to reflect on the material. IDL includes three major components: in-class sessions, asynchronous on-line modules, and hands-on laboratories. Asynchronous activities were specifically added as part of the revision of the course to simulate and model on-line teaching experiences.

FACULTY PERSONNEL ISSUES

Beyond the need for faculty development, several other significant issues regarding distance learning have emerged in recent years. In developing or advancing distance learning programs, these issues should be discussed and resolved by all involved parties.

Faculty Preparation

Mention was made earlier that developing and preparing distance learning courses can be a very time-consuming activity for faculty who are doing so for the first time. However, even faculty with experience indicate that developing and preparing for distance learning courses requires additional time (Graf, 1993; Hanson et al, 1997; Cyrs and Conway, 1997).

To some degree, the amount of time depends on the distance learning delivery system. If we consider two of the most popular technologies, namely point-to-point video and on-line computer courses, there is little question that additional organizational and planning time is required on the part of faculty to develop distance learning lessons using either of these technologies. In point-to-point video classes, faculty frequently work with technical staff to prepare and test their delivery systems prior to their scheduled classes. This may take from thirty to sixty minutes. Faculty also are encouraged to develop back-up plans and materials for each lesson should a video or network connection be lost or disrupted during a class. In on-line computer courses, the same preparation, testing, and back-up planning described above are required if the course is being taught in a synchronous mode, that is, at the same time.

In asynchronous courses, faculty find that students feel free to send questions via e-mail almost anytime and on any day of the week. Furthermore, in a typical asynchronous course, questions are more numerous and in many cases more substantive because students can devote more time to formulating their thoughts. A conscientious teacher will make every attempt to respond to student queries as quickly as possible. While this might be a labor of love for many dedicated teachers, it definitely takes more time than answering similar questions in a traditional classroom where faculty can better control the amount of time devoted to student questions. Furthermore, answering an ad hoc question verbally generally takes less time than writing an e-mail response. Just as the students are more deliberate in developing questions, teachers must be more deliberate in formulating written responses.

Lastly, one of the most time-consuming activities in distance teaching that uses current audio-video and computer technologies is the need to devote more time to practicing with new features and keeping up with upgrades as the technology associated with these delivery systems evolves. This is especially true with on-line and Internet-based computer software, which is undergoing rapid change. These changes also involve substantial discussion and committee work with administrative, technical, or teaching staff, particularly when changes or upgrades to the fundamental instructional delivery technology are being considered. In a traditional class, with the exception of science, engineering, or other technology-dependent disciplines, faculty do not have to keep up with a technology unless they choose to do so.

Distance Learning Class Size

Class size is another important faculty personnel issue. For their traditional courses, educational organizations generally establish standard class sizes that have a pedagogical basis for effective instruction. To a degree, smaller classes tend to allow faculty to provide more time for a variety of individual student needs including answering questions, providing comments on assignments, and being available for course advisement, all of which can lead to improved instruction. Standard class sizes also reflect and are limited to physical seating capacity of classrooms. Class enrollments may vary a bit from semester to semester but generally there is an average class size that faculty are accustomed to teaching. Collective bargaining agreements, where they exist, frequently have negotiated class size clauses.

In distance learning, the nature of a "classroom" can fundamentally change. Certain distance learning delivery technologies such as broadcast television or on-line computer networks establish a "classroom" as a virtual entity not dependent on a physical space. Hence enrollments in distance learning courses are not dependent on the size of rooms and can vary significantly. Technically, there is little difference in broadcasting a lecture to thirty homes versus one hundred homes versus one thousand homes. However, instructional activities such as grading tests, correcting written assignments, or answering student questions will increase in direct proportion to the number of students receiving the broadcast. Highly interactive distance learning technologies such as on-line computer networks can generate a good deal of student activity in the form of comments and questions as mentioned earlier. Large class sizes in such an environment can easily overload a teacher's ability to respond to queries.

When considering distance learning, class size must be discussed by administrators and teachers and appropriate support provided where necessary. One common practice is to have teaching assistants provided for every "so many" students enrolled in a class. Team teaching using two or more faculty members can reduce the burden. Automatic test scoring equipment might be employed to reduce the need to grade examinations manually. However, in these situations, consideration also must be given to the quality of instruction. An overdependence on teaching assistants or the use of short-answer questions when written compositions or essays might be more appropriate can jeopardize the quality of a distance learning class.

Faculty Compensation

Because of the need for an investment in training, increased preparation time, and the potential for teaching to large numbers of students, incentives such as release time or additional financial remuneration might be needed. Without incentives, senior faculty may be reluctant to invest their time and efforts in distance learning. Cyrs (1997) commented that institutions rely more on new faculty to teach distance learning courses and even may require it as a condition of employment. Regardless of whether distance learning courses are taught by senior, junior, or adjunct faculty, institutions should consider some form of additional compensation. This may be difficult, especially in environments where salary structures are uniform or pay differentials nonexistent.

Furthermore, if Cyrs is correct in his observation, junior faculty should receive recognition for their efforts in distance learning. Willis has expressed concern that in some institutions the work of the distance learning teacher is "forgotten" or discounted during promotion and tenure proceedings (Willis, 1993, p. 47). If this is the case, then mounting a distance learning program in these institutions will be very difficult. How does one ask instructors, especially junior faculty, to teach a regular course load, to conduct research, to publish, and to develop and teach distance learning courses? Lisa Guerney (1997), in an article titled "Scholars Who Work with Technology Fear They Suffer in Tenure Reviews," reports that this is a serious issue on American college campuses, especially for junior faculty working on technology-based teaching and research projects. Enlightened administrations should recognize the unfairness here and develop mechanisms for evaluating and rewarding these faculty accordingly.

Intellectual Property Rights

For decades, teachers in traditional educational institutions have prepared handouts and other materials for their courses or developed lecture notes without ever considering who owned them. The assumption always has been that the professor owned these materials as his or her intellectual property. Even in situations where schools or colleges provided some assistance such as purchasing a computer software program or making available media equipment, they rarely assumed ownership of course materials developed by their faculty. This has begun to change and is becoming problematic as more institutions become involved in distance learning.

In schools and colleges dedicated to or established for distance learning, such as the Open University of the United Kingdom, course materials meant for wide distribution, such as printed study guides and accompanying audio or video materials, are developed for the institution and continue to be used after a faculty developer(s) leaves. Where course materials are particularly successful, agreements for the sharing of revenue or profits with the faculty developers are a common practice. However, in organizations where the development of distance learning materials is a more recent phenomenon, ownership agreements are frequently neglected or nonexistent. This can become especially complicated where a school or university has provided extensive assistance, such as in developing costly multimedia materials for distribution over the Internet, via broadcast television, or on videocassettes.

A recent case at Athabasca University in Canada illustrates the complexity of the problem. Athabasca offers distance learning courses and programs to more than 12,000 students annually. At Athabasca, it was assumed that the university and the faculty developers jointly owned distance learning course materials. Thirty percent of any profits or additional revenue generated by sale of these materials to other colleges or universities was given to staff and faculty developers either individually or through a faculty organization. The remaining 70 percent of profits went to the university's administration. In 1994, however, Athabasca decided to change its policy unilaterally and to return 25 percent to the administration of the departments where the distance learning materials were developed and keep 75 percent for the university's administration. The faculty association protested the change in policy and Athabasca reverted back to its previous policy, at least until a new ownership agreement/policy could be negotiated. Unfortunately, the debate has been so intense that some faculty at Athabasca believe that the issue can only be resolved in the courts (Guerney & Young, 1998). Since its inception in 1970, Athabasca University has enjoyed an excellent reputation as a school that has evolved and matured in the delivery of distance learning. Yet it has not been able to resolve fully the intellectual property rights issue. At hundreds of other colleges that are only recently starting to develop distance learning courses or programs, this issue has emerged as a major stumbling block.

The American Association of University Professors appointed a committee to consider a number of faculty issues related to distance learning. Among the conclusions in the committee's report was that the "ownership of intellectual property is among the most widely debated issues on university campuses today" (American Association of University Professors, 1997, p. 7). Past practice in this regard is in most cases unclear or inconsistent. Faculty who write textbooks or curricular guides for publication rarely, if ever, share royalties with their colleges. On the other hand, most research universities own the patent rights to inventions developed in their laboratories and other facilities by their professors and generally develop an income-sharing agreement with them. The development of distance learning course materials such as CD-ROMs or videos do not fit neatly into either of the above categories. Teacher groups such as the National Education Association insist that the faculty own their course materials. Administrators question faculty ownership in cases where a good deal of technical support in developing course materials has been provided by the school or college. Assume, for instance, that a faculty member provides guidance and voiceovers for a series of multimedia lessons developed by a team of technicians employed by a college. Assume also that the multimedia lessons required expensive digital video equipment, facilities for copying CD-ROMs, and hundreds of hours of staff time to produce, all supplied by the college. Who owns the final product?

The resolution of the intellectual property issue is not simple and will only be resolved by mutual agreement, discussion, and negotiation between faculty and administrators. Schools that have such policies in place are far ahead of most other institutions. Schools that do not have such policies in place should begin the process of adopting such a policy before proceeding with any major new distance learning initiative. Graham B. Spanier, the president of Pennsylvania State University, a major distance learning provider, has indicated that a college or university without a policy on intellectual property and course ownership will likely encounter "major dysfunction in the years ahead" (Guerney & Young, 1998, p. A22).

COPYRIGHT ISSUES

Copyright relates directly to the issue of intellectual property rights. Faculty or institutions that develop original instructional materials such as video, text, images, and so forth are entitled to copyright protection. By the same token, faculty and instructional developers need to be aware of copyright infringement when selecting materials developed by others for use in their classes. As we will see in the following sections, this has particular ramifications for distance learning where materials are broadcast, copied, or otherwise transmitted from one location to one or more other locations.

Copyright refers to the body of legal rights that protect creative works from being copied, reproduced, or disseminated by others without the permission of the creator or owner. The creator of a work can give or sell his or her copyright to someone else who then becomes the owner of the work. The work, as used here, refers to original creations such as literary pieces, music, drama, dance, images, paintings, video, television and radio programs, sound recordings, and the like. Copyright protects only the way in which an author has created an idea but not the idea itself. It is not an infringement of copyright to express the same idea in a different format.

Almost every nation has some form of copyright protection for creators of original works. The degree of protection varies significantly from one country to another. The Universal Copyright Convention (UCC) is an international treaty organization that has approximately eighty member nations, including the United States and Great Britain. Its major agreement is that every member nation gives foreign works the same copyright protection that the home nation gives its authors. A number of similar international treaties and agreements have been developed including the Berne Convention and the Buenos Aires Convention.

Fair Use

In the United States, the Copyright Act of 1976 stipulates that the owner of a work has the exclusive rights to reproduce, change, distribute, or copy the work. However, Section 107 (see Figure 6.5 for actual text) provides for limited or fair use including copying of works under certain circumstances for teaching, research, and scholarship. As a result, teachers in traditional classrooms have been allowed to make copies, with limitations, of various creative works for discussion and critical analysis.

The limitations or circumstances under which teachers can use copyrighted works depends on four factors, namely the purpose of the use, the nature of the copyrighted work, the amount or portion of the work used, and the effect of the use upon the potential market or value. Numerous court cases have been heard and decided on these factors. Many legal experts consider the fourth factor, the effect of the use upon a potential market, as being the most critical. However, fair use as stipulated here is a very flexible doctrine that is open to various interpretations in courts of law. A variety of arguments can be made based on any of the above factors that might sway a judgment one way or the other. One important bottom line is that fair use applies only to nonprofit activities. Any attempt to use a copyrighted work for a commercial enterprise is generally viewed as an infringement of fair use and the copyright law.

FIGURE 6.5   Text of Section 107 of the U.S. Copyright Act of 1976

Section 107 of the Copyright Act of 1976. Fair Use.

"Notwithstanding the provisions of sections 106 and 106A, the fair use of a copyrighted work, including such use by reproduction in copies or phonorecords or by any other means specified in that section, for purposes such as criticism, comment, news reporting, teaching (including multiple copies for classroom use), scholarship, or research, is not an infringement of copyright.

In determining whether the use made of a work in any particular case is a fair use the factors to be considered shall include:

1). the *purpose and character* of the use, including whether such use is of a commercial nature or is for non-profit educational purposes;
2). the *nature* of the copyrighted work;
3). the *amount and substantiality* of the portion used in relation to the copyrighted work as a whole; and
4). the *effect* of the use upon the potential market for or value of the copyrighted work.

The fact that a work is unpublished shall not itself bar a finding of fair use if such finding is made upon consideration of all the above factors."

Fair Use and Distance Learning

Are the stipulations established in Section 107 applicable in distance learning environments, where works may be broadcast or otherwise transmitted over wide or even limited area networks? Section 110 of the U.S. Copyright Act reiterates the importance of educational activities and the need for teachers to have access to and to use copyrighted works in the classroom. However, Section 110 also stipulates that the classroom involves face-to-face instruction and specifically excludes distance learning, especially of the broadcast television variety that is delivered into student homes. The only exception involves disabled students whose conditions prevent their attendance in a regular classroom. The underlying argument made by the owners of copyrights is that to allow fair use by distance learning providers infringes on their ability to sell copies of their works to the recipient sites, which is protected by the fourth limitation in Section 107 mentioned on the previous page.

As of this writing, the U.S. Congress was reviewing these issues and several bills were being debated (i.e., Digital Millennium Copyright Act) that might change the stipulations regarding fair use and distance learning. However, it is unclear whether new legislation would be less or more restrictive for distance learning providers. While educators surely would like to see less restriction, major holders of copyrights, such as book publishers, film producers, and television networks, would prefer more stringent restrictions.

Guidelines for Fair Use in Distance Learning

Schools and colleges would be wise to establish a set of guidelines on copyright and fair use in general and especially as applied to distance learning. These guidelines might include the following:

1. Identify a person(s) or office at the institution who has and maintains expertise in copyright law.
2. Make the copyright policy and institutional guidelines available in manual or pamphlet form to all faculty.
3. Delineate the differences in fair use for traditional face-to-face instruction and distance learning.
4. Acknowledge and place copyright credit on all legally made copies.
5. Encourage faculty to obtain permission to use copyrighted work.
6. Provide an institutional form letter for seeking permission (see Figures 6.6A and 6.6B).
7. Develop awareness and expertise with copyright in academic support offices such as media centers, libraries, and reproduction services.
8. Develop expertise in academic support areas to assist faculty in locating legitimate materials copyrighted or otherwise.
9. Conduct occasional audits of classes and Web sites to determine if any infringement of copyright is occurring in the institution.

FIGURE 6.6A A Form Letter for Requesting Permission to Use Copyrighted Materials

---

Kepler University
Collegetown, Illinois

Date: _____

Name and address of the owner of the copyrighted material:

_____

_____

_____

_____

Dear _____:

Describe the work with full citation for which permission is being sought. If possible, attach a copy of the material for which permission is being sought.

_____

_____

_____

_____

Identify the course, enrollment, number of copies, any student fees to be charged for materials, and the nature of the copies to be made (i.e., handouts, digitized images, 35mm slides, etc.) and how copies will be distributed.

_____

_____

_____

_____

Please sign and complete the information below. Enclosed is a self-addressed, stamped envelope for your convenience. If you have any questions, please feel free to contact me at your convenience.

Thank you for your attention to this matter.

Sincerely,

_____

- -

I (we) grant permission for the use requested above.

Name/Title_____ Date: _____
Company _____
Address _____

- -

In addition to making any guidelines developed available to the school and college community in text form, because copyright law is so inherently complex, forums should be made available in which faculty and others can ask questions. A discussion of copyright is an excellent topic for a faculty training program and might even be considered a requirement for faculty involved with distance learn-

FIGURE 6.6B   A Sample Letter to Obtain Permission to Use a Copyrighted Work

---

Kepler University
Collegetown, Illinois

January 1, 2000

ABC Publishers, Inc.
535 Broadway
New York, New York 10022
ATT: Permissions Department

Dear Permissions/Media Editor:

I would like to use excerpts and two images from the following book for a distance learning course I teach in Art History (ART 106).

> Sanders, J.K. (1991). *Sculpture from the Ancient World.* New York: ABC Publishers.

The excerpted sections and two images are attached.

Copies of the excerpted text will be distributed at no cost to each student as part of a distance learning coursepack. Approximate enrollment is fifty students per year. The two images will be scanned and copied onto a password-protected computer network accessible only to students in the course.

Please sign and complete the information below. Enclosed is a self-addressed, stamped envelope for your convenience. If you have any questions, please feel free to contact me at your convenience.

Thank you for your attention to this matter.

Sincerely,

Joyce James
Professor
Department of Art

I (we) grant permission for the use requested above.

Name/Title_____ Date: _____
Company _____
Address _____

---

ing. In recent years, especially with the proliferation of the Internet, institutions need to be ever more scrupulous about where and how faculty are acquiring course materials. Penalties for copyright infringement can be substantial. Neither the institution nor the faculty would want to go through the legal process of defending themselves, let alone be found liable for hundreds of thousands of dollars in damages.

SUMMARY

This chapter examines faculty issues associated with distance learning. Teachers, as the main catalysts for any instructional program, are perhaps the most important contributors to its success. Their experience and expertise provide important insights into any discussion on academic program development. However, distance learning and its associated technologies are evolving rapidly. Good distance learning programs do not simply take existing courses and conduct them in the same fashion using a distance learning technology. On the contrary, distance learning pedagogy requires a close re-examination of courses, lessons, and components of lessons to determine how they can be *converted* into new distance learning formats.

For faculty to use distance learning effectively, training and development is a necessity. The pedagogy and technology of distance learning is different from traditional instruction. Faculty who are successful in a traditional format can become successful in a distance learning format if provided with the appropriate training and support. A staff development training model is presented, which is integrated with other distance learning planning activities. The main components of the model are as follows:

Assess needs
Design program
Provide incentives
Implement program
Evaluation and review

Training and staff development should be designed to meet specific needs. Various techniques have been used successfully in training faculty to use distance learning. These include traditional seminars and workshops as well as "one-on-one" coaching and using the "training the trainer" technique to build a cadre of expert faculty who can assist other faculty. Hands-on activities and access to equipment and facilities are also required for developing familiarity with distance learning technologies.

Beyond faculty development, several other significant issues involving distance learning have emerged in recent years. Preparation time, course enrollments, special compensation, and personnel decisions may have to be reconsidered for faculty who develop and teach in distance learning programs. Intellectual property rights is a growing area of concern and interest as faculty develop media-intensive courses.

The chapter concludes with a discussion of copyright issues. This topic has particular ramifications for distance learning where materials are broadcast, copied, or otherwise transmitted from one location to one or more other locations.

CASE STUDY

Lubastat University Year: 2000

Setting

Lubastat University is located in a multilingual country in Eastern Europe. Lubastat University enjoys an excellent reputation as the premiere seat of higher education in the country and traces it beginnings to the seventeenth century. It offers a variety of programs in the liberal arts and sciences and employs a well-respected faculty, several of whom enjoy international reputations in their disciplines.

The Issue

A major concern at Lubastat in recent years has been the inability of the faculty to keep up with the latest worldwide developments in science and technology. The chancellor of Lubastat University has been in contact with two institutions in the United States for assistance in training its faculty in science and technology. There is general agreement that a relationship can be developed, however the cost of sending American faculty to Lubastat and vice versa for extended periods of time appears prohibitive. Furthermore, with the rapid changes in science and technology, there is a sense that a long-range, on-going program is more desirable than a one-time faculty exchange program. One of the American universities has suggested that distance learning courses be developed using video and Internet technologies. The idea would be for a small cadre of faculty from all three institutions to develop jointly the distance learning courses.

There are several issues associated with this approach. First, the American faculty who are most conversant in the areas of science and technology that are of interest to Lubastat University speak only English. Some of the faculty at Lubastat are multilingual, but their English needs further practice and development. Second, while several of the faculty at one of the American universities have extensive experience in developing distance learning materials, the faculty at the other American institution and at Lubastat have never taught in a distance learning environment. Third, while both of the American institutions have extensive access to Internet technology, Lubastat University has just begun to bring its faculty on-line. Substantial infrastructure costs are associated with advancing this technology, and it may be several years before most of the faculty have access to the Internet in their offices.

To solve the need for financing, proposals have been submitted for an American aid program that might provide at least an initial infusion of funding. While both governments have indicated a willingness to support the activity and are clear on the need for infrastructure support at Lubastat, several questions have been raised regarding the ability of the American universities to deliver effective distance learning courses. The chancellor of Lubastat has been requested by his government's American liaison to develop a detailed plan of the design and implementation of the distance learning courses, including an analysis of faculty development needs.

Assume you are a member of a consulting firm hired to assist in developing the aid proposal and in responding to the questions above. What do you see as the major areas of faculty training needed both at Lubastat and at the American universities? How would you prioritize these training needs? What type of training program(s) would you recommend?

REFERENCES

American Association of University Professors (1997, November 14). *Committee R on Government Relations Report on Distance Learning.* Presented by the Subcommittee on Distance Learning.

Cyrs, T. E., & Conway, E. D. (1997). *Teaching at a distance with the merging technologies: An instructional systems approach.* Las Cruces, NM: Center for Educational Development, New Mexico State University.

Davis, S., & Botkin , J. (1994). *The monster under the bed: How business is mastering the opportunity of knowledge for profit.* New York: Simon & Schuster.

Graf, D. (1993). *Teleteaching: Distance education planning techniques & tips.* Ames, IA: Media Resources Center, Iowa State University.

Guerney, L., & Young, J. R. (1998, June 5). Who owns on-line courses. *The Chronicle of Higher Education,* A21–A23.

Guerney, L. (1997, June 6). Scholars who work with technology fear they suffer in tenure reviews. *The Chronicle of Higher Education,* A32–A33.

Hanson, D., Maushak, N. J., Schlosser, C. A., Anderson, M. L., Sorenson, C., & Simonson, M. (1997). *Distance education: Review of the literature* (2nd ed.). Washington, D.C.: Association for Educational Communications and Technology.

Hartman, J. L, Dzubian, C., & Moskal, P. (1999, August). *Faculty satisfaction in ALNs.* Paper delivered at the Sloan ALN Summer Workshop, Urbana, Illinois.

Lenzer, R., & Johnson, S. S. (1997, March 10). Seeing things as they really are. *Forbes,* 122–128.

Noam, E. M. (1995). *Electronics and the dim future of the university.* Unpublished manuscript.

Rogers, E. M. (1995). *Diffusion of innovation* (4th ed.). New York: The Free Press.

Tapscott, D. (1996). *The digital economy: Promise and peril in the age of networked intelligence.* New York: McGraw-Hill.

Viau, E. A. (1994, Autumn/Winter). The mind as channel: A paradigm for the information age. *Educational Technology, 3,* 5–10.

Willis, B. (1993). *Distance education: A practical guide.* Englewood Cliffs, NJ: Educational Technology Publishing, Inc.

CHAPTER SEVEN

Administrative Support Services, Facilities, and Finances

Libraries have evolved for thousands of years in concert with centers of learning. The earliest libraries in the Middle East began as repositories of clay tablets. Ramses II formed one of the first Egyptian libraries with 20,000 papyrus scrolls in 1250 B.C. The Moors, using Chinese methods of papermaking, established a library of more than 400,000 volumes in the tenth century in Cordoba, Spain. The Bibliotheque Nationale de France in Paris traces its origins to

King Charles V in the fourteenth century and now houses more than ten million books. In 1638, John Harvard bequeathed 300 books to start the library at the university in Cambridge, Massachusetts that now bears his name.

For centuries, scholars from around the world traveled to these libraries to explore the knowledge that existed on their shelves. Universities could not exist without these informational treasures. Today in every college library, students can be seen studying, writing, and searching for information. An issue on many campuses is how long the library should stay open, especially during final exam periods. Teachers and students need the place we call the library. Indeed, the success of an academic program depends on the library as well as on well-equipped science laboratories, computer and media centers, and various other support services. In this chapter, we consider the support services and facilities needed for a distance learning program.

SUPPORT STAFF—THE SILENT HEROES

While watching the nightly television news, viewers take for granted that the program starts exactly on time, that the voice or audio is synchronized with the images, and that the camera pans to another location only when appropriate activity is occurring. This happens night after night, but viewers associate the entire broadcast with the one or two individuals who deliver the news. Occasionally a problem occurs; the TelePrompTer does not work properly or an expected video clip is not available. Viewers can see the look of concern on the newscaster's face as he or she depends on some behind-the-scenes individual to correct the situation. The deliverer of a nightly news program actually requires an extensive support staff of reporters, writers, audio and video technicians, a group of dedicated individuals whose names might appear in the closing credits but are rarely seen or known to the audience.

In a school or college, students enroll in countless classes, each led by an instructor who is expected to guide them through a body of material that will add to their knowledge. Classes are conducted several times a week with little interruption unless there is some problem such as the instructor is ill, the bulb on the overhead projector blows out, or a student must drop a course because of a financial aid glitch. When this happens, faculty or students seek the assistance of some support person to assign a substitute teacher, to find a new bulb, or to counsel the student on financial aid options. During times of need or when problems occur, the importance of support staff and the services they provide become apparent. Schools and colleges have established offices such as media services, academic computer support centers, registrar, and student counseling that faculty and students alike can seek out when they have a question or problem. These support services are just as important in a distance learning environment as they are in a traditional environment. The difference, however, is that in a traditional environment most instructional activity occurs in the same general place as support service activity. In distance learning, this is not the case and can present some unique logistical problems.

DEVELOPING DISTANCE LEARNING FACILITIES: START WITH AN ADMINISTRATIVE ORGANIZATION

Depending on the technologies used in distance learning, different facilities and the appropriate support staff may be required. If distance learning is provided via broadcast television, a studio with transmission facilities is needed. If point-to-point videoconferencing is used, classroom facilities that are set up to both send and receive video signals are required. If the Internet is being used for asynchronous learning, a computer network with database, World Wide Web software, and dial-in modem capabilities must be provided. Each of these technologies has different needs and will require different facilities and different support staffs. Furthermore, all of the distance learning technologies mentioned above are inherently complex and will require well-trained technicians to insure that the equipment works reliably and without substantive problems. Schools and colleges that have already invested in these technologies are able to build incrementally on existing facilities and staffs. Those that have not must make a substantial initial investment to establish them. Regardless of whether the plan is to expand existing facilities or to build new facilities, a significant investment of resources for equipment and staffing will be required. In a national survey of post-secondary education in the United States conducted by the National Center for Education Statistics, the three major reasons why institutions were not expanding existing distance programs or starting new ones were as follows:

1. Program development costs
2. Equipment cost and maintenance
3. Limited technological infrastructure
   (U.S. Department of Education, 1997)

In primary and secondary schools, most distance learning activities have evolved through governmental arrangements, especially statewide and consortia, since individual school districts generally lack the resources to do so themselves.

In developing new facilities, some distance learning administrative organization has to be established. If existing facilities are expanding, an administrative organization should already be in place. Providers whose sole mission and instructional delivery are based on distance learning naturally have the entire educational organization devoted to it. In environments where the primary mission and delivery is traditional instructional delivery, organizational and administrative decisions will have to be made as to how distance learning will be integrated with other departments and offices.

Many organizational structures exist that have proven to work well in educational enterprises. Figure 7.1 shows an organizational chart of a typical college with four major functions beneath the president. Distance learning (in brackets) in this scenario relies on the services of departments or offices in each of the four major administrative areas. Academic departments, registrar, library, academic computing services, telecommunications, student services, and continuing education

FIGURE 7.1 Traditional College Organization

Typical College/University Organization Chart
President

Vice President for Academic Affairs	Vice President for Administration	Vice President for Student Affairs	Vice President for External Affairs
Academic Departments/Schools	Comptroller	Admissions	Public Relations
Academic Advisement	Budget Office	Counseling	Annual Giving
Academic Computing	Personnel	Financial Aid	Community Affairs
Media/TV Services	Telecommunications	Recruitment	Continuing Education
Library	Campus Facilities	Student Activities	Gifts & Grants
Institutional Planning	Administrative Computing	Residence Life	College Publications
Registrar	Campus Security		
•			
•			
•			
[Department/School of Distance Learning]			

could all provide support to or otherwise be involved with distance learning. It would be difficult and perhaps very costly to duplicate all of the services provided by these offices in one distance learning department. As a result, the major functions (see Figure 7.2) of the distance learning department here are to plan, develop, and coordinate distance learning activities with the rest of the college. Degree programs need to be developed with the academic departments. Proposals for new equipment might be discussed and agreed upon jointly by academic computing or telecommunications offices. Specialized outreach programs to the community or local businesses may need to be coordinated with community affairs or continuing education. What is most important here is that the appropriate planning, support, and coordination occur.

Figure 7.3 provides an alternative to the typical structure that recognizes the growing influence of information, computer, and other technologies in all aspects of an organization. Private corporations, especially service-oriented businesses, have popularized this type of organization. Here a chief information officer reports to the president and has responsibilities for a full range of information technology resources including academic and administrative computing, library, and media services. A department of distance learning can be included under the responsibilities of the chief information officer. This structure eases the integration and coordination of distance learning with the other technologies such as computing, telecommunications, and media. Additional coordination with academic departments, registrar, and student services is still necessary.

FIGURE 7.2   Functions/Responsibilities of an Office/School of Distance Learning

Department/School of Distance Learning
Director/Dean

Functions/Responsibilities:
  Conduct market research studies/needs for distance learning.
  Propose new courses, programs, and other distance learning initiatives.
  Establish program quality standards for distance learning.
  Evaluate existing distance learning activities.
  Conduct cost and benefit analysis of distance learning programs.
  Develop the schedule of classes for distance learning.
  Design and implement faculty and staff development programs.
  Coordinate technical, student, and academic support services for distance learning.
  Coordinate/recommend new hardware and software acquisitions for distance learning.

FIGURE 7.3   Information-Services-Emphasized College Organization Chart

		President		
Vice President for Academic Affairs	**Vice President for Administration**	**Vice President for Student Affairs**	**Vice President for External Affairs**	**Chief Information Officer**
Academic Schools/ Departments	Comptroller	Admissions	Public Relations	Academic Computing
Academic Advisement	Budget Office Personnel	Counseling Financial Aid	Annual Giving Community Affairs	Administrative Computing
Registrar	Campus Facilities	Recruitment Student	Continuing Education Gifts & Grants	Library Media/TV Serv.
Research Institutional Planning	Campus Security	Activities Residence Life	College Publications	Telecommunications
				•
				•
				[Distance Learning]

Regardless of the organizational structure that has evolved or is already in place, competent people are needed to plan, design, implement, and coordinate distance learning services. If this is not happening, an evaluation is needed to determine whether the cause is the organizational structure or the people in the positions of responsibility. In addition, a department of distance learning will need the support of senior administrators. Given that distance learning is still something new and different in most institutions, success may very much depend on the moral, symbolic, and financial support of the president or vice president(s).

ADMINISTRATIVE SUPPORT SERVICES

In one survey of distance learning students, the most common criticisms made by the respondents were related to basic services such as knowledge of the institution's policies and procedures, overall communication, and material distribution (Hardy & Boaz, 1997). Academic and student services as provided by a library, media center, counseling, and advisement services are as critical to the success of a distance learning program as they are to a traditional program. How well they are delivered at a distance will depend on the coordination and monitoring done by the administrative personnel in a distance learning department or office. Readers may wish to review the material in Chapter 5 where issues associated with academic and student services were first introduced.

Earlier in this chapter, the functions and responsibilities of an office or school of distance learning were discussed (see Figure 7.2). Some of these responsibilities, such as developing a semester or yearly schedule of distance learning classes, are substantial and perhaps self-contained undertakings. However, many of the functions and responsibilities involve working with and coordinating distance learning activities with other offices. It would be inefficient and costly for a distance learning office to try to duplicate all the services provided by these offices. Additionally, regardless of where the responsibility for providing these services lies, the distance learning office must monitor the services to its students and make recommendations for improving or expanding them if needed. To do so, the distance learning office should have some monitoring mechanism in place that alerts staff to problems, issues, and the overall quality of the delivery of services to students. While feedback from students in the form of surveys and evaluations can yield important information about services, a more proactive approach is recommended.

The concept of a "help line," which is used extensively by many service industries, has a good deal of applicability in a distance learning environment where students are separated and physically not located at a school or college. Help lines are generally provided via routine telephone services such as toll-free "800" numbers. When a problem occurs, it is likely that the distance learning student is alone and the security of knowing that there is somebody to talk to is very reassuring. For distance learning applications based on computer networks, the telephone help line can be supplemented by an e-mail or an on-line help center. The purpose of this help line is not necessarily to answer every question but to direct student inquiries to the proper office or individual. In fact, it is unlikely that there are any single individuals at a school who know enough about academic matters, advisement, financial aid, or the availability of reference materials, among other things, to provide all the proper and informed responses.

In addition to providing an important service to students, the help line will also serve as a monitor for problems and issues as they arise. Queries from students should be logged for patterns or common issues that might need closer scrutiny. Areas that generate many student inquiries may need to be reviewed more carefully and discussed with the appropriate department or personnel. An instructor who is not responding to students, the unavailability of reference material at an off-campus library, and technical problems with computer on-line services are just some of the problems that might arise. If sporadic, these are not major problems. However, if a pattern develops, then more aggressive action might be needed to correct the problem.

How well a help line works will depend on its availability (hours of operation and number of staff answering telephone calls), the expertise of the staff on the help line, and the competence and efficiency of the various services that support the distance learning program. The larger the program, the greater the required availability. While a problem may cause anxiety or frustration for some students, receiving a constant busy signal on a help line only adds to the frustration. The distance learning office or department should staff this help line with knowledgeable individuals who are sensitive to the needs of distance learning students as well as familiar with the support services that are available at the institution. The help line staff need to know who or what office can answer a question, as well as when and how they can be reached. Ultimately, the success of the help line depends on the abilities and responsiveness of the staffs of the various services to whom students will be directed. While the point has been made that the distance learning office cannot assume responsibility for all the services that a school or college provides, nevertheless it has to do everything it can to ensure the success of its program. Ongoing discussion, building a relationship, and coordinating activities with service areas such as the library, computer center, registrar, or counseling offices are important. The distance learning office should be responsible for ensuring that these service areas are familiar with its programs and especially with the needs of distance learners, many of whom work full-time, have families, and lead busy lives.

TECHNICAL SERVICES

A well-trained technical support staff is critical to the initial development of courses as well as the ongoing delivery of classes. The size, qualifications, and nature of the technical support staff is dependent on the size and nature of the distance learning program. For instance, schools whose primary missions are entirely related to distance learning will have large technical support staffs developing materials for courses. Distance learning courses that depend extensively on graphical or video content will need specialists (artists, editors) to assist in developing quality educational materials. Distance learning programs that use computer networks will need data communications specialists, programmers, and other technically trained individuals. In sum, for major distance learning projects, a development team that includes various levels of technical expertise and assistance will be necessary. If this expertise is available within the organization, it needs to be redirected or partially directed to the distance learning program. If it is not available, then this expertise must be secured through new hires, consulting, or other contractual arrangements.

Once courses have been developed, ongoing support will be necessary for testing, preparing, and modifying existing materials. Again, the nature of this support will depend on the size and nature of the distance learning program. Economies can be realized by using graduate assistants and other part-time staff with skills or interest in distance learning and the associated technologies.

Later in this chapter, a typical videoconferencing classroom design (see Figure 7.5) will be discussed. Such a classroom contains specialized equipment (cameras, monitors, and communications connections) that requires ongoing maintenance and testing. Faculty generally do not have the time or training to maintain and troubleshoot this equipment. Common practice is for a technician to be available throughout a distance learning class to assist the instructor in setting up materials and more importantly to be available in case of any technical difficulties. Without such assistance and support, most faculty would feel too uneasy and vulnerable to teach in this environment.

Developing materials for delivery over a communications network may also require periodic modifications and upgrading. Analog or digital networking technology is highly complex and rapidly evolving and changing. Well-trained staffs that are able to keep up with technological changes become critical to the ongoing success and development of a distance learning program. Not only are they able to upgrade hardware or software but they also can assist faculty and students who have to use the new technology.

A critical issue in technical support staffing is their relationship with the faculty. It is incumbent upon the administration or management of the distance learning program to ensure that technical staff are oriented to distance learning instructional needs. Faculty training programs, where discussions of content and material development naturally evolve, can be especially effective when technical support staff are included. The success of a distance learning course is dependent on both the content and delivery. While faculty possess content expertise, a good technical support staff can ensure the delivery. Distance learning programs that are successful have established a good working relationship between the two.

BUILDING A TECHNOLOGY INFRASTRUCTURE

Increasingly, distance learning depends on the availability of modern, high-speed data communications systems. Many organizations have devoted a good deal of study and subsequently resources to developing the infrastructure for such systems.

The term *technology infrastructure* was popularized in the 1990s. To prepare for the twenty-first century, government officials, corporate leaders, and educators called for the building of a national, corporate, or school technology infrastructure. Technology infrastructure generally refers to computer networking facilities that can deliver data at high speed and high capacity reliably throughout an organization. A faculty member at his or her desk, a lab assistant developing a laboratory experiment, or a student doing an assignment in a dormitory would have access to a computer workstation and be able to connect to a college network and, via the network, to the Internet or other external networking systems. Buildings and offices are wired, preferably with fiber-optic or coaxial cable, and equipped with the necessary message-handling facilities so that faculty, students, and others can communicate with one another. The ability to do so easily, reliably, and extensively is called "connectivity."

The technology infrastructure is based on digital networks that can handle data, audio or voice, and video signals. In the past, separate facilities were frequently developed to deliver data, audio, and video; this is no longer the case. In developing an infrastructure, the concept of a common networked environment that integrates data, audio, and video for the entire organization (i.e., teachers, students, libraries, and other support areas) is recommended. Such an environment would be able to support both analog (i.e., telephone, television) as well as digital (i.e., computer, Internet) applications. A major decision involves planning the appropriate mix or combination of technologies that will support not only the present but the future needs of the organization.

It is critical that the digital network have the capacity to convert and deconvert analog transmissions such as those used for basic audio and video activities. While virtually all future communications technologies will be based on digital networking and transmission, a need for analog communications will exist into the early part of the twenty-first century. For the present, digital networks should be developed that include conversion/deconversion hardware and software to handle analog communications. To connect digital computers to analog telephone lines, for instance, modems (modulator/demodulators) are routinely used to convert digital or computer signals into analog electromagnetic sound waves and vice versa. Codec (coding/decoding) equipment is also used in the same fashion to convert and compress analog video signals into digital formats and vice versa.

Figure 7.4 provides a conceptual design for a network based on a communications distribution system that handles analog and digital transmissions for a variety of activities. While the network provides high-capacity transmission paths to and from analog and digital sources, users can connect to and access the network from various locations. Teachers and students can use computer workstations to connect to the network for individual activity. Classrooms connected to the network can be set up with videoconferencing capabilities for group activities. Broadcast television and satellite transmissions also can be received and distributed on the network.

Building a technology infrastructure requires a good deal of planning and expert knowledge. Some organizations have developed the expertise within their own environment, while others rely on outside consultants. The technologies associated with computer networks, data conversion, and video compression are complex and rapidly evolving. It is likely that any organization that is planning to build a new infrastructure or expand an existing one will require some outside expertise. The expenditure for such a consultancy is necessary and appropriate.

FIGURE 7.4 Technology Infrastructure

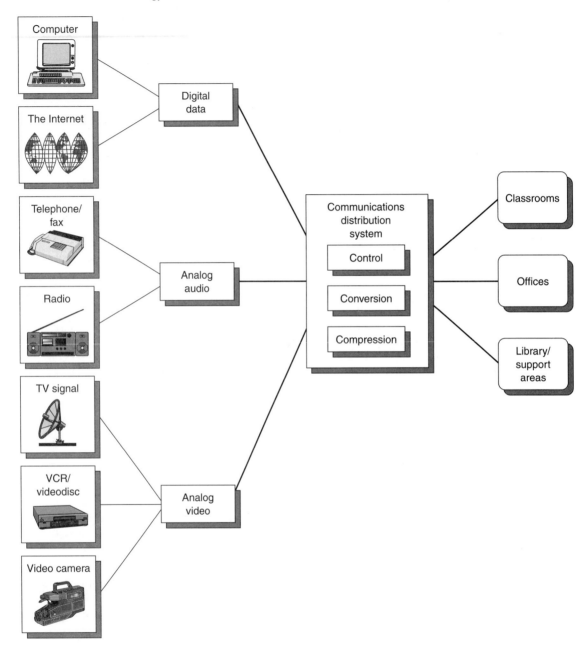

DESIGNING CLASSROOMS FOR DISTANCE LEARNING

Classrooms for distance learning also need to be well planned. Ergonomics, floor layouts, furniture, electrical distribution, and media locations are critical factors to the success of a distance learning program. Depending on the nature of the distance learning application (videoconferencing, broadcast television, or computer network), the physical requirements differ. What is important is that the people who will use these facilities are provided with a physical environment that is conducive to learning. This is especially important for classrooms that are used by large numbers of faculty and students. Many factors, such as physical dimensions, electrical power, ventilation, location of equipment, sight lines, and so forth, have to be considered when developing a distance learning classroom. It is impossible to provide details for every type of distance learning facility here, but perhaps a brief example of the kinds of issues that arise might provide enough insight to appreciate and understand the importance of good classroom design.

When designing point-to-point videoconferencing facilities, at least two locations are needed. In the sending location, an instructor can deliver a lecture or lead a discussion for a "live" class while students at a second, or third, or fourth receiving location can see and hear the instructor, ask questions, and make comments. Assume that major considerations such as the seating capacity, electrical supply, and temperature control are appropriate for the rooms. If we consider the actual teaching/learning activity, a number of other important physical considerations become apparent. For example, lighting controls can be very helpful, especially for media-based lessons, so that students at the remote location can see the instructor and media material as needed and vice versa. More important than seeing is the absolute need to hear properly. Acoustics in both rooms should be tested, and the ability to adjust volume adds immensely to the success of a lesson. Consider in a traditional class what would happen if the instructor could not hear a student's question or, worse yet, the students could not hear the instructor. Lighting and acoustic controls should be easy to use and located in close proximity to the instructor. This will help avoid perhaps several trips to the back of a lecture hall to adjust lights for playing a short video clip or showing a collection of slides.

Assuming that lighting and acoustical controls are available and function easily, instructor knowledge that he or she is being seen and heard properly at the remote location is essential. A common design technique is a three-part (instructor, student, media) monitor system located away from and facing the instructor. An instructor can view the monitors and see exactly what the students at the remote location are seeing—generally either the instructor or a media presentation. The third monitor is for the instructor to see the students at the remote location and to control for closeups of specific students asking questions or making comments.

In recent years, microphones have been developed with sensors that automatically adjust cameras at a remote location to focus immediately on students who are speaking, thereby negating the necessity for manual control. These microphones can be located on desks where students simply push a button to ask a question. In more sophisticated designs, microphones are hung from the ceiling and automatically activate cameras when someone speaks.

While controls for lighting, acoustics, and camera angles are best located in the front of a class, preferably on a teacher's desk or workstation, the location of the recording camera and monitors for viewing activities at remote sites are best located toward the rear of the classroom and facing the instructor. As much as possible, while delivering a lecture or leading a discussion, instructors should be able to face into the camera and look at their audiences at the same time. Therefore, monitors for viewing remote activities should be located in close proximity to the instructor's camera. Teachers should not need to turn their backs frequently to look at monitors to see what is going on at the remote locations. A secondary problem is how do the students at the sending location (live audience) see their counterparts at the remote location. There is no simple solution here other than to have two sets of monitors: one for the students located at the front of the room, and one for the instructor located in the rear. This duplication may seem to be an unnecessary expense, however instructors who teach in videoconferencing classrooms find the convenience of being able to view their remote audiences without turning away from the live audience very helpful for delivering their lessons.

Figure 7.5 is a floor plan for a sending distance learning classroom that incorporates the approaches described in the above paragraphs. Monitors for the students are located in the front of the room along with a student camera. Instructor monitors and camera are located in the rear of the room. While the depiction is of separate monitors, new technology is available that can provide one large monitor with the ability to "split the screen," thereby providing multiple images or video feeds on one monitor. With small modifications, the design considerations discussed in this example can also be applied to receive other types of distance learning and media-based classrooms.

FINANCIAL ISSUES

While considering the administrative support, facilities, and technical assistance needs discussed in the previous paragraphs, policy makers and educational administrators can easily conclude that developing a major distance learning program is an expensive undertaking. For some, the financial commitment may prove daunting. In the following paragraphs, issues related to financing and budgeting for distance learning programs will be discussed in greater depth.

The cost-effectiveness of distance learning and technology-based instructional programs has been widely debated for several decades. Keegan (1996) examined the issue of cost effectiveness, especially in large-scale distance learning programs using mass media such as television or radio, and whether economy can be achieved by reducing labor costs and increasing enrollments. In particular, he traced the history and debate of cost effectiveness research at the Open University of the United Kingdom. Citing the work of Wagner (1972), Laidlaw and Layard (1974), Carnoy and Levin (1975), Mace (1978), and Rumble (1982), he observed that their conclusions conflicted

FIGURE 7.5 Videoconferencing Classroom

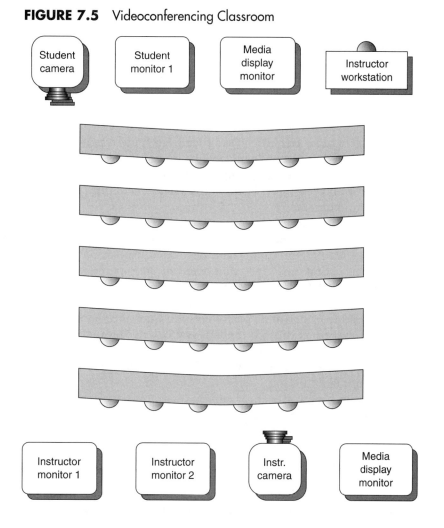

significantly. While some evidence was presented that the Open University was more cost effective than traditional universities, other evidence indicated that it was not. In these studies, Keegan pointed out that significant disagreement existed on how to assess the costs and outcomes in a media-intensive distance learning environment versus a traditional education environment.

Whether used in distance learning or in traditional environments, the cost of technology generates a good deal of interest. For years policy makers, administrators, and faculty have all questioned whether investments in new communications or computer equipment lead to better learning. The simple but popular notion that properly designed equipment or machines can replace people and thereby save money has not been accepted in educational settings, as it has in other industries such as automobile assembly lines, telephone communications, and printing/ publishing. Furthermore, as Keegan concluded, one fundamental problem in conducting cost-effectiveness analyses in education is that extensive disagreement exists on what constitutes effectiveness. Unlike goods and services in many commercial industries, outcomes in education are not precisely measurable by quantifiable data. While testing can measure the degree of mastery of subject matter at a particular time, other educational outcomes such as emotional maturation, critical thinking, future career or academic preparation, social contacts, and appreciation for culture and the creative arts are more difficult. Even identifying the cost of an education, while less complicated than agreeing on outcomes, can also be a complex undertaking and open to disagreement. Regardless of this complexity, a propensity exists to conduct cost-effectiveness analyses in media and technology-based distance learning programs.

In addition to its dependence on expensive technology, distance learning has been subject to a greater degree of cost-benefit study for other reasons. First, many distance learning programs have been conducted or offered experimentally in traditional institutions. One component of an experiment is to evaluate carefully whether or not it has been successful and has achieved its objectives. Distance learning as an experiment has come under scrutiny and in some instances has struggled to establish its parity with traditional programs. In addition, many experimental programs are funded temporarily through grants or other means. A careful accounting of expenditures and evaluation of outcomes are frequently required by the granting agency at the end of the grant cycle and as a requirement for continued funding.

Second, many distance learning programs have evolved from continuing education or adult education programs that are designed to be self-sustaining. These programs typically offer a menu of courses but only actually conduct those courses or programs where fees or tuition from the students cover all expenses. As a result, basic cost and enrollment data have been more routinely evaluated here than in traditional programs.

Third, the majority of distance learners are mature adults seeking to upgrade skills. Many have families and provide financial, emotional, and social support to spouses, children, and others. Their priorities and expectations in seeking an education are more clearly defined in terms of mastering subject matter. Assessing outcomes through easily quantifiable data such as test scores, course attrition, or program completion rates may be more acceptable here than in traditional programs geared to younger students, where outcomes such as emotional maturity or social integration are less easily quantifiable.

Over the years, a number of studies have been published reporting substantial savings in distance learning applications. Chute, Hulik, & Palmer (1987) for instance, reported savings of $1,810,000 per year in travel, meals, lodging, and employee time by AT&T for corporate training as a result of converting a traditional staff development and training program to teletraining. Fredrickson (1990) reported that distance learning applications in rural Alaska using audiographics were four to five times less expensive per course than when using live teachers. Hosley and Randolph (1993), in a study for Lockheed Space Operations Technical Training Department, reported a one-year savings of $50,000 in travel expenses by using a videoconferencing system.

Vigilante (1996) studied the costs and benefits of four different (see Figure 7.6) on-line computer delivery systems used in a graduate program in information systems analysis at New York University. He concluded that among these, delivering hypertext tutorials were the least expensive while asynchronous computer conferencing moderated by faculty was the most expensive. Vigilante also concluded that digital video, while the most expensive to produce, was actually less costly in its delivery than computer conferencing because of the communications efficiency of viewing video as opposed to the labor–intensive (faculty) nature of electronic bulletin board and group e-mail discussions. In terms of instructional benefits, Vigilante determined that digital video was the most effective of the delivery systems. However, his final recommendation was to blend several technologies, because distance learning using audiographics, computer conferencing, and video offered the "just right" combination of higher instructional benefits and reasonable costs.

Caution should be exercised in generalizing individual case cost-benefit studies. Commonly used criteria for cost evaluation such as student contact hours, faculty workload, or the use of part-time or full-time faculty may vary from one environment to another. Distance learning programs use a myriad of delivery technologies, and costs associated with one technology may have little relationship to another technology so that generalization about distance learning can easily become confused and conflicted. While distance learning providers may be able to reduce costs in certain situations, some of these costs, such as the expense of purchasing and maintaining computer equipment, actually are being passed on to students.

FIGURE 7.6 Distance Learning Delivery Systems Used in a Graduate Program in Information Systems at New York University.

Hypertext Readings: Online readings with dynamic cross-references to all text materials.

Audiographic Tutorials: Tutorials that provide course instruction in the form of graphic images and audio presentations.

Computer Conferencing: Asynchronous student-faculty discussions of topics, projects, case studies, and assignments.

Digital Video: Videos consisting mostly of computer animations, faculty demonstrations, and simulations. Each session included approximately one half-hour of video files.

SOURCE: Vigilante, R. (1996). *Semesters in CyberSpace.* New York: New York University Office of Continuing Education, p. 9.

Cost must always be carefully considered in relation to the quality of a program. This discussion on cost-effectiveness began by referencing Keegan's study of whether large-scale distance learning programs using mass media such as television or radio could effect significant economies by reducing labor costs and increasing enrollments. As the demand for educational opportunity increases, the potential economies of distance learning has an appeal to educational policy makers around the world. These economies should be welcomed in any environment, so long as the quality of the instruction has not been compromised. Hiltz (1997) offered a caution on the issue of economy in distance learning. In an evaluation of asynchronous learning (ALN) using computer networking at the New Jersey Institute of Technology, she concluded that if administrators think that ALN courses are a "cheap" way to offer distance learning, they should be aware that if they are developed for instructional quality and conducted by full-time faculty, these courses can in fact be more expensive.

BUDGETING A DISTANCE LEARNING PROGRAM

Budgeting for distance learning should be done as carefully as it is for any other major administrative or academic program. The basic funding components (see Figure 7.7) that exist in traditional educational environments provide appropriate starting points. In a traditional educational organization, expenditures are devoted to people-costs and non-people or "other than personnel" costs such as equipment, supplies, and contractual and facilities services such as electricity, telephone, heating, and cooling. In a basic operating budget, people-costs, especially full-time salaries, are almost always the major expenditure and can easily exceed 70 percent of the total budget. This occurs because the highest other-than-personnel expenditure, the construction of new buildings and facilities, is frequently financed and funded separately as a capital expenditure using long-term bonding amortized over many years. Depending on the nature of the institution (public, private, proprietary), certain revenue streams such as tuition, government subsidies, or special taxes are used to repay bondholders. Distinguishing the operating budget from the capital budget has relevance to distance learning. Examples of capital projects that can support distance learning include building and equipping television production facilities, upgrading and equipping the technology infrastructure, and wiring buildings with fiber optic cable.

In developing a funding plan for a distance learning program, a starting point might be determining if any capital expenditures are required for facilities. If so, capital funds should be secured first with the remainder of the financing to follow. This determination depends on what facilities exist and the nature of the proposed program. Constructing buildings and studios or wiring campuses easily costs millions of dollars. Organizations that have previously invested heavily in facilities that support technologies such as communications and computers may be in a better position to expand or initiate new distance learning programs. Many more ed-

FIGURE 7.7 Major Funding Components for an Educational Enterprise

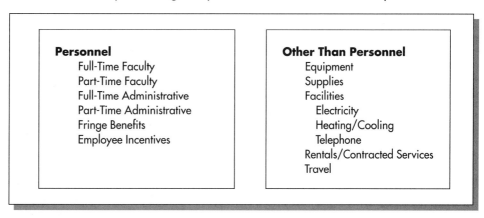

ucational institutions are making significant investments in digital communications to access informational resources such as the Internet for their traditional academic programs. Therefore, it is increasingly likely that facilities already exist and are available for distance learning.

Once capital costs are accounted for, the operating budget for a distance learning program should provide for extensive technology support and continued upgrading, since a fundamental characteristic of communications and computer technologies is that they are constantly evolving. Figure 7.8 identifies most of the major funding components of a distance learning program. Personnel costs for administrative services, technical support, and faculty are the major expenditures. Other than personnel, costs include equipment, software, supplies, furnishings, specialized communications such as high-speed telephone lines, and contractual services. The distribution of the funding for these expenditures can vary significantly depending on the nature of the program, the instructional delivery technologies, and faculty deployment and productivity. For example, programs that use satellite communications for a world audience are more expensive than programs using local telephone connections within a limited geographic area. Internet technologies are less expensive than point-to-point videoconferencing facilities. Broadcast television reaching thousands of students will have higher delivery costs than courses delivered on videocassette. All of the above are readily ascertained once the decisions have been made regarding the nature of the program and the delivery mechanisms. However, this is not necessarily true for faculty costs. In fact, the most complex variable in determining the costs of a program will be the faculty.

Turoff (1997), in a cost analysis for developing a "virtual university" for 2,000 students using an asynchronous computer network calculated the yearly non-faculty costs as $1.8 million including the following: administrative/support staff

FIGURE 7.8 Funding Components for a Distance Learning Program

Personnel
  Program Administration
    Scheduling
    Training
    Marketing
    Material Distribution
    Record Keeping
  Technical Support Services
  Faculty
    Release-Time Reimbursement

Other Than Personnel
  Equipment
    Purchases
    Major Repairs
    Upgrades
  Software
  Communications
    Telephone
    Satellite
  Supplies/Furnishings
  Contractual Services
    Equipment Maintenance
    Training
    Printing

($1.5 million), facilities ($150,000), and computer hardware/software ($150,000). For the faculty, he presented eight separate scenarios varying from a low of $7.5 million to a high of $60 million. Critical variables included the faculty course workload per year, students per class, number of majors and unique courses offered, and faculty personnel requirements for teaching versus research and scholarship. For $7.5 million dollars, faculty would teach eight courses per year with an average enrollment of fifty students per course. For $60 million, faculty would teach four courses per year with an average enrollment of thirteen students per class. Turoff determined that utilizing the middle range costs for faculty, a virtual university for 2,000 students could be developed for between $15 and $30 million. An important assumption in Turoff's analysis was that the faculty be full-time and well-paid at approximately $150,000 per year for salary and fringe benefits in recognition of the additional preparation and training time needed to be effective in this environment. Naturally, substantial savings can be realized by lowering full-time faculty salaries or by using part-time or adjunct faculty who generally are paid less on a course-by-course basis and receive minimal fringe benefits.

The use of full-time versus part-time faculty in post-secondary education and especially in programs oriented for adults, such as continuing education and distance learning, is becoming a major issue. More and more institutions are relying on part-time instructors, mainly because of the economies that can be realized. It is incumbent on each institution to examine its own policies with regard to the percentages of courses taught by full-time versus part-time faculty. The recommendation here is that the proportion of full-time versus part-time faculty teaching traditional courses should be maintained for distance learning courses also. If not, concerns for the academic quality of the distance learning program would be justified.

REVENUE AND FUNDING SOURCES

Once a budget plan is in place, determining revenue and funding sources becomes the major focus in mounting a distance learning program. Most distance learning providers (colleges, educational consortia, private corporations) rely extensively on student fees and tuition. Even state-subsidized consortia supporting primary and secondary schools frequently charge annual fees to school districts for providing distance learning services. If student fees and tuition will be the major revenue source for the distance learning program, then a careful analysis of projected enrollments and tuition per course must be undertaken.

The starting point for determining fees and tuition for a distance learning course will likely be the fee structure established for traditional courses within the institution. Publicly subsidized universities and community colleges have much lower tuition and fee structures (i.e., several hundred dollars per course) than prestigious, private, research universities (i.e., several thousand dollars per course). For educational providers whose sole program will be distance learning and who do not offer traditional courses, some type of market analysis should be undertaken. This can be especially complex for programs hoping to attract students worldwide whose individual incomes will vary significantly.

In determining and estimating fees and tuition, consideration should be given to the goals and objectives of the distance learning program. If the goal is to expand student access and educational opportunity, consideration must be given to establishing an affordable fee structure. If the program is expected to be self-sustaining, then the costs for offering the program serve as the basis for the fee structure. If the goal of the program is to generate a profit, then an analysis of the market and what students are willing to pay becomes a determining factor. In this regard, some institutions such as Penn State's World Campus and Stanford University's on-line Masters in Business Administration Program actually have established a higher fee and tuition rate for distance learning courses than for their comparable traditional courses. In estimating fees and tuition, generally an important, albeit complex, factor is whether or not financial aid is available for the intended student population.

Financial Aid

Financial aid regulations vary significantly from country to country and from state to state. In the United States, general principles for estimating financial aid possibilities for students include the following:

1. Aid is based most often on student need.
2. Loans are more readily available than grants.

3. Full-time students have greater access to aid than part-time students.
4. Government-based or guaranteed programs are primarily available to citizens and/or residents.

However, these principles may or may not apply to distance learners. Cheryl Leibovitz (1997), Senior Policy Specialist, U.S. Department of Education, cautioned that many distance learning providers are not fully aware of some of the stipulations associated with the major financial aid programs funded by the U.S. federal government. For example, correspondence courses that include many video-based, home-study courses may not be eligible for federal financial aid. This is especially true if such courses are non-degree or certificate courses and not part of an associate, bachelor, or graduate degree program. Even if some of these courses do qualify, for purposes of receiving financial aid, such study is considered no more than half-time regardless of the number of courses for which the student is enrolled.

Some distance learning providers may or may not meet the institutional eligibility requirements for federal financial aid. Generally, an institution will not qualify if a majority of its courses are correspondence or based on telecommunications. Furthermore, regardless of its courses, if 50 percent or more of its students are enrolled in correspondence or telecommunications-based courses, the institution does not qualify for federally funded financial aid programs.

In light of the growing popularity of distance learning in the United States, some of these regulations are undergoing a reevaluation. Nevertheless, in developing or expanding a program, distance learning providers should be aware of whether and how these regulations will affect student financial aid eligibility. Furthermore, while a great deal of variability exists, most state financial aid programs follow federal guidelines. Hence, students who might be eligible for both federal and state financial aid programs in a traditional school, may find themselves eligible for neither in a distance learning environment.

Consortia and Cooperative Arrangements

References have been made several times in this chapter to consortia and cooperative arrangements in establishing and developing distance learning facilities. Such arrangements can be cost-effective and can provide opportunities for organizations with limited resources or limited technological expertise. Smaller colleges, and primary and secondary schools, in particular, find these arrangements appealing; they may be their only pathway to offering or participating in distance learning. Costs that can be shared include those for building an infrastructure and for providing technology assistance in establishing and maintaining distance learning facilities throughout a geographic area. Such arrangements may also include coordinating responsibilities to minimize duplication of effort, and as a result, cost.

Within the United States, a number of states have established such systems. In 1980, Learn/Alaska became the first state educational satellite system operating in the United States. The Georgia Statewide Academic and Medical System (GSAMS) is also proving to be successful in providing highly interactive distance learning activities. Walsh and Reese (1995) describe the GSAMS as the largest interactive distance network in the world, reaching hundreds of classrooms and other sites. The Iowa Communications Network (ICN) has established one of the most extensive fiber optic educational networks in the country. The plan is for all school districts, colleges, and public libraries in Iowa to be connected to the ICN. The ICN model is being considered or duplicated in other states because it provides full-motion video, two-way interactive communications, and digital (Internet) and voice services. All of the above involved a significant financial commitment on the part of the states for the initial development of the delivery systems and administrative organization. Once established, participants pay fees or make other contributions for whatever use they make of the facilities.

Outside of the United States, where central ministries govern educational policies and programs, distance learning consortia and cooperatives tend to be countrywide. Some follow a British Open University model or a French Centre National D'Enseignement a Distance (CNED) model, with a central college or university developing and offering distance learning programs for entire populations. Other countries such as Finland (Finnish Association for Distance Education), Sweden (Swedish Association for Distance Education), and China (DIANDA—Radio and Television Educational Network) have established truer consortia arrangements with a central administrative structure providing services to many schools and organizations.

States and countries that have established consortia arrangements have created desirable cost-effective environments in which their schools and other organizations can develop distance learning programs. Those that have not should consider doing so. Even if not designed specifically for distance learning, much of the required technology infrastructure supports other desirable educational technology needs such as access to the Internet and data resource sharing.

Gifts and Grants

Any discussion of funding sources for distance learning would not be complete without some discussion of gifts and grants. Distance learning and related instructional technology projects are of significant interest to both public and private granting agencies. While some gifts and grants can support distance learning programs for an extended period of time, most are designed for start-up activities. Organizations considering new programs or significantly enhancing existing programs should investigate whether grants or other outside funding are available.

The U.S. Department of Education and the National Science Foundation have several major grant programs designed to provide funds for distance learning projects. Many of these projects favor consortia and cooperative arrangements above individual schools or colleges. Several states such as Wisconsin (Wisconsin Advanced Telecommunications Foundation and Educational Technology Board) have also established grant programs for funding distance learning and other technology-based programs. Excellent sources of information regarding federal and other public grants and funding include the following:

- *The Federal Register,* Office of the Federal Register, National Archives and Records Administration, Washington, D.C. 20408
- *Education Daily,* Capital Publications, Inc., 1101 King St., Alexandria, VA 22313-2053
- *Federal Grants and Contracts Weekly* (also published by Capital Publications, Inc.)

The U.S. Department of Education and the National Science Foundation also provide complete and updated information on their grant programs at their Web sites.

Private foundations such as the Alfred P. Sloan Foundation and the Annenberg Foundation have well-established major grant programs for distance learning activities and disburse millions of dollars per year. Private corporations such as computer manufacturers, telephone companies, book publishers, and other media-related enterprises also have grant programs designed to support distance learning. Frequently these programs require the use of equipment or services provided by the companies. Following are three excellent sources of information on grants from private corporations and foundations.

- Sloane Reports, Inc., P.O. Box 561689, Miami, FL 33256
- The Foundation Center, 79 Fifth Ave., New York, NY 10003-3050
- The Grantsmanship Center, P.O. Box 17220, Los Angeles, CA 90099-4522

In addition, standard search engines on the World Wide Web such as *Yahoo, Altavista,* or *Excite* can provide a good deal of information. One caution, however—in seeking grants, faculty and other initiators should share their proposals and ideas with experienced grant administrators at their colleges and school districts. Competent personnel in grants administration can save enormous time by assisting in searches for information and steering faculty in the right direction. They may also be able to provide assistance in developing proposals and assessing the possibilities for funding.

SUMMARY

This chapter examines the administrative aspects, physical facilities, and financial requirements for distance learning. To be successful, all instructional programs depend on a number of services for support. Libraries, media centers, and computer laboratories directly contribute to the academic experiences of students. Registrars, counselors, and advisors likewise provide critical behind-the-scenes support. In distance learning, these support services are just as important as they are in traditional programs. In fact, because distance learning relies more on advanced technologies and facilities, competent and reliable technical support services are an absolute necessity.

Administrative organization is an important starting point for providing support services for a distance learning program. As much as possible, a distance learning office should work with other support services already established and required for traditional programs. An office or school for distance learning, while providing vision and direction, most efficiently operates by securing the cooperation of the many other support areas in the educational organization. This office should also establish administrative mechanisms such as "help lines" to ensure that distance learners are receiving the proper support from other areas.

Depending on the technologies used in distance learning, different facilities with appropriate support staff may be required. In recent years, digital and analog video technologies have become the basis for many distance learning programs. In addition, the Internet and other computer networking services have required all education providers to consider making major investments in a technology infrastructure to support the overall enterprise. This infrastructure should be well planned and carefully designed to support a wide range of informational needs for the entire educational organization. Distance learning is but one important activity that can flourish where a modern technology infrastructure is in place or evolving. Once a plan for the infrastructure is established, attention to other facilities such as distance learning classrooms is required. Because of their reliance on technology, distance learning classrooms should be carefully designed to ensure that the instructional delivery is comfortable, and easy for teachers and students alike.

Modern technology, whether intended for distance learning or not, can be expensive and is a major financial consideration for even well-financed educational organizations. The cost-effectiveness of distance learning and technology-based instructional programs in general has been widely debated for several decades. Extensive literature exists addressing this issue. Perhaps most important to these analyses is that cost always be carefully considered in relation to the quality of a program.

Budgeting for distance learning should be done carefully. The basic funding components that exist in traditional educational environments provide appropriate starting points. In a traditional educational organization, expenditures are devoted to people costs and non-people or "other-than-personnel" costs such as equipment, supplies, and contractual and facilities services such as electricity, telephone, heating, and cooling. The major funding components of a distance learning program include personnel costs for administrative services, technical support and faculty, and other-than-personnel costs including equipment, software, supplies, furnishings, specialized communications such as high-speed telephone lines, and contractual services. The distribution of these expenditures can vary significantly depending on the nature of the program, the instructional delivery technologies, and faculty deployment and productivity.

The chapter concludes with a discussion of revenue and funding sources for establishing and advancing a distance learning program. Issues associated with student tuition, fees, financial aid, consortia, and grantsmanship are discussed.

CASE STUDY NO. 1

Bowdain College Year: 2000

Setting

Bowdain College is a private college located on the west coast of the United States. It offers a variety of undergraduate and graduate (masters degree) programs in liberal arts and professional programs. Bowdain is organized into six schools: Humanities, Social Sciences, Mathematics and Science, Business, Education, and Nursing. The total enrollment is 7,000 students, approximately half of whom live on campus. In 1996, the college made significant capital improvements at its campus including substantive improvements to its telecommunications infrastructure. Faculty offices, laboratories, and student dormitories are all wired in a fiber-optic network with easy access to Internet and other computer networks. Many of the faculty in each of the schools have begun to integrate the Internet and other computer networks into their courses. Three faculty in the School of Business have been offering Internet-based distance learning courses.

The Issue

For the past three years, the school of business has received $50,000 a year in grants from the James P. Clonen Foundation to offer Internet-based, distance learning courses in its undergraduate international business program. These funds have been used to provide computer equipment, faculty training, and faculty release time. Three of the full-time faculty in the program have been heavily involved in this grant and now offer more than half of the courses in the international business major via the Internet. The number of majors has increased from 110 to 130 full-time-equivalent students since the Internet-based courses were introduced.

Donald Landon, the Dean of the Business School, is engaged in discussions with the program officer from the Clonen Foundation regarding a new grant in the range of $200,000 a year for three years. Dean Landon originally approached the Foundation for another modest grant of $50,000 to expand the distance learning program in international business to other programs in the School of Business such as finance, marketing, and accounting. However, after discussion with the program officer at Clonen, he is now considering the more ambitious project of offering the entire international business undergraduate program, including all required liberal arts and sciences courses, via distance learning. The academic requirements for the international business program are as follows:

- 60 credits in liberal arts and sciences distributed in humanities, social sciences, and mathematics and science
- 33–36 credits in the major (all courses taken in the School of Business)
- 12–15 credits in a minor (many students opt to minor in another program in the School of Business)
- 15 credits in electives

The three full-time faculty in the international business program would like to see their program expanded and favor offering an entire degree program via distance learning. While very positive about the project, they are concerned about whether or not their colleagues in the other schools share their enthusiasm.

Assume you are Dean Landon and have been requested to present the Clonen Foundation proposal to the provost of the college and the deans of the other schools. You have also been asked to provide a detailed budget analysis of the use of the grant funds, as well as college resources, if required. Assuming the grant is for $200,000 a year for three years, prepare a budget analysis for offering an entire undergraduate degree in international business via distance learning at Bowdain College. Also determine what other significant issues should be discussed at the meeting with the provost and other deans. Lastly, what other information, if any, do you feel you need to do the presentation and budget analysis?

CASE STUDY NO. 2

Northwest University Year: 1999

Setting

Northwest University is a private university with an enrollment of 13,000 students. It was founded in 1911 and offers undergraduate programs in the liberal arts, business administration, and education. Its most important graduate programs are in business administration and education. In 1994, Northwest started a distance learning program called LearningNET. Two graduate degrees have been developed and now are offered entirely via the Internet. In addition, LearningNET also offers a College by Video program using videocassettes. Enrollment in both distance learning programs is 900 students per semester with 400 in asynchronous Internet courses and 500 in the College by Video courses.

The Issue

In June, John Decker, the director of LearningNET since its inception, left for a similar position at another college. A search committee has reviewed applications, conducted the first round of interviews, and submitted the resumes of three finalists to the provost. The three finalists all have advanced degrees, some experience with grantsmanship, and entrepreneurial attitudes. However, their technical backgrounds are somewhat different. Jane Leslie has an extensive background in video production and has participated in developing two award-winning documentaries for public television. She also has many contacts at the local public television network. Bob Sanders has a background in computer science and has been a director of telecommunications for a nearby public university for ten years. He was a member of the coordinating committee that established a statewide educational computer network in 1988, presently being updated with fiber-optic technology. Loretta Strand started her career as a librarian but for the past five years has been the director for media services at Northwest. She was directly involved with the production of several of the videocassettes used in the College by Video program.

Assume you are the provost. Based on the information provided, which of the three finalists, on the surface, appears to be the best candidate for the position? What rationale or priorities form the basis for your selection?

REFERENCES

Carnoy, M., & Levin, H. (1975). Evaluation of educational media: Some issues. *Instructional Science, 4,* 385–406.

Chute, A. G., Hulik, M., & Palmer, C. (1987). *Teletraining productivity at AT&T.* Presentation at the International Teleconferencing Association Annual Conference, Washington D.C.

Fredrickson, S. (1990). *Audiographics for distance education: An alternate technology.* Paper presented at the Annual Conference of the Alaska Association for Computers in Education. (ERIC ED345711)

Hardy, D. W., & Boaz, M. H. (1997). Learner development: Beyond the technology. In T. E. Cyrs (Ed.). *Teaching and learning at a distance: What it takes to effectively design, deliver, and evaluate programs.* San Francisco: Jossey-Bass Publishers.

Hiltz, S. R. (1997). Impacts of college-level courses via asynchronous learning networks: Some results. *Journal of Asynchronous Learning Networks, 1*(2), 1–19.

Hosley, D. L., & Randolph, S. L. (1993). *Distance learning as a training and education tool.* Kennedy Space Center, Fl: Lockheed Space Operations Co.

Keegan, D. (1996). *Foundations of distance education* (3rd ed.). London: Routledge.

Laidlaw, R., & Layard, R. (1974). Traditional versus OU teaching methods: A cost comparison. *Higher Education, 3,* 439–468.

Leibovitz, C. (1997, October). *How do federal laws and regulations address distance education?* Paper presented at the Quality Assurance for Distance Learning Conference sponsored by the Middle States Commission on Higher Education. Philadelphia, Pa.

Mace, J. (1978). Mythology in the making: Is the OU really cost effective? *Higher Education, 7,* 295–309.

Rumble, G. (1982). The cost analysis of learning at a distance. *Distance Education, 3*(1), 116–140.

Turoff, M. (1997). Costs for the development of a virtual university. *Journal of Asynchronous Learning Networks, 1*(1), 28–38.

U.S. Department of Education, National Center for Education Statistics (1997). *Distance education in higher education institutions* (NCES 97–062). Washington, D.C.

Vigilante, R. (1996). *Semesters in cyberspace: Evaluation of the 1995 Virtual College teleprogram.* New York: New York University Office of Continuing Education.

Wagner, L. (1972). The economics of the Open University. *Higher Education, 2,* 159–183.

Walsh, J., & Reese, B. (1995). Distance education's growing reach. *Technological Horizons in Education Journal, 22*(11), 58–62.

CHAPTER EIGHT

Web-Based Distance Learning: The Virtual Model

Franco Zeffirelli is a world-renowned producer and director of opera, film, and theater whose productions have won almost every possible award. When the curtain goes up on a Zeffirelli opera, the beauty and magnificence of his set designs provoke "oohs" and "ahs" from normally reticent and critical audiences. He has worked with many of the great performers of our time including Maria Callas, Luciano Pavarotti, and Placido Domingo. At a Metropolitan Opera lecture in 1998, he was asked these questions: How does he start a new production? Does he start with the music, the story, the performers, or the sets? He immediately, and perhaps surprisingly, responded that he starts with the audience, whom he visualizes as an "ensemble" of individuals each with unique expectations and needs for coming to his production. As a result, his production becomes a struggle to address these individual expectations.

In developing and designing a distance learning course, instructors likewise should not necessarily start with the curriculum, the course materials, the technology, or the delivery mechanisms but with the individual needs of their students. Designers would also do well to think of these students not just as a singular group or class but as individuals with individual needs and expectations. In World Wide Web-based distance learning, where most students participate in the privacy of their homes or offices, designing courses to meet individual needs becomes even more important. Course designers must try to see Web courses through the eyes of individual students whose basic interactions will be through a computer work station. The challenge in creating these learning environments is really to determine what individual learners need and how to accommodate these needs reasonably (Chute, Sayers, and Gardner, 1997).

In the previous chapters, various models of distance learning have been presented and discussed within the context of the emergence of a virtual model independent of space and time. In this chapter, a virtual model based on the Internet and World Wide Web technology is examined. Several issues related to student needs, pedagogy, and the technology are also examined with the understanding that this model is still evolving and has not yet matured.

VIRTUAL SPACE AND TIME

The term "virtual" has been defined in this book as "functional and effective without formally existing in a traditional mode." Virtual learning, for example, is learning that can functionally and effectively occur in the absence of traditional space, such as a classroom environment, or a specific meeting time. Virtual learning assumes that teachers and students are free to engage in instructional activities at any place and at any time. Not all of the distance learning models presented in the earlier chapters of this book are virtual learning models. Some, such as point-to-point videoconferencing, assume that teachers and students will be in specific places at specific times. Broadcast television likewise requires participants to be viewing a television program at a certain time. Other models, such as printed study guides or courses on videocassettes, are more "virtual" in that they allow students to learn at any place and at their own pace or time. However, printed study guides and videocassettes, while economical and easy to use, do not take advantage of current technology that provides for timely interaction and engagement with other students and a teacher. The model that comes closest to operating in virtual space and time while allowing for timely interaction is based on Internet and World Wide Web technology. While generically referred to as computer-mediated instruction, the terms "virtual learning" and "asynchronous learning network" (ALN) have become popular and are commonly being used. This model uses modern computer networking systems to link students and teachers in an electronic community designed to provide and enhance the basic instructional functions that exist in a traditional classroom. All activities take place at a computer work station connected to the ALN at times when it is convenient for both students and teachers. A valid caveat to this Web-based model is that teachers and students can engage in instruction at any time or any place *where access to a computer network* is available. However, with the proliferation of portable computing and telephone devices, it will not be long before accessing a computer network can be done at any place and at any time.

THE MAIN COMPONENTS OF WEB-BASED LEARNING

Web-based learning relies on using the Internet as the primary communications vehicle for collecting and disseminating instructional resources. Computer work stations designed to store billions of bytes of information on networks distributed throughout the world provide the materials, instructor notes, student assignments, and "blackboard" illustrations that exist in a typical course of instruction. These work stations also provide the communications vehicles through which students and teachers engage in ongoing discussions on instructional topics.

Figure 8.1 illustrates the main components of Web-based learning, which depends on the networking capabilities of the Internet to connect the distance learner

FIGURE 8.1 Web-Based Distance Learning

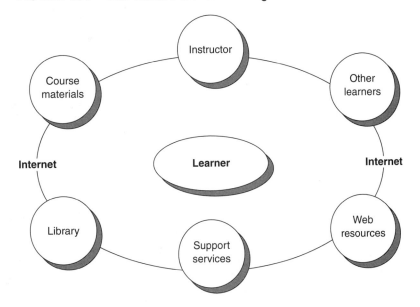

with course materials, the instructor, other learners, library and support services, and other Web resources. The Internet, fondly referred to as the "mother of all networks," is a global digital resource that connects millions of people through computer communications systems. In developing a Web-based course, designers might want to view the student at the center of a variety of digital resources, all of which are readily available on the Internet through a computer work station.

LEARNER NEEDS IN VIRTUAL SPACE AND TIME: A SCENARIO

Jane Simpson lives in New York City with her husband Greg and their two children, James and Karen. James is eight years old and attends a nearby primary school. Karen is three years old and attends a day care center. Jane is a full-time language arts teacher who is taking the graduate courses she needs to receive permanent certification in her teaching specialization. Jane takes one course a semester and one each summer offered by a local college over the Internet. A typical day for Jane starts at 6:00 A.M. She goes to her desktop computer and checks her e-mail for the latest messages from her instructor and from two other students with whom she is collaborating on a group project. She has one message from one of her fellow students asking her opinion about their joint project. Jane responds. She gets herself and her children ready for work and school. James gets on the bus to go to school and Greg drops Karen off at the day care center. Jane arrives at her school at 8:00 A.M.

Once at school, most of Jane's day involves preparing for and teaching five classes. During the lunch hour, she manages to check her e-mail again to see if there are any messages from her instructor or fellow students. There is one message from her instructor reminding the class that their group assignment is due the following week. When the school day ends, Jane picks Karen up from the day care center and heads home to find James snacking on some cookies, which, with mom's encouragement, he reluctantly shares with his sister. Until seven o'clock, Jane is involved with mother and wife chores (straightening up the house, helping James with homework, preparing dinner, and so on). After dinner, she and her husband get the children ready for bed and then spend some quality time with each other.

At ten o'clock, Jane goes back to her computer, reviews the assignment that is due, and sends e-mail messages to her fellow students suggesting that they engage in a real-time chat about their assignment the following night at 9:00 P.M. She also posts a response on the electronic bulletin board to a question that the instructor had posed to the class the previous day regarding language arts curricula and multicultural issues. Jane goes to bed at 11:00 P.M.

At about the same time that Jane is going to bed, Danielle is starting her day and arriving at Johannes Kepler University in Graz, Austria. Danielle is a full-time graduate student specializing in business education. In addition to her regular classes, Danielle and four other students at Kepler University are auditing the course that Jane is taking in New York City. Danielle and her colleagues' purpose in auditing this course is to familiarize themselves with American educational systems and to establish contacts with American educators. Their hope is to teach in the United States as part of an exchange program after finishing their graduate studies.

Danielle goes to one of the university's computer centers and checks her e-mail. As she reads her mail, she is especially interested in the recent posting Jane has made in response to the instructor's question of the previous day. Danielle sends a message agreeing with Jane's point of view and provides an example from the Austrian schools to support her comment. Danielle then goes to class and, while waiting for the instructor to arrive, shares her recent e-mail exchanges with other students.

This scenario is based on actual course activities. Web-based distance learning is being used to meet the needs of many students but particularly those whose studies may be impeded by time or space. Jane is a woman who combines her mother, wife, and professional responsibilities into an incredibly busy day. Her time is very valuable. By taking a Web-based course, she is able to make the time to fit graduate studies into her day. Attending a traditional class would include traveling one or two nights a week and hiring a babysitter at least until her husband returned home from his job. The Web-based course allows her to spend more time with her children and provides them with a consistent daily routine with Mom around on a regular basis.

Danielle and her colleagues in Austria have overcome the impediment created by space. Being thousands of miles from the United States, the Web-based course allows them to familiarize themselves with American education without incurring the expense of traveling and living in another country. They are also finding that, while not the same as actually visiting the country and observing schools and classes, collaborating and exchanging ideas with American educators for months or longer prepares them well for the day they may actually come to the United States to teach.

Designers of Web-based distance learning applications have to understand the needs of a Jane or a Danielle. For example, course materials and the basic communications systems have to be available every day on a twenty-four-hour basis. The computer hardware and software systems therefore must be stable and not prone to "downtime," which can be very frustrating to distance learners. Students who are paying a high tuition rate for a course will become resentful and frustrated when the course is experiencing technical difficulty. To appreciate this, consider your own response when a favorite television program is experiencing technical difficulty.

The distance learning technology must also be simple, and easy for students to use. Neither Jane nor Danielle are high-end computer users. They have basic computer skills, know how to send and access e-mail, and can navigate on the World Wide Web. Requiring students to understand a great deal about software can limit enrollments or frustrate students who do not possess enough technical knowledge. Requiring the average distance learning student to download and install a number of software packages or "plug-ins" may be intimidating if not overwhelming. This may not be true for instructional programs such as engineering, information systems, or computer science, where students are expected to possess above-average technical skills, but it is true for many other programs. As discussed in Chapter 7, an on-line "help" facility becomes indispensable to assist students having any technical difficulties.

In Web-based applications, students will be using a variety of computer configurations. Some may have access to the latest and fastest microprocessors, while others may be a generation or two behind. Some may be using simple, single computer work stations with slow-speed modems in their homes while others may be using computers connected to sophisticated, high-speed communications networks in their places of employment. It is difficult, if not impossible, to control the technology environment of the average distance learning student. Web-based course designers should design course activities to operate on the lower end of the hardware/software configuration spectrum if the goal is to enroll and reach as many students as possible. Web-based course materials such as full-motion video that require a good deal of processor or modem communication speed, do not run very effectively on lower-end configurations and can frustrate students. For distance learning programs designed for a select student population, this may not be a problem as long as information is clearly available specifying the minimum computer configurations required to participate effectively.

A BRIEF LOOK AT SOME ISSUES

The needs of a Jane, a Danielle, and many other students like them are real and are being met through opportunities provided by Web-based distance learning. Though relatively new, the literature and research support this approach and see it evolving as the dominant distance learning application in the years to come.

The U.S. Department of Education indicates that in the two-year period between 1995–96 and 1997–98, the number of postsecondary institutions offering Web-based distance learning courses had tripled, far exceeding the growth of any other distance application. (U.S. Department of Education, 1999, p. vi.) Khan (1999) provides an excellent compilation of articles and research on Web-based distance learning and is highly recommended for additional reading. Professional journals such as *The American Journal of Distance Education, The Journal of Distance Education, Research in Distance Education, The Journal of Computer-Based Instruction,* and *The International Journal of Educational Telecommunications* are also excellent sources. Another readily available source is the on-line *Journal for Asynchronous Learning Networks* (http://www.aln.org). Much of this literature focuses on individual faculty and course studies. It indicates that both teachers and students are satisfied with their experiences, that student performance is comparable to that in traditional settings, and that the interest and demand for additional courses are growing. However, a good deal more research is needed using broader faculty and student databases and measuring outcomes and performance over a longer time period. Gladieux and Swail (1999), in a study titled, *The Virtual University and Educational Opportunity,* cautioned that there is not enough experience and much less "systematic data" upon which to assess the future. Phipps and Merisotis (1999), in a review of "several hundred studies and articles," likewise lamented the "paucity of true, original research" related to distance learning.

Quality Assurance

The need for quality assurance has always been a major theme for American education but especially since the publication in 1985 of *A Nation at Risk: The Imperative for Educational Reform* by The National Commission on Excellence in Education. While directed at primary and secondary education, *A Nation at Risk* and many spin-off reports have also highlighted the need for greater educational accountability at all levels. Federal, state, and local government officials, whether driven by genuine concern or by political ideology, are asking educators to measure clearly and demonstrate the outcomes of their enterprises. The scrutiny of Web-based distance learning has been particularly close as governmental and other educational organizations struggle to endorse and to support an approach where faculty and students do not physically meet. The two studies referenced in the above paragraph are typical of this scrutiny and were commissioned by the College Board (Gladieux & Swail, 1999), the National Education Association, the American Federation of Teachers, and the Institute for Higher Education Policy (Phipps & Merisotis, 1999).

Technology-based instruction that appears less rigorous than traditional education raises concerns. Likewise, the increasing number of new Web-based distance learning providers, many of whom have little or no experience, is another cause for concern among regional accrediting and other regulatory agencies. The global nature of the Internet complicates accreditation issues because Web-based distance learning providers are not limited by state, regional, or national boundaries. Schools and colleges in the United States have traditionally been accredited, chartered, or sanctioned by the agencies in the states and regions in which they are physically located. This is no longer always the case and may be less so in the years to come as Web-based distance learning continues to expand beyond state and regional boundaries. To ensure educational quality, many accrediting and regulatory agencies are re-evaluating their processes. Meanwhile, these accrediting and regulatory agencies have been slow to endorse fully Web-based distance learning programs, especially those provided by new and out-of-state or out-of-region schools and colleges.

Web-Based Technology and Reduced Educational Costs

As discussed in Chapter 7, instructional technology does not have an established track record of cost reduction. In fact, instructional technology has been used mainly to add educational value to courses and in the process has added to the cost. Web-based distance learning surely has the potential for reducing costs. Because of its newness and the need to invest in developing materials and training faculty, however, it is unlikely that any savings will be realized in the short term by traditional institutions that are converting their existing programs. At its core, however, Web-based distance learning is cost effective, because it builds on the technology infrastructure already established for Internet and other data communications applications. This is also an important consideration for distance learning providers who have relied on and already invested in other (e.g., point-to-point video) distance learning technologies. While the research is sparse, the technology of Web-based distance learning is less expensive than other distance technologies such as point-to-point video. Colleges and other providers that have already established distance learning programs based on more expensive technologies may find savings by switching to the less expensive Web-based technology.

Experimental Courses Versus Entire Academic Programs

Phipps and Merisotis (1999), in the study mentioned earlier, concluded that a major shortcoming of the distance learning research to date was the emphasis on student outcomes for individual courses rather than for total academic programs. This is valid but to be expected. In any new technology, experimentation should start with individual courses and, if successful, expand to entire programs. New research will likely evolve as entire programs are delivered on the Web. In the meantime, concern exists about large programs at the undergraduate level where social, cognitive, and attitudinal development are as important as academic achievement in assessing a program's quality. Research on long-term student development in these areas will surely be needed if the Web-based approach is to evolve into a major instructional delivery application. Later in this chapter, pedagogical and technical issues related to the expansion of experimental courses into full programs will be discussed.

DESIGNING EFFECTIVE WEB-BASED APPLICATIONS

As previously discussed in Chapter 2 and elsewhere in this book, the main instructional benefits of Web-based instruction are asynchrony, high interactivity, and graphics/multimedia capability. The virtual model by definition relies extensively on an asynchronous and highly interactive instructional environment as provided in Web-based distance learning applications. This model also is making greater use of the graphics and multimedia capabilities of the Web. However, achieving instructional benefits is not automatic and sound pedagogical approaches designed to take advantage of the capabilities of the technology have to be carefully developed. In the remainder of this chapter, techniques and approaches are considered in designing effective and pedagogically sound Web-based distance learning applications. Readers should refer to the material in *A Guide to Designing a Web-Based Distance Learning Course* at the end of Chapter 9 in this book, which provides a detailed description of a typical Web-based course.

COURSE MANAGEMENT SYSTEMS— TO CMS OR NOT TO CMS

Up until a few years ago, a Web site for a distance learning course would have been developed in the native HTML (Hypertext Mark-Up Language) that is the software base for creating all Web pages. Figure 8.2 is an example of the HTML language for a simple course home page (Figure G.2A). HTML is not a difficult language to use, but because of its cryptic style that makes use of various special characters, tags, and two-character instruction codes, it might prove difficult to the average instructor. In the past, instructors who wanted to teach on the Web either learned this language to produce the Web content or were provided with the technical assistance to do so.

Web developers now have the option of using an HTML filter or conversion software program such as Netscape's *Composer,* Microsoft's *FrontPage,* or Softquad's *Hot Metal Pro,* to develop HTML documents. These filters generally provide a menu-driven, relatively easy-to-use interface for developing Web pages in HTML. They are continually evolving so that even sophisticated routines such as those generally provided by more advanced software languages such as Java and JavaScript are now becoming available by pointing and clicking on a menu. Learning to develop relatively straightforward Web pages is now no more difficult than learning an advanced feature on a standard word processing software package. In fact, the latest version of Microsoft *Word* allows the user to save automatically any word processing document in HTML format. Even electronic presentation software packages such as Microsoft's *PowerPoint* or Gold Disk's *Astound*, which are designed to integrate images, text, sound, and animation into digital slide shows, have "Save as HTML" features for automatically converting these shows into Web pages. The point here is that developing HTML documents is becoming relatively easy and, with a little bit of guidance, requires about the same technical skill as using a standard word processing program.

Recently, a number of course management software (CMS) packages designed specifically for teaching on the Web have become available. Figure 8.3 is a list of some popular CMS products. These CMS packages provide a complete set of software tools for creating Web-based courses including home pages, electronic bulletin boards, e-mail systems, test generators, chat areas, and multimedia facilities. Almost all of these packages provide a course template that makes developing a Web course no more difficult than filling in the blanks and selecting menu options. Most of the course facilities identified in the sample Web pages in the Guide at the end of Chapter 9 are available on CMS packages on a template or as menu selections.

FIGURE 8.2 HTML Code (For the Course Home Page in Figure G.2A)

```
<!DOCTYPE HTML PUBLIC "-//SQ//DTD HTML 2.0 + all extensions//EN" "hmpro3.dtd">
<HTML>
<HEAD>
<TITLE>ED722 - Fall 1998</TITLE></HEAD>
<BODY
BGCOLOR="#FFFFFF" TEXT="#0000A0" LINK="#0000FF" BACKGROUND="webback.jpg"
VLINK="#FF0000">
<P ALIGN="CENTER"><IMG SRC="hunter.gif" ALIGN="MIDDLE"></P>
<P ALIGN="CENTER"><B>National College, School of Education</B></P>
<H2><A NAME="Return"></A>EDUC 722 - ISSUES IN CONTEMPORARY EDUCATION</H2>
<H3><B>Instructor: Dr. Lynne Jones, </B><A
HREF="mailto:antho13926@aol.com"> e-mail address: ljones@national.edu</A></H3>
<H3><B>Course Description</B></H3>
<P><B><FONT SIZE="+1">This course is designed to provide a forum wherein issues in contemporary
education will be presented and discussed. It is also designed to provide future administrators with an
appreciation of differences in points of view and to have them consider how they would approach issues that can
be divisive in a school or community. </FONT></B>
</P>
<H3><B>Below are the resources and information you need to participate in this course. If this is the first time
you are accessing this Web page, please select &quot;Getting Started /Help Desk.&quot;</B></H3>
<P></P>
<TABLE
WIDTH="600" BORDER="7" ALIGN="CENTER" CELLPADDING="20" CELLSPACING="20"
BGCOLOR="#C0C0C0">
<TR ALIGN="LEFT" VALIGN="TOP">
<TD><IMG SRC="bullet.gif"><A HREF="a722cout.html"></A><B>Course Outline</B></TD>
<TD><IMG SRC="bullet.gif"><A HREF="a722read.html"></A><B>Reading List</B></TD>
<TD><IMG SRC="bullet.gif"><A HREF="a722conf.html"></A><B>Student
Assignments/Evaluation</B></TD></TR>
<TR ALIGN="LEFT" VALIGN="TOP">
<TD NOWRAP="NoWrap"><IMG SRC="bullet.gif"><A HREF="a722conf.html"></A><B>Topic
Presentations</B></TD>
<TD NOWRAP="NoWrap"><IMG SRC="bullet.gif"><A HREF="a722link.html"></A><B>Web
Resources</B></TD>
<TD><IMG SRC="bullet.gif"><A HREF="a722supp.html"></A><B>Library &amp; Media
Resources</B></TD></TR>
<TR ALIGN="LEFT" VALIGN="TOP">
<TD NOWRAP="NoWrap"><IMG SRC="bullet.gif"><A
HREF="a722week.html"></A><B>Communications
Center</B></TD>
<TD><IMG SRC="bullet.gif"><A
HREF="http://listserv.cuny.edu/archives/ADSUP-722.HTML"></A><B>Archives</B></TD>
<TD NOWRAP="NoWrap"><IMG SRC="bullet.gif"><A HREF="a722pics.html"></A><B>Getting
Started/Help Desk</B></TD></TR></TABLE>
<P><B>Figure 10.A - Sample Course Home Page </B></P></BODY></HTML>
```

FIGURE 8.3 Popular Course Management Software Systems

Product	Vendor
Authorware	Macromedia, Inc.
CourseInfo	Blackboard, Inc.
IconAuthor	Aimtech Corp.
LearningSpace	Lotus Development Corp.
Phoenix for Windows	Pathlore Software Corp.
QuestNet+	Allen Communications, Inc.
ToolBook	Asymetrix Corp.
TopClass	WBT Systems, Inc.
Web Course in a Box	madDuck Technologies
WebCT	University of British Columbia

While CMS software surely makes developing a course Web site easier, evaluating these systems for adoption can be time-consuming and, in some cases, difficult. McCollum (1997) describes the situation as a "new industry that offers faculty a dizzying array of tools for developing Web courses." Figure 8.4 provides a list of some of the more important criteria for evaluating a CMS.

Most of the general criteria in Figure 8.4 is subjective in nature depending on the evaluator's experience and level of expertise and cannot easily be quantified or reduced to a "Yes–No." Even a relatively straightforward criterion such as cost can become complicated when evaluating a CMS. Some of the packages have complex pricing structures that depend on a variety of factors including several levels of site licensing, how many servers will be allowed to house the CMS, the number of course developers, the number of students who will be enrolled, the maximum number of developers and/or students at any one time, and so forth.

In selecting a CMS, good practice suggests that a committee or task force be established that includes teachers, technical support staff, and students. Criteria should be established on which all faculty users and support staff can agree. Those outlined in Figure 8.4 provide good starting points, but local committees should determine and prioritize criteria that will best meet their needs in the long run. Ease of use, training and staff development requirements, and software stability and reliability may be more important in certain environments than more advanced technical features or capabilities.

In adopting a CMS for a school, college, or program, evaluators should also keep in mind that they are dealing with a rapidly evolving if not volatile technology. The Internet burst on the technological scene in the 1990s and is redefining digital communications in ways that were undreamed of as recently as five years ago. The software systems, including CMS, that support applications on the Internet are being pioneered by small companies where competition is fierce and unpredictable. To remain competitive, software products are being upgraded and

FIGURE 8.4 Criteria for Evaluating Course Management Software Packages

General Criteria

Cost (Total including Ownership, Site Licensing, Maintenance)
Ease of Administrative Management (Stability, Reliability, Performance)
Ease of Use (Faculty and Students)
Level of Vendor Support
Software Platforms (Windows, UNIX, Macintosh) Supported
Standards-Based
Training Opportunities

Features/Capabilities Provided

Chat (IRC)—Synchronous Discussions
Conversion Tools (i.e., from word processing files)
Desktop Videoconferencing
Discussion Groups
Electronic Mail
Grading
Indexing of Course Material by Instructor, Major, Field, Course Name
Individualized Student Assignments
Multimedia Support
Related Resources
Sharing Materials across Courses
Standard Design with Flexible Customization
Student Progress Reporting
Template Development Tools
Test Generator

enhanced with new features every few months. While desirable with respect to improving a product's capability, this rapid change can be unsettling for long-range course planning where design, development, and evaluation can take several years. Web-based course designers and planners have to be prepared to be flexible and open to new products and/or changes to existing products.

DIGITAL MEDIA AND WEB-BASED DISTANCE LEARNING

The asynchronous, Web-based model that has been the focus of the discussion in this chapter has been evolving for several years. For most distance learning applications, this model relies extensively on text (e-mail, discussion groups, bulletin boards, and such) for instruction and communication. In the early 1990s, there would not have been much point in extending this discussion into other media (see Figure 8.5) such as audio or video, because the Internet did not handle media beyond text very well. However, as we enter the twenty-first century, multimedia ap-

FIGURE 8.5   Multimedia and the World Wide Web—Some Background

Multimedia and the World Wide Web

The term "multimedia" refers to many types of communication processes, delivery systems, and events. It is a popular word used in connection with entertainment, advertisement, museum exhibitions, theme parks, video games, and dozens of other areas of human endeavor. The term "multimedia" connotes a certain technological "chic" and conjures up images of color, movement, dazzling special effects, and provocative sounds. Because of the variety of ways in which the word has been used, multimedia has come to mean different things to different people.

Generically, multimedia can be defined as any combination of two or more media such as text, images, animation, sound, and video. When used with computer technology, multimedia refers to a variety of applications that combine media and utilize CD-ROM, video, audio, and other digital equipment.

In addition to this basic definition, multimedia when used with computer equipment also implies interactive navigational (hypermedia) capabilities that can be invoked and controlled by the user. Hypermedia is the integration of sights, sounds, graphics, video, and other media into an associative or linked system of information storage and retrieval. Hypermedia allows users to navigate in a nonlinear manner from one topic to another by the use of information linkages built into the associative system. These linkages are usually presented in the form of active screen areas or buttons that, when clicked on by a mouse, transfer or link the user to some other material. Examples of these linkage techniques are found in many menu-driven software products. Hypermedia is an extension of the concept of hypertext, which linked text information in an associative system. The term hypertext was coined in 1965 by Ted Nelson, an engineer, to describe computer-based document retrieval systems that could be used in a nonlinear fashion as opposed to the traditional linear format of other document retrieval systems such as books and microfilm. For educational technology purposes then, multimedia refers to computer-based systems that use associative linkages to allow users to navigate and retrieve information stored in a combination of text, images, animations, sounds, video, and other forms of media.

The World Wide Web is the software system that introduced hypermedia capabilities to the Internet. Originally developed in the early 1990s at CERN, the European Laboratory for Particle Physics, in Switzerland, the Web was designed to provide hypertext and full multimedia support in a relatively easy-to-use hypertext mark-up language (HTML) for physicists and other scientists using the Internet. This concept of a hypermedia-based software system for the Web is generally credited to Dr. Tim Berners-Lee, who envisioned an Internet that would be much easier to use and would stimulate users with sights and sound. Web-based distance learning relies extensively on the hypermedia-based software techniques first envisioned by Berners-Lee and his associates at Cern.

plications on the Internet are becoming commonplace. In teaching and learning, "a picture can be worth a thousand words." Full-motion video capable of transmitting thousands of pictures in minutes accompanied by an audio track can be worth much more. However, while pedagogically important, producing high-quality multimedia material for the Internet is not yet easy and can be expensive. Gerald Heeger, dean of New York University's School of Continuing Education, which has a successful history for delivering and developing multimedia-based distance learning, estimates that producing high-quality digital animation and video for a single Web-based course costs approximately $50,000 (Arenson, 1998). This might be beyond the budgets of many distance learning providers. Regardless, the potential of multimedia for Web-based distance learning cannot be ignored.

Five Levels of Digital Media

There are essentially five major levels of digital media: text, still images, animation, audio, and full-motion video. A brief review of these will be helpful in discussing the use of digital media in distance learning applications.

Text (letters of the alphabet, numbers, special characters) is handled very efficiently in any digital form, whether on stand-alone or networked computers, or the Internet. By far, the most popular applications on computer equipment worldwide are text-based and include word processing, e-mail, and database/data file manipulation.

Still images and photographs likewise are handled well in digital format. Standard word processors such as Microsoft *Word* or Lotus *WordPerfect* have made adding an image or photograph to a text document a routine, click-the-menu item. Internet service providers such as America Online or Compuserve likewise encourage subscribers to attach photographs to their e-mail messages. Digital cameras, which were rare and quite expensive several years ago, can now be purchased for less than $300. They attach to a computer or produce images on a floppy disk for immediate use in any digital-based application. Kodak and other major camera companies routinely develop a roll of 35mm film into digital format on a CD-ROM for approximately the same price as standard three-inch by five-inch snapshots. In sum, still images and photographs have become standard accompaniments to text on all types of digital applications and are important enhancements to Web-based learning.

Animations are still images to which some motion has been added. Digital animation as a field has grown considerably in the 1990s. Major film producers such as Disney and Lucasfilms, Incorporated depend extensively on digital animations for special effects. In 1997, the highly acclaimed movie, *Titanic,* relied almost exclusively on digital animation for the sequences where the doomed luxury liner was seen cruising the Atlantic. For the average individual, developing good-quality animation is not easy unless one is willing to devote many hours to editing and refining the images and sequencing flow. On the other hand, with some technical assistance and expertise, developing a good animation can significantly enhance a presentation, including a class lesson. Where technical support is available, animations have been used very successfully to add meaning and understanding to complex processes in many disciplines, especially in the sciences, engineering, and medicine. For students, viewing an animation on a stand-alone or locally networked computer is relatively simple and works well. Downloading or playing an animation from the Internet can be effective assuming sufficient modem speeds and other communications facilities are available.

Digital audio and sound files without images is also becoming easier to develop. An inexpensive microphone (less than $20) can be attached to an input jack on the back of almost any computer and a decent-quality lecture can be converted into digital form. If done in an acoustically controlled environment with more sophisticated recording equipment, the quality of a digitally-produced sound file can be superb. Playing the sound file of a lecture on a stand-alone or locally networked computer is easy and can be more effective than reading a comparable amount of text. To enhance understanding, instructional applications can combine the two (text and audio). On the Internet, "streaming" technologies such as those used with *RealAudio* applications have significantly improved the quality and timing of audio transmissions. Downloading or playing audio files from the Internet can be effective if sufficient modem speeds and other communications facilities are available.

Thirty frames (still images) per second accompanied by a sound track is the recognized standard for full-motion video digital or analog productions. Less than thirty frames per second provides a jerky and poorer quality video with the accompanying audio frequently out of synchronization with the images. Producing high-quality, full-motion video in digital format, while becoming easier, is beyond the technical expertise and ability of the average computer user. Technical support staffs that spend many days editing the digital video footage are needed to produce an acceptable product. Playing digital video on a stand-alone or a locally networked computer works well, and while streaming technologies on the Internet are also being used with video, they need further development to be effective for applications that require high quality. Full-motion video requires extensive digital storage, easily running into hundreds of millions of bytes or more. Students or other users attempting to download or play large video files need substantial computer capability (disk space, processor speed, and input-output transfer rate) as well as high-speed modem and communications capabilities. This may be beyond the financial means of the average home computer user.

Designing Multimedia for Web-Based Distance Learning

In developing multimedia for Web-based distance learning applications, course designers should start with a consideration of student access to the Internet. As indicated above, the effective transmission of sound, animation, and full-motion video on the Internet depends on computer hardware resources and communications capabilities. If the goal of a distance learning program is to reach out and provide learning opportunities to students in their homes, then course designers should carefully consider the extent to which multimedia can be effectively used, since student access will likely be through slow-speed modems or communications facilities. Providing a good deal of multimedia content requiring students to download large media files might be frustrating if hardware capability or transmission speeds are not available in the home environment or if they are unaffordable to the targeted population. On the other hand, where course developers control their students' computer environments such as in a distance learning program for a particular industry or organization, then multimedia-based distance learning can be very successful. If the student computer environment cannot be controlled, then designers would do well to use multimedia carefully.

Besides modem speed and communications facilities, another significant issue is media file formats. Unlike text, which has a standard digital format (ASCII), multimedia materials such as images, animation, audio, and video can be stored in dozens of different formats. Students using these materials will have to have the right "players" or software packages to read these files. Frequently referred to as "plug-ins" for Web-based applications, students will have to have access to these packages on their home computers. Distance learning providers therefore can give directions to students on how to download these plug-ins, or they can supply the students with a standard suite of software tools when they register for a Web-based course. In either case, these procedures will add to the technical support requirements of a distance learning program and should be considered accordingly. This issue of technology and media standards is serious enough that a number of government, business, and entertainment organizations have various groups studying it and making recommendations. The United States' National Governors' Association held a conference in June 1998 titled *Technology Standards for Global Learning*. Figure 8.6, an excerpt from a working paper that was used to establish and focus the conference's agenda, clearly presents the extent of the problem.

In developing multimedia materials for distance learning, course designers must strive for high quality. A video that has the look or feel of amateurism will not be effective in any learning environment, distance or otherwise. Given the superb quality of the media that students are accustomed to viewing on television, in films, and in video games, educators have found it difficult to compete. In traditional classrooms, instructors rely on materials such as videocassettes or films that they have purchased or rented from commercial or other professional producers. Delivering these same materials over the Internet may be impossible since they may not be available in digital form and/or it may be a serious infringement of copyright laws to copy them for use on a computer network.

Given the issues of student access to technology, technical support requirements, and the cost of producing or the difficulty in obtaining high-quality multimedia materials, course developers should only consider providing substantive animation, audio, or video material if it in fact adds to the instructional value of a course. This should not be done merely to add "pizzazz" or technological "glitz" to the course content. Certain subject matter is significantly enhanced when multimedia illustrations, animation, or video are added to the presentation. Surely the sciences and engineering make extensive use of computer simulations to conduct experiments and should seek to continue to do so in distance learning applications. High-quality documentaries such as those produced by educational television, National Geographic, or The Annenberg Project can add significant pedagogical value to a class presentation. Duplicating some of these for distance learning would be appropriate but may be difficult or costly. Distance learning providers will have to

FIGURE 8.6 Excerpt from Working Paper Presented at a Conference on Technology Standards for Global Learning, Salt Lake City, Utah, April 27–28, 1998.

Overview

This is a white paper to be shared with conference speakers, panel members, moderators and the conference steering committee. . .

Purpose of the Conference on Technology Standards for Global Learning

The purpose of the standards conference in April is to first identify the current state of standardization relative to functional and technical educational aspects of electronic education. Based on the current state of affairs, it will then strive to develop a consensus among educators, public officials and representatives from the Information Technology (IT) industry regarding an action plan to accelerate the development, acceptance and/or deployment of global standards that can facilitate a global common market in education . . .

The Current Technology Environment

Education and related services are delivered today utilizing many technologies. They include, but are not limited to: broadcast television; cable television; satellite television; interactive video networking; audio conferencing; and increasingly, digital networks such as the Internet, which traverse every medium from phone lines to high-speed fiber optic networks. The digitization of communications and convergence between computing and telecommunications allows voice, data and video to travel on any digital transport technology, providing a wide range of flexible and powerful means of delivering education.

The other side of this flexibility is that very often the new and improved technologies are not compatible with previously developed technologies. The analog satellite receivers that have been receiving educational programming for many years cannot receive programming delivered via the new digital medium.

To further complicate matters, there are multiple incompatible standards for digital satellite systems that have been deployed over the past several years which have resulted in numerous different receiving configurations. Similarly, interactive video networks may use H.261, MPEG, or H.323 technologies, none of which are compatible or interoperable. This problem afflicts the software used to support education as well. The faculty and students must learn to exchange files between Word and WordPerfect, email gateways are needed to link proprietary LAN email systems with the Internet, instructional content developed with WebCT cannot be used with TopClass, students must often learn how to use a different chat room and conferencing system for each course, and a new plug-in may be needed for each new multimedia format used in every new course.

What is missing is a common set of guidelines for the delivery of education via technology. The entertainment market and electronic commerce may eventually drive the emergence of technology standards which education will adopt in some areas, but it is important that educators' voices are heard to express their requirements to ensure the availability of technology standards which accommodate the delivery of pedagogically-sound instruction. Agreement in areas where multiple standards have emerged will help education be delivered more economically.

The desired end-state is the availability of widely accepted, vendor-independent (i.e., Open) standards for the technology-based delivery of instruction. Such standards will enable the education provider community to reach students anywhere, and for students to understand what they need to do to access educational content and services from multiple providers. This will provide economy of technology requirements for students and providers, and reduce unnecessary duplication of hardware, software, networks, interfaces, training and support.

Literally hundreds of different groups are working on technology standards which are necessary for this free exchange of education. Some are education-related, but many are not. The major questions before us are:

Assessing the state of this work;
Identifying what can be leveraged for educational delivery; and
Developing an action plan for standardization in areas where progress is not being made to meet the needs of education.

consider these issues carefully as they attempt to provide content and learning experiences on the Web comparable to those provided in the traditional classroom. Good design of any instructional activity recognizes the importance of diversity in the presentation of content. This holds true for distance learning.

Digital Videoconferencing

Point-to-point videoconferencing using analog television transmitters or receivers has been and will continue to be an important element of distance learning. This format, however, does not fit our Web-based virtual time and space model. Most point-to-point analog videoconferencing systems operate in dedicated spaces or distance learning classrooms where students meet at specific times. On the other hand, digital videoconferencing systems using the Internet have the potential of operating at any place and any time but will need some maturation before they are used extensively in people's homes. In addition to modem speed and other communications limitations, digital videoconferencing systems can be expensive and will require higher-end technical support services deployed over a wide geographical area. Currently, digital videoconferencing systems are working best in Local Area Networks (LAN) environments where all elements of transmission, communications, and end-user equipment can be controlled and maintained by technical staff. These systems are also being used at a distance to dedicated sites such as a company's training facility, where again technical staff are available to maintain the hardware and software.

In our Web-based model, digital videoconferencing could be used, for instance, to replace synchronous chat areas in which students and/or instructors establish a specific time to be available to each other to answer questions or to collaborate on a project. Rather than being limited to text messages, digital video-conferencing would allow participants to see and speak to each other. This would be more efficient and more personal. When used in conjunction with other delivery systems and media, videoconferencing can add significantly to the basic asynchronous model.

Internet videoconferencing technology is evolving rapidly. The popular *CUSeeMe* technology developed at Cornell University and now available as a commercial product from White Pine Software, has advanced beyond the first postage-stamp-size, jerky image of several years ago. Streaming audio techniques have advanced to include streaming video capable of providing relatively high-quality images in synchronization with the audio track. *RealAudio, RealVideo, RealSystem G2* (RealNetworks, Inc.); *NetShow* (Microsoft); and *QuickTime* (Apple) are examples of highly rated streaming video software packages (McMakin, Murphy, and Sauer, 1999.) The caveat once again involves access to sufficient computer and communications facilities. The standard microcomputer capable of transmitting and receiving high-quality video is available and affordable for many students. The same is not true for communications facilities. Slower-speed telephone lines are still the norm for the average home computer users. Using the newest video streaming,

Comcast, a major American cable company, established a new Web site (www.TheBitScreen.com) in 1998 to provide quality video clips produced by major film companies from around the world. In reviewing this site, Peter Nichols (1999), a *New York Times* film critic, commented that while each clip pushes the boundaries of the technology, poor picture quality caused by a slow-speed modem on the receiving end hinders the most creative efforts of these Web site developers. Nichols further mentioned the need for image smoothing, larger frames, and the elimination of streaming interruptions that may make a "shambles" of the picture. Regardless, as communications technology advances, digital videoconferencing will play a more significant role in Web-based distance learning, and course designers would do well to keep abreast of the potential of this technology.

VIRTUAL PROGRAMS, SCHOOLS, AND COLLEGES

Much of the discussion in the section above was devoted to the instructional design issues associated with developing Web-based asynchronous learning courses. However, designing a course or two is far different from developing an entire program, school, or college. In addition to faculty development, academic and student support services, and costs discussed earlier in this book, there are several "scalability" issues that relate to establishing virtual programs, schools, and colleges.

Common Interface

Faculty in traditional courses develop a teaching style based on their experience, expertise, and personalities. One instructor is effusive and lively, and demonstrates his or her sense of humor, while another is serious and straightforward. One instructor makes extensive use of multimedia and another does not. One is an excellent questioner and is able to engage students in discussion without any difficulty, while another delivers a lecture filled with kernels of important information but rarely engages students in discussions. All of these styles can be effective for instruction. Students recognize different teaching styles and adjust accordingly. However, all of these styles generally operate within a common environment, which we call the classroom. Students understand classroom protocol such as knowing where to sit; knowing how to take notes from a blackboard, overhead projector screen, or video presentation; knowing how to ask questions by raising their hands; and so forth. In an asynchronous program, while individual teaching styles surely evolve and develop and should be encouraged, the basic Web environment in which instruction is delivered should be somewhat standardized.

When designing courses for entire programs, schools, or colleges, distance learning providers should develop some common interface with which students are familiar for finding and accessing the basic components of their courses. The first page(s) of the course Web site is a likely candidate. This common interface provides a consistent layout that students use to access e-mail, to send messages to the discussion group or bulletin board, to access library or other informational resources, and so on. The basic functions of every course in the program, school, or college should use this common interface. While students are enormously capable of adapting to the individual needs of courses, presenting them with different layouts or procedures for engaging in basic instructional functions can hinder their participation and learning. This level of course activity should become second nature and be akin to raising one's hand or taking notes from a blackboard.

While designing a basic course interface may seem like common sense, in large programs or schools, instructors and designers will have to discuss and come to an agreement about what this common interface should look like and provide. In most cases, the common interface should provide for all possible basic course functions, even though most instructors will not use every function. Course management systems (CMS) discussed earlier in this chapter generally provide for a common interface and can help resolve this issue.

Course Enrollments

One of the most important aspects of instructional design in any environment, distance or otherwise, is student-to-faculty ratio. In primary and secondary education, school districts try to establish a standard class enrollment for the various grade levels. Colleges, universities, and adult education providers likewise establish course enrollment standards that depend on the discipline, nature of the course (lecture, discussion, laboratory), level (graduate, undergraduate), and so on. Generally, low student-to-faculty ratios are desirable, however, the economics of higher and adult education require provision for larger size sections as typified in college lecture halls holding hundreds of students. While discussions regarding class enrollments in higher education environments can sometimes be likened to a "contact sport" with faculty generally vying for lower enrollments and administrators pushing for higher enrollments, disagreements are always resolved. Standards adopted for traditional, face-to-face courses provide a starting point for establishing standards for Web-based courses, but some additional consideration will also have to be given to the instructional features of Web courses.

A Web-based course designed to be highly interactive with a good deal of faculty-to-student or student-to-student e-mail or bulletin board exchanges will put significant demands on the instructor's as well as on the students' time and therefore should have a lower enrollment. On the other hand, courses designed to be self-paced with student-to-faculty e-mail exchanges only as needed, will put fewer demands on the instructor's time and can accommodate a larger enrollment. Web-based courses that require extensive start-up costs for multimedia materials will likely either have to have increased enrollments or charge students higher tuition or additional fees to enroll. The bottom line is that the nature of the Web-based course has to be added to the criteria and procedures/mechanisms that are in place for determining the class sizes for traditional courses.

For example, in large traditional lecture courses of perhaps 500 students, the faculty, department chairs, and other administrators frequently agree that teaching assistants will be employed to conduct short recitation sections with small groups of students to review the material presented in the large lecture halls. This makes good pedagogical sense, because students are able to ask questions and to share views in recitation sections that logistically would not be possible in a large lecture. The use of teaching assistants also makes good economic sense, because their salaries are much lower than that of a full-time faculty instructor. The same approach can be taken in highly interactive Web-based courses. A faculty member may lead a discussion on the Web, but teaching assistants or tutors can be assigned to smaller groups of students to handle individual questions. The point is that faculty and administrators working together should be able to resolve any issue involving class size. Ultimately, the fundamental consideration is to provide a learning environment that is effective as well as affordable.

Guidelines with Respect to Instructional Activities

Virtual programs, schools, or colleges should consider establishing some basic guidelines for instructional activities. It is not the intent here to consider guidelines for the entire virtual enterprise but to provide some examples of where they may be appropriate. For example, take the issue of expected response time in a Web-based course. That is, if a student asks an instructor a question via e-mail, how long should he or she be expected to wait for a reply? A student who pays tuition for a Web-based course is entitled to expect an answer within a reasonable time. Establishing a guideline for the entire program, school, or college might be worth discussing among administrators, faculty, and support staff.

It is likely that a discussion of expected response time could lead to defining the responsibilities and operations of an on-line and/or telephone Help Desk. Which questions should the instructor refer to the Help Desk? Does the Help Desk provide technical support (hardware and software), referral support for administrative (registration, financial aid) services, referral support for academic services (library), tutoring services, or all of the above? Does the Help Desk ever attempt to answer questions related to course content? Probably not, but again, some guidelines clarifying responsibilities would help smooth the instructional pathway.

Processes for submitting and returning graded assignments such as written essays or take-home examinations should be consistent for all courses in a distance learning program. Again, this is rarely an issue in face-to-face classes but can be problematic for the program as a whole if students are expected to submit assignments one way for one course and another way for another course. There are several options such as e-mail, regular mail, fax, or all of the above. Establishing guidelines for submitting assignments as well as how faculty are expected to return graded assignments would help.

Students' use of college e-mail services is becoming an important issue for both face-to-face and distance learning programs. In face-to-face courses, e-mail usage may or may not be integral to instruction. In a Web-based course, students will likely have to use their own or a college-supplied e-mail address to participate. When college-supplied, are e-mail addresses to be used only for course-related activities, or can they be used for social, political, or other personal activities? Most schools would probably allow a certain amount of e-mail usage beyond strictly course-related matters. However, what if the usage related to activities that the school found questionable, such as hate mail, prurient subject matter, or running a home business? Standard guidelines for the proper use of college e-mail should be established for use in all courses.

In a traditional college environment, students are not expected to provide a home address or telephone number to other students in a class. In fact, the federal Family Educational Rights and Privacy Act (FERPA) stipulates procedures for disclosing data that give students the option of not allowing their personal information to be disseminated to third parties. In a distance learning course that makes extensive use of e-mail, do students using their personal e-mail addresses relinquish some of their rights in terms of privacy? The answer is probably yes and may subject students to unwanted solicitations from other students or others who have received their e-mail addresses as a result of participation in a course. This is not a problem in most situations but, again, some policies, guidelines, procedures, and prior disclosure might be appropriate.

The issues discussed in the above paragraphs can all be resolved through discussion leading to appropriate guidelines and policies. If distance learning providers are experiencing success with individual courses, they should consider introducing larger scale programs. Proper planning and inclusive decision making that will bring to the fore issues such as those discussed in the above paragraphs are a must. Enterprises that expand after some success in a limited market must enhance services, develop new policies and procedures, and protect themselves in exceptional situations. As programs grow, the providers, the faculty, and the students they serve become more vulnerable to the occasional or unique circumstance or misuse of services. These issues should not be ignored until a problem or breach occurs. On the contrary, they should be considered and resolved as part of the move from limited or experimental course offerings to more extensive, full programs.

VIRTUAL SPACE AND TIME WITH OTHER MODELS

The techniques associated with developing a Web-based, asynchronous course can be extended to other instructional models. Elements of virtual space and time can now be added to traditional courses as well as to the various distance learning models discussed in this book. E-mail, discussion lists, and Web-enabled courses are becoming commonplace in all types of instruction to enhance communication, to facilitate collaborative projects, and to extend reflective practice beyond the confines of a fifty-minute class session. Students in large lecture courses can ask questions of an instructor or teaching assistant at any time of the day or night by e-mail. Broadcast television and other one-way distance learning technology can evolve from a passive to an interactive model by adding a discussion group or electronic bulletin board component. Slides, illustrations, and other graphics used in any instructional activity can be duplicated on Web pages for students to review and study.

The Internet and World Wide Web has provided the gateway to virtual space and time that humankind has been seeking from its earliest stirrings. The Web-based, asynchronous learning model presented in this chapter is here and now. However, the Internet is in its nascent stages. Some speculation on its future will be discussed in Chapter 9.

SUMMARY

In this chapter, Web-based distance learning is presented as the virtual model in which learning can take place at any place and at any time. An examination of some of the issues involved in designing and implementing this model is provided. As part of the presentation, the definition of virtual is reexamined.

In developing and designing virtual courses, instructional designers start by considering the individual needs of their students. The Web-based virtual model is built on students and instructors using the Internet as the main vehicle for sharing and interacting with instructional resources. The course Web site provides the organizational foundation for the model, while software tools such as e-mail, electronic bulletin boards, and discussion lists provide the interactivity.

The software tools for developing Web materials are discussed, with the understanding that these tools are becoming easier for the average person to use. A number of techniques including the use of standard word processing packages, electronic presentation packages, and HyperText Mark-Up Language filters are suggested. Course management systems (CMS) designed specifically for developing course materials on the Web are becoming very popular and represent the most advanced software tools available for this application.

Multimedia and videoconferencing technologies for Web-based distance learning are examined. While potentially very important pedagogically, these technologies should be carefully considered in terms of student access to appropriate hardware and software. While basic computer work stations are becoming more powerful and more affordable, the communications facilities available in the average person's home limits the widespread use of multimedia for many Web-based distance learning activities. However, where student computer environments can be controlled, such as on a company's local area network, multimedia technology can be used most effectively.

As distance learning providers achieve success with individual courses, a natural progression to offering entire programs on the Web should be considered. The

1990s saw the emergence of schools and colleges whose entire offerings are Web-based. When expanding courses into programs, a number of issues including common course interfaces, class enrollments, and guidelines and policies will have to be considered. Planning processes should be established that are inclusive and that help bring scalability issues to the foreground where solutions can be sought and mutually agreed upon by all parties.

The chapter concludes with the suggestion that the virtual time and space model presented in this chapter can and is already being extended to other instructional models, both in traditional and distance learning environments.

CASE STUDY

NetSafe Incorporated Year: 2000

Setting

NetSafe Incorporated is a successful software provider in the southwest United States. NetSafe develops and maintains several software products designed to monitor computer network activity. These products have proven successful and attractive to high-end commercial users who are dependent on stable computer networking environments. NetSafe's customer base is located entirely within a five-state region. NetSafe employs approximately eighty full-time and fifty part-time employees. Most of them are technicians who, in addition to general expertise, are highly trained to understand the dynamic world of computer network hardware and software. James Kierson, the president of NetSafe, believes his company's success is due in part to having an excellent training program that develops and hones the technical expertise of its staff. Mr. Kierson is convinced of the need to develop a staff that knows networking technology as well as, if not better than, any other company. NetSafe's training consists of a program developed at its headquarters by the managers and staff, which is free to all employees. Training is provided by a combination of in-house experts and outside consultants. Traditional face-to-face training sessions are frequently supplemented by on-line follow-up activities designed to relate real-life work experiences with the subject matter.

The Issue

In January, Mr. Kierson announced the merger of NetSafe with National Supervision, Incorporated, a facilities management company that assists in administering and managing computer facilities for corporate and other clients. National Supervision has an extensive client base with customers in forty-two states. The merger provides National Supervision with an attractive software product line that could feed the facilities management business. The merger also allows NetSafe to evolve from a regional to a national company.

In analyzing the strengths and weaknesses of the two companies, Mr. Kierson sees a need for a new strategy for staff training and development in the merged company. National Supervision's approach has been to provide a generous tuition assistance program to its employees to take courses at colleges and universities of their choice. Mr. Kierson would like to see a more focused, targeted approach similar to that established at NetSafe. However, with branch offices and employees distributed throughout the country, such a program could prove quite expensive. Mr. Kierson has asked his head of training, Carol Stams, to develop a proposal to provide a cost-effective approach to staff training and development that builds the NetSafe model into a program that can be delivered nationally.

Assume you are Ms. Stams. How would you proceed to gather data to develop a plan for a new training program? What would be some of the key elements of your study and/or proposal? Consider especially the technical skills of your employees and their access to technology.

REFERENCES

Arenson, K. (1998, October 7). N.Y.U. sees profits in virtual classes. *The New York Times*, p. B8.

Chute, A. G., Sayers, P. K., & Gardner, R. P. (1997). Networked learning environments. (T. E. Cyrs, Ed.). *Teaching and learning at a distance: What it takes to effectively design, deliver, and evaluate programs.* San Francisco: Jossey-Bass, Inc.

Gladieux, L. E., & Swail, W. S. (1999). *The virtual university & educational opportunity.* Washington, D.C.: The College Board.

Khan, B. H. (1999). *Web-based instruction.* Englewood Cliffs, NJ: Educational Technology Publications.

McCollum, K. (1997, October 21). Colleges sort through vast store of tools for designing Web courses. *The Chronicle of Higher Education.* http://chronicle.com/data/internet.dir/itdata/1997/10/t97102101.htm

McMakin, M., Murphy, S., & Sauer, J. (1999). Showtime for streaming video. *NewMedia* 9(1), 60–69.

The National Commission on Excellence in Education. (1985) *A nation at risk: The imperative for educational reform.* Washington, DC: Superintendent for Documents, U.S. Government Printing Office.

Nichols, P. M. (1999, January 17). The newest wave: Made-for-the-Internet movies. *The New York Times*, p. AR27.

Phipps, R., & Merisotis, J. (1999). *What's the difference: A review of contemporary research on the effectiveness of distance learning in higher education.* Washington, D.C.: The Institute for Higher Education Policy.

U.S. Department of Education, National Center for Education Statistics, Distance Education at Postsecondary Education Institutions: 1997–98. NCES 2000–013, by Laurie Lewis, Kyle Snow, Elizabeth Farris, and Douglas Levin. Bernie Green, project officer. Washington, DC: 1999.

Zeffirelli, F. (1998, November 9). Lecture at Lincoln Center, New York City.

CHAPTER NINE

A Glimpse at a Future in the Making

Humankind has been on a knowledge quest since the dawn of recorded history. Education systems including distance learning are evolving to support and continue this quest into the first part of the twenty-first century. Networking technologies such as the Internet and World Wide Web, which revolutionized many aspects of creating, storing, and disseminating information, now provide the vehicle for teachers and students to journey through and connect across virtual space and time. In the next twenty-five years or so, the Internet and

World Wide Web as we know them will be gone, replaced by newer networking technologies designed to enhance these journeys. In this chapter, we take a look at the future and speculate on the possibilities and implications for distance learning.

SHAPING OUR WORLD: LEARNING AND LIVING WITH TECHNOLOGY

Webster's Third International Dictionary defines ubiquitous as "existing or being everywhere at the same time." Historically, ubiquity referred to the religious doctrine of omnipresence or a God who is everywhere. Technologically, the word ubiquitous is frequently used to describe wide-area digital networks that can be accessed everywhere. James Dunderstadt (1997), president emeritus of the University of Michigan, in discussing the future of education, envisions a ubiquitous university where "the constraints of time and space—and perhaps of reality itself—are relaxed by digital networks." Dunderstadt's vision provides an appropriate base upon which to begin a discussion of distance learning in the twenty-first century. He sees technology as a major tool for meeting what will be an unprecedented demand for education as the world's population continues to grow, and as learning becomes a life-long activity. While much discussion of the future is speculative, several social and technological trends can be cited that support Dunderstadt's vision of the ubiquitous university.

Education for Young and Old

One of the most significant demographic trends during the past century has been an increase in the number of people seeking higher levels of education. In countries all over the world, the major issue for ministries of education is the expansion of educational services to growing populations. This issue involves broadening opportunities to a larger percentage of the population while the population itself experiences unprecedented growth. The world population of approximately six billion people is increasing at a rate of slightly more than 1 percent per year or seventy-five to eighty million people. While the most densely populated countries such as China and India, each with more than one billion people, will face the most severe shortages of schools, other countries must also develop and expand educational facilities.

The population of the United States will increase from 275 million people in the year 2000 to almost 300 million by the year 2010. This predicted growth is due in part to greater longevity and increased immigration, but to a greater extent to a demographic phenomenon called the "baby boom echo" or the children of "baby boomers." Figure 9.1 provides data on the number of births in the United States from 1948 to 2018, clearly demonstrating the effect of the baby boom and its echo. While school enrollments are at an all-time high already, the early part of the twenty-first century will see significant increases, particularly at the secondary and post-secondary levels. Figure 9.2A through 9.2C provide the projected enrollment

FIGURE 9.1 Number of Births in the United States: Years 1948–2018

SOURCE: U.S. Department of Education/National Center for Education Statistics

Number of births (in millions)

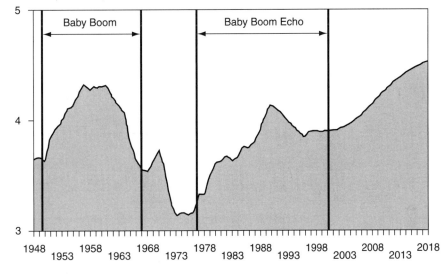

FIGURE 9.2A Projected Primary School Enrollments

SOURCE: U.S. Department of Education/National Center for Education Statistics

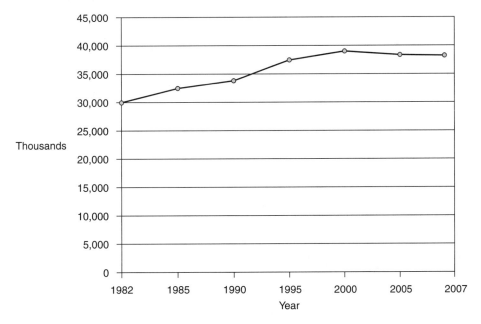

FIGURE 9.2B Projected Secondary School Enrollments

SOURCE: U.S. Department of Education/National Center for Education Statistics

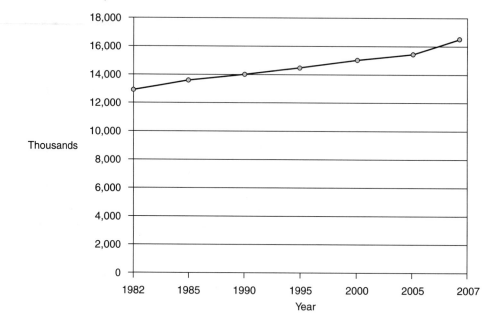

FIGURE 9.2C Projected Two-Year and Four-Year College Enrollments

SOURCE: U.S. Department of Education/National Center for Education Statistics

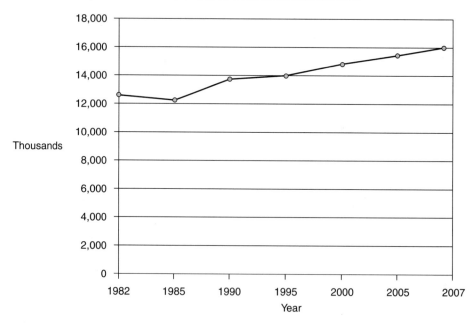

FIGURE 9.3   Excerpt from a report entitled, *A Back to School Special Report on the Baby Boom Echo: Here Comes the Teenagers*

This year (1997) . . . .

Total public and private school enrollment will rise to a record 52.2 million;

Between 1997 and 2007 . . . .

Public high school enrollment is expected to increase by 13 percent, while elementary enrollment is projected to increase by less than one percent;

The number of public high school graduates will increase 18 percent;

About half of the states will have at least a 15 percent increase in the number of public high school graduates, with an 80 percent increase projected for Nevada, 49 percent for Arizona, and 41 percent for Florida;

Largely because of the high school enrollment increase, over 150,000 additional public and private high school teachers will be needed—a 14 percent increase;

Full-time college enrollment is projected to rise by 21 percent.

Beyond 2007 . . . .

Unlike the decline after the previous baby boom, where births dropped down to 3.1 million in the early seventies, the number of births is not projected to fall off, but remain fairly stable at around 4 million. Long-range projections by the U.S. Bureau of the Census indicate a rising number of births thereafter, rising to 4.2 million in 2010 and 4.6 million in 2020.

SOURCE: National Center for Education Statistics. 1997. U.S. Department of Education. Office of Educational Research and Improvement. Released: August 1997, http://oeri.ed.gov/pubs/bbecho/

data for primary, secondary, and post-secondary schools through the year 2007. Figure 9.3 is an excerpt from the executive summary of a report prepared by the U.S. Department of Education's National Center for Education Statistics on projected enrollments in the United States for primary, secondary, and post-secondary education. By the year 2007, high school enrollments are expected to increase by 18 percent and college enrollments are expected to increase by 21 percent. Some states such as Nevada will experience a growth rate in excess of 80 percent in their primary and secondary schools.

These projections are based on mathematical formulae that examine and weigh enrollments from previous years. However, educational reforms and socioeconomic conditions may further accelerate enrollments in schools, colleges, and universities.

For example, half-day kindergarten, heralded as a major reform in the late 1940s, gave way to the need for universal all-day prekindergarten in the 1990s. Numerous studies of *Headstart* and other early childhood programs have convinced most policy makers that starting education early is an important determinant for future achievement. In the late 1990s, many states implemented policies mandating all-day prekindergarten classes for all children. Not only will this put greater demands on primary schools, but in all likelihood it will lead to greater persistence in upper grades, especially in secondary schools.

In post-secondary education, the percentage of high school graduates continuing on to college steadily increased throughout the latter half of the twentieth century. In addition to the major increases in enrollments after World War II as a result of the GI Bill and again in the 1960s and early 1970s when the baby boom generation went to college, the demand for post-secondary education in the 1990s appears to be accelerating without precedent. Secretary of Education Richard Riley (1998), in a report issued on September 8, 1998, commented:

> "This year marks a new college enrollment record. . . . We project that college enrollment will jump from 14,350,000 in 1997 to 14,590,000 [1998]—an increase of 240,000 students. This should not come as a surprise, with 65 percent of all high school graduates now immediately going on to college and millions of adult Americans going back to college to brush up on their skills." (Riley, 1998)

The increase (240,000 students) in college enrollments referred to by Secretary Riley was in fact 25 percent higher than that projected by the U.S. Department of Education in 1996.

Secretary Riley noted that the increase in college enrollments was due in part to the number of adults "going back to brush up on their skills." Indeed, the number of older students in colleges and universities has been growing more rapidly than the number of younger students even though larger percentages of high school graduates have been entering college immediately upon graduation. Between 1985 and 1995, the enrollment of students under age 25 increased by 13 percent. During the same period, enrollment of persons 25 and over rose by 22 percent (U.S. Department of Education, NCES, 1997b). This trend is expected to continue into the early part of the twenty-first century.

Almost all segments of the job market have been affected by technological and other advancements that are requiring workers to maintain and upgrade their skills on a regular or "life-long" basis. As economies in many countries have advanced and shifted, workers have been forced to advance or shift their skills in order to maintain their marketability. In the United States, the economy has been moving from an industrial base to a service (technical, financial, health, legal) base for several decades. Workers have learned new job skills in order to be employed in the new service sectors.

While some people enroll in adult, continuing, and other types of professional or job skill courses in the hope of making a career change, many are doing so to maintain or upgrade their skills for current positions. Employees in every segment of the economy—the assembly line worker learning the dynamics of a new industrial process, the doctor learning a new medical procedure, the attorney brushing up on new regulations, or the teacher learning how to use technology in the classroom—must upgrade skills to maintain and improve current operations. The latter half of the twentieth century provided many lessons on the importance of keeping skills well-honed. The closings of outdated industrial plants and the consolidations of operations into new, more modern facilities have been numerous. The stories of displaced blue-collar workers, many of whom gave lifetimes to their companies, have been well-publicized. Likewise, white-collar workers who had dedicated their careers to companies with excellent reputations such as IBM, AT&T, and CITICORP have experienced a number of downsizing changes, resulting in tens of thousands of retirements or other job losses. While devastating for those directly involved, other workers have observed the changes and come to realize the importance of maintaining their skills and job marketability.

The Information Age and Beyond

With the introduction of the digital computer in the 1950s, the Information Age emerged and will continue well into the twenty-first century. In the 1960s and 1970s, all segments of business, government, and education embraced the new information technology in order to streamline operations, improve record-keeping, and serve better their clientele. Complex mathematical formulae, impossible to calculate by hand, were done routinely on advanced high-speed computer processors. Database management systems capable of storing trillions of characters were being developed by major business and non-profit information providers. Services such as automatic teller machines (ATMs), intelligent cash registers, and express checkout counters that automatically read bar codes on merchandise and calculated bills became commonplace.

Until the late 1970s and 1980s, information was the domain of highly trained computer analysts and programmers. But with the introduction and proliferation of microcomputers, the Information Age began to spread into the schools and workplaces. Children in primary schools were using software packages such as *Logo* to develop computer programs to solve simple geometry problems. Secretaries traded in their typewriters for word processing machines. The desktop computer became an indispensable tool for economic analysts, attorneys, researchers, and others as they sought out the latest information on stock market activity, commodity futures, government regulatory decisions, or census data. Every desk and table suddenly had a display monitor situated off to one side.

The 1990s brought the Information Age directly into people's homes. The Internet and World Wide Web turned the desktop computer into every person's home information helper. Everything that was being done in the workplace with computers could now be done at home: looking up a customer profile, purchasing airline tickets, or faxing a new order to a supplier. E-mail established a faster and less expensive way of maintaining relationships with family, friends, and colleagues. Working at home took on a whole new meaning as more and more people found themselves able to access company data files, communicate with associates, and develop memoranda without changing out of their pajamas and bathrobes.

The largest segment of the population buying computers for the home were households with children (see Figure 9.4). Parents wanted to assure themselves that their children would not be at a disadvantage in learning their ABC's, in writing a composition, or in collaborating with fellow students on developing a Web page for their class project.

Social scientists are studying the nature of home Internet use in all segments of the population including children, home workers, and senior citizens. While some concern has been expressed that social and human interaction may be waning, others see many positive developments. The interactive use of digital technology is more intellectually and socially stimulating than passive activities such as viewing television. Writing e-mail messages requires children and adults to write words, to spell, and to use noncolloquial grammar, while talking on the telephone does not. Participating in electronic bulletin boards, discussion groups, or other group e-mail activities actually increases interaction among people over wider geographic areas.

As we enter the twenty-first century, the evolution of the Internet will surely shape the Information Age. When one considers that only a handful of academics, researchers, and engineers were accessing the Internet in the early 1990s, and that more than 40 percent of American households had home access by the year 2000, the acceptance and importance of this technology is clear. While most other coun-

FIGURE 9.4   Projected Percentage of Households in the United States with Internet Access
SOURCE: Nielsen Media Services Home Technology Report (Tapscott, 1998).

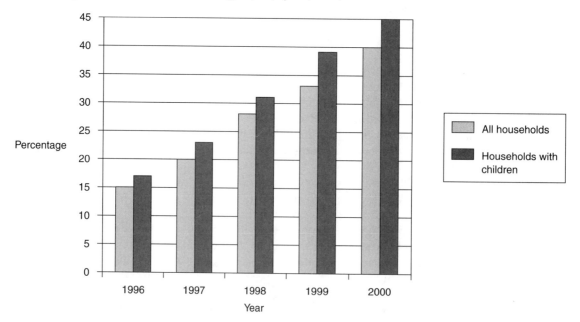

tries lag behind the United States in home Internet access, some such as Finland and Iceland actually have higher percentages of the population connected to the Internet (Ibrahim, 1997). In the twenty-first century, the home digital computer in various shapes and sizes will become as common as the television for communicating with and learning about our world. Furthermore, this computer will be connected to a worldwide network that is much faster and more powerful than the Internet of the twentieth century.

The Convergence of Technologies

William Gibson (1996), the futurist who coined the term *cyberspace* in 1981, sees the Internet as being in its "larval stage," a "test pattern" for whatever will become the dominant global medium. The new global medium will be based on a technology that gracefully merges communications, digital computing, and high-quality audio/video. As discussed in Chapter 8, the Internet presently used by most people in their homes is excellent for text and limited graphics but is too slow for more advanced communications requiring high-quality audio and full-motion video. The next global medium will provide affordable, high-speed communications comparable to that presently available only through dedicated telephone lines with speeds in the range of one million bits per second. This medium will connect to very high-speed and high-capacity computing devices that will come in various sizes and have high-quality digital audio/video record and playback features. The global medium described here is not available yet but will be in the early part of the twenty-first century.

The convergence of technologies progressed steadily during the second half of the twentieth century. Digital technology, which has been the basis for computing devices since their inception, is becoming widely accepted and used by other technologies, namely communications and audio/video. Digital technology is broadly defined as any technology that uses electronic "on-off" impulses to store, transmit, and receive data. Audio compact discs, digital video, digital communications switches, and digital television are examples of communications and audio/video equipment that use digital technology.

The technology that is slowing down the emergence of a digitally based global medium is communications. More advanced telephone equipment using digital technology is too expensive for the common home user. A number of major communications, media, and computer companies are actively engaged in research and development of an inexpensive digital alternative for the home user. Most home users of the Internet operate with modems over standard telephone lines at speeds rarely in excess of 56,000 bits per second. Newer broadband lines or other communications conduits that operate at speeds closer to a T1 service (1.5 million bits per second) are needed in order to send and receive high-quality audio/video signals. This requirement is being intensely studied and tested by satellite, fiber optics, cable television, and telephone providers around the world. While doable, cost is the issue.

The next global medium will also be truly accessible in any place and at any time. Digital devices that will serve as one's computer, telephone, television, and other communications links will come in various sizes, but will be especially popular in portable and handheld sizes. A device combining the features of a laptop computer, a cellular telephone, and a Sony Walkman will be available in the first quarter of the twenty-first century.

Figure 9.5 provides a timeline of the evolution of digital computing machines. In the second half of the twentieth century, digital computing has been steadily progressing by providing greater capacity at lower cost and in smaller sizes. As a result, more and more people have been able to purchase and acquire computing equipment. In the twenty-first century, this progression is leading toward an inexpensive, palm-size information appliance that will allow anyone to look up a bank statement, compose and forward e-mail, view a television program, or call mom. Such a device does not yet exist, but prototypes such as the Motorola *Pagewriter,* Nokia *6160,* and 3M *Palm Pilot* do. Furthermore, these devices will be so inexpensive that every household will own several. If there is any doubt, just consider how Americans have moved from one piece of furniture containing a television in the living room to a TV in every room—or from one telephone on the wall to a telephone in every room, a portable for the patio, and a cellular in the car or in one's pocketbook.

The convergence of computer, communications, and audio/video technologies resulting in inexpensive, portable information devices will have a major impact on all aspects of information-related activities, including education. Distance learning will be more convenient and affordable, and will allow teachers and students to connect more gracefully in virtual space and time.

EDUCATION'S RESPONSE TO SOCIAL AND TECHNOLOGICAL CHANGE

The social and technological changes described above will affect many aspects of society. In education, the increased number of people going to school combined with a greater understanding and ease of access to information and communications technologies bodes well for distance learning. Responding to these trends will be a challenge for educational policy makers and planners.

Projects are beginning now that provide a glimpse of future possibilities. Large university systems such as those in California, Texas, New York, and Maryland that did not have extensive experience in distance learning embarked on distance learning initiatives in the 1990s. Other schools with long histories of providing successful distance learning programs such as Penn State University began to redirect much of their efforts to Internet-based applications. A number of new distance learning providers such as Magellan University and the Mind Extension University have been created that do not have classrooms or laboratories and only exist as entities on the World Wide Web. In all instances, these initiatives direct or redirect distance learning efforts to using digital networking technology.

FIGURE 9.5   The Evolution of Digital Computing

	1940s **Pre- Mainframe**	1950s **Mainframe**	1960s **Minicomputer**	1970s ➡ 1980s **Microcomputer**	1990s ➡ 2000 **Post- Microcomputer**
Machine	Experimental machines such as ENIAC	IBM 700, 360, 4300 Series	Digital Equipment PDP Series	PC, Macintosh	Digital information appliances
Cost	Unaffordable	Affordable to large businesses	Affordable to large and small businesses	Affordable to individuals	Inexpensive—individuals will own several
Size	Large room	Room	Large Desk	Desktop, Laptop	Palm-size
Distribution	One in existence	Thousands sold	Hundreds of thousands sold	Hundreds of millions sold	Billions will be sold

While some of these efforts required major new funding, others represent modest investments that will increase as the student demand grows and the technology advances. An evolutionary approach is recommended and desirable where possible. On the other hand, not all policy makers or planners will be in a position to take a slower evolutionary approach, and a bolder decision or plan may be necessary.

The Western Interstate Consortium on Higher Education (WICHE) facilitates resource sharing and cost-effective services among fifteen western states and their public and private colleges and universities. As indicated earlier in this chapter, an 18 percent increase in high school graduates is anticipated nationally, but this number will be far higher in several of the WICHE-affiliated states. In Nevada, for example, from the 1995–1996 to the 2011–2012 school year, the high school graduating class is projected to more than double (134 percent increase). Large increases in the number of graduates are also expected in Arizona (62 percent), Colorado (36 percent), Washington (36 percent), California (28 percent), and Oregon (26 percent) during the same period. In 1998, WICHE issued a report titled *Is Access to College in Jeopardy in the West?* that described three major strategies for dealing with rapid growth, namely building new facilities, developing joint-use facilities, and providing electronic access (see Figure 9.6).

These three strategies represent the cornerstone of a plan for accommodating unprecedented increases in the number of students seeking higher education. Building new facilities makes sense but it is costly and takes a good deal of time. California is moving rapidly in this direction, but as the WICHE report indicates,

FIGURE 9.6 Excerpt from the Report of the Western Interstate Commission on Higher Education (1998), *Is Access to College in Jeopardy in the West?*

Is Access to College in Jeopardy in the West?
Strategies to Increase Capacity

1. New Facilities.

California is increasing its capacity through the addition of new educational facilities. Over the past decade, two new California State University campuses have been built and state officials are considering adding one more California State University campus and an additional University of California campus in the near future. Even with these new facilities, the California Postsecondary Education Commission reports that public institutions in the state are filled to capacity.

2. Joint-Use Facilities.

Rather than investing in new facilities, other states found ways to more fully utilize existing facilities. Nevada has formed partnerships among community colleges and the K–12 system to share facilities. Local high schools are offering classes on community college campuses in both Las Vegas and Reno. These high school students can take community college courses while completing the requirements for their diplomas. Nevada gains by both making dual use of existing facilities and shortening time to degree for newly matriculating students.

3. Electronic Access.

New information technologies, such as the World Wide Web, offer people who are place- or time-bound access to a full range of educational options. Students enrolled in distance learning programs made up 5 percent of all enrollments in 1994–95. The Western Governors University, the California Virtual University, and other distance learning networks throughout the country may lead to increases in enrollment through distance learning.

The capacity of campus-based programs may benefit from the use of information technologies. At Northern Arizona University, for example, students enrolling in some large lecture classes may attend a lecture face-to-face or access the course by way of the World Wide Web from their dormitory. These arrangements enable students to successfully negotiate schedule conflicts and free course registration from the limitations of available classroom space.

SOURCE: Western Interstate Commission on Higher Education.
http://www.wiche.edu/rapa/PolicyInsights/Access/Strategies.htm

---

even with two new campuses and a third on the way, the state is already filled to capacity and will need to do much more. Joint sharing of facilities with other entities such as occurs in primary and secondary schools of Nevada also makes good sense. But this approach is expected to alleviate, not solve, the problem. The third strategy, electronic access, is most pertinent to our discussion. The use of Web-based distance learning in major new undertakings such as the Western Governor's University and the integration of Web-based distance learning techniques into traditional classes at Northern Arizona University also make sense. While no single strategy will solve the entire problem, the three strategies in combination provide the basic framework for a plan that might. What is important here is that Web-based distance learning is considered an important strategy comparable to building new colleges and sharing facilities. In the twenty-first century, policy makers and planners throughout the world will routinely be including network-based distance learning as part of their overall strategies for providing educational services and opportunities.

NEW SCHOOLS, STRUCTURES, AND ENTERPRISES

The beginning of the twenty-first century will see a number of new approaches to higher and adult education. The 3,000-plus decentralized, self-contained colleges and universities in the United States will be challenged by new schools, structures, and commercial enterprises. The concept of a traditional college governed and controlled by local administrations and faculty where eighteen to twenty-two-year-old students go for four years has been changing since the end of World War II as large public university systems, community colleges, adult extension centers, and employee training programs developed and grew. At the close of the twentieth century, the college student population consisted largely of adults over the age of twenty-five, part-time, or non-residential full-time students. Less than 15 percent of the college student population fit the profile of "young, full-time and living on campus" (Connick, 1997). Governance and policy making, particularly in the publicly supported schools, has increasingly been shifting from local college to statewide structures. Distance learning may accelerate these trends, since it extends the college enterprise beyond local environs. New educational entities and structures may come to the forefront. In the following paragraphs several such entities, primarily based on Internet-based distance learning programs, will be presented.

The For-Profit Distance Learning Provider

Traditionally, most of the providers of education at all levels have been publicly funded or nonprofit enterprises. A number of for-profit proprietary schools have always existed but generally have served a very small percentage of the school-going population. The 1990s saw the emergence of for-profit education providers such as Sylvan Learning Systems, the University of Phoenix, and Real Education, Inc., which rely extensively on technology for delivering part or all of their services. Many of these providers have targeted a particular niche such as remedial education, technology-oriented courses, or career programs for adults for development.

Magellan University, for example, operates out of 600 square feet of office space at 4320 N. Campbell Ave., in Tucson, Arizona. William R. Noyes, with twenty-six years at the University of Arizona as a professor and administrator, started Magellan University in 1996 with $1 million, provided for the most part by Research Corporation Technologies. Former University of Arizona President John Schaefer heads Research Corporation Technologies, a nonprofit group that moves inventions from the lab to the marketplace. Schaefer is also chairman of Magellan's board.

Noyes has stated that bricks and mortar have nothing to do with his university's capacity or capabilities. "All students need are a videocassette player, computer, modem and access to the Internet" (Christman, 1998). Magellan has directed most of its courses to adults in areas such as basic mathematics, engineering, and systems design. It enrolled its first twenty-five students in 1998 and hopes eventually to have an enrollment of 12,000.

Noyes considers carefully the academic quality and rigor of the program at Magellan. By design, class size is small, tutors are always available, and writing is an important component of all courses. Interestingly, Noyes favors the conventional university setting for an eighteen year old, because of the social interaction and "the breadth of the educational experience" that extends beyond one's major course of study. But for working adults who are attempting to advance in a career or launch a new one, the flexibility and intensity of on-line courses such as those offered at Magellan will be a boon in the twenty-first century (Christman, 1998).

For-Profit Subsidiaries

In the past, a number of colleges and universities have established separate profit centers in conjunction with products or inventions that emanated from research and development efforts. Frequently, part or all of the initial funds for these for-profit efforts were supplied by corporate partners. It is rare for traditional colleges to create for-profit subsidiaries for instructional activities.

New York University (NYU), the largest private, nonprofit university in the state of New York, has an enrollment of approximately 45,000 students in its undergraduate and graduate programs. NYU also operates a very large continuing education program encompassing all aspects of adult learning. In October 1998, NYU announced plans to create a for-profit subsidiary that will develop and then sell specialized on-line courses to other colleges and corporate training centers, and will offer them directly to students who prefer to attend class at home. In a sense, NYU would put itself in the position of both wholesaler and retailer of on-line distance learning. The move is in direct response to "what many educators see as the biggest challenge to higher education, the rise of profit-making institutions using the Internet to siphon off some of academia's most profitable courses, namely continuing education for adult learners" (Arenson, 1998).

NYU's subsidiary will have its own board of directors and will receive $1.5 million in start-up funds from NYU. However, much of the approximately $20–$30 million dollars needed for the endeavor will come from commercial investors or from a public stock offering. Gerald Heeger, dean of NYU's School of Continuing and Professional Studies will run the new subsidiary. Initially, courses will be offered in subjects that typically appeal to adult learners, namely business administration, management, information technology, and computer languages.

Sheldon Steinbach, general counsel for the American Council on Education, considers NYU's for-profit venture "brilliant" and believes that it places the University in a flexible position to market and maneuver in the dramatically expanding world of distance learning (Arenson, 1998).

Other colleges and universities with substantive adult and continuing education programs are likely to follow NYU's lead or at least follow its development. Martin Lipton, NYU's chairman of the board of trustees, indicated that in order to compete with other services and to cover the start-up costs, most traditional nonprofit colleges and universities attempting to move into large-scale distance learning will have to consider doing so on a for-profit basis (Arenson, 1998).

Large Statewide Coordinating Bodies

States that had historically established and supported major distance learning programs such as Alaska, Hawaii, Iowa, Pennsylvania, and Wisconsin usually either designated a particular distance learning institution or established some coordinating or other statewide body to support distance learning operations in several institutions. In recent years, large public systems, namely the California state system (California Virtual University), the State University of New York (SUNY Learning Network), and the City University of New York (CUNY On-Line), all of which had modest distance learning programs, established system-wide coordinating bodies in an effort to support distance learning at all campuses and to minimize the costs that would result from many colleges attempting to mount individual distance learning programs.

The SUNY Learning Network (SLN) was established in 1994 to meet the needs of the 400,000 students projected to enter New York's public higher education system in the early part of the twenty-first century. The conceptual design for SLN was not to create a new virtual university but "to virtualize the existing university system" (Fredricksen, Pickett, Pelz, Swan, and Shea, 1999). The design called for SLN to serve as the marketing and operations facilitator for all SUNY colleges wishing to offer Web-based distance learning courses. The SLN is responsible for developing a semester course schedule of on-line course offerings; for facilitating admissions, registration, and other student services related to SLN courses; for providing faculty training and development; for maintaining the technical infrastructure; and for providing a student help center.

Under SLN, each campus is responsible for determining the nature and scope of its on-line distance learning offerings, academic terms, faculty workload, student admission, and degree requirements. In essence, each college involved with SLN retains it own political, regulatory, and fiscal environment and is subject to the established administration and faculty governance of each campus. The goal is to allow students the opportunity to choose among a wide range of institutions and courses of study and to benefit from the overall quality of the combined offerings of the colleges participating in SLN. SLN offered its first courses in 1995–96 enrolling 119 students. By 1998–99, 400 courses were offered, enrolling more than 6,000 students. Present projections indicate that enrollments will double in each of the next three years to approximately 40,000 students by 2003–2004.

Mega Universities

Large universities that operate beyond state boundaries are not as common in the United States as they are in other countries. The United States does not have a history of strong federal or central control of education. Schools at all levels receive their charters and are subject to regulations and guidelines established by state and local entities. In most other countries, a central ministry of education is frequently the major educational policy-making and administrative body and, as a result, large-scale initiatives can be undertaken that affect the country's entire educational enterprise. This centralized control has resulted in several large-scale distance learning colleges or mega universities in countries such as China, Turkey, Great Britain, France, India, and Pakistan, where national programs have been established that enroll hundreds of thousands of students.

In June 1995, the idea for a western virtual university was born at the annual meeting of the Western Governors' Association. Under the leadership of Michael Leavitt, Governor of Utah, and Roy Romer, Governor of Colorado, a proposal was made that western colleges and universities, in anticipation of a dramatic increase in student enrollment in the twenty-first century, should consider collaborating on the development and delivery of distance learning courses and programs. This would avoid unnecessary duplication and would allow all the member states to pool resources. The proposal was studied and in June 1997, a new virtual university, the Western Governor's University (WGU), was approved by the governors of ten western states.

The WGU is designed to expand access to post-secondary education by means of Internet and other networking technologies. To accomplish this, WGU will add to the instructional offerings of existing higher education institutions, corporate training, and other education providers. WGU will also provide access to a central electronic course catalog, and will provide support for admissions, registration, and bursaring operations. WGU appears to be a larger version of the SUNY Learning Network except that one of its goals is "to provide the means for students to earn competency-based credentials including degrees up to the masters level and vocational/professional certifications" (http://www.wgu.edu). The inclusion of competency-based credentialing adds significantly to its mission and clearly establishes WGU as something beyond a coordinating body. In evaluating and awarding degree credits for courses, life experiences, and other expertise, WGU in fact, becomes a higher education degree-granting institution in its own right. The SUNY Learning Network, while coordinating distance learning, maintains that students meet admission and degree requirements of individual colleges and universities. SLN does not award degrees or certificates; the participating colleges do. WGU awards degrees and certificates.

The performance of WGU will be followed closely in the early part of the twenty-first century. John Daniel, Vice Chancellor of the Open University of the United Kingdom, commented:

"As you would expect, the universities in the western USA are not sure what to make of their governors' enthusiasm for this idea. They think some of the assumptions behind it are naive, but they don't want to get left behind." (Daniel, 1997, http://www.leeds.ac.uk/educol/documents/000000087.htm)

In 1998, WGU signed preliminary agreements of collaboration with the Open University of United Kingdom, the Open Learning Agency in British Columbia, Canada, the Tokai University System in Japan, and the Universidad Virtual del Instituto Technologico y de Estudios Superiores de Monterrey in Mexico. In November 1998, Michael Leavitt, Governor of Utah, announced that the Western Governors' University and The Open University of the United States had formally established a joint partnership to create the Governors' Open University System, offering competency-based and credit-based distance learning opportunities worldwide. The Open University of the United States is a private American university established with the backing of the Open University of the United Kingdom.

SPANNING THE GLOBE

In 1998, the first two modules were launched and fitted into what is perhaps the most extensive international collaborative project ever conceived, the building of a new space station. Over the next several years, astronauts are to assemble the station from components made by sixteen countries and carried into space by more than fifty rocket or space shuttle flights. Major partners in this venture, which is expected to cost at least $30 billion, are the United States, the European Space Agency, Russia, Japan, and Canada. When completed, this station will be the first stop for astronauts on humankind's exploration of the heavens. It is a credit to the cooperative spirit of our world leaders that such a venture involving so many countries is possible.

In the late 1980s and 1990s, with the end of the Cold War and the easing of East-West tensions, international exchange and cooperation in science, technology, commerce, and education blossomed. While Coca-Cola and Pepsi vied to be first in China, and Burger King and McDonald's sought to open in Red Square, major new venues for cooperation were being explored by world leaders, governmental agencies, and big businesses. General Motors Corporation, Ford Motor Company, and IBM have opened new facilities and offices in Eastern Europe. Major banks and financial services firms in Europe, the United States, and Japan are pursuing investment opportunities in the former Soviet republics. The Earth has suddenly become much smaller as advances in communications have opened up all types of information and social exchange. We also have become much more dependent on one another. Financial crises in world stock exchanges in 1998 and 1999 were clear evidence of this dependence. Pertinent to the topic of this book is the role that networking technology will play as a communications vehicle for developing and sustaining relationships with partners, colleagues, and friends around the globe.

Historically, educational institutions confined their international experiences to study-abroad programs and student/faculty exchanges. As part of the new world spirit of cooperation in the 1990s, this expanded to include the establishment of education branch campuses, educational alliances, and technical assistance programs in other countries. In the twenty-first century, the Internet and other network-based distance learning will extend and enrich these exchanges as students from almost any country will be able to register for courses in other countries. Distance learning will become part of the mainstream of every country's educational services. As commerce and enterprise expand from industrial nations to less developed nations, the need for sustained technical and business-related skills development will expand. Corporations around the world will require more and better trained workers, technicians, and managers everywhere on the planet.

Higher and adult education, as presently constituted around the world, is not in the position to provide major new or additional services and is already in a crisis. The world's population is increasing and the demand for greater educational access is growing. However, the resources to educate the world's increasing population are simply not available and will not be available during the early part of the twenty-first century unless a more effective means of sharing educational facilities and services is developed. For the industrial countries of Europe such as Great Britain, France, and Italy, the issue is essentially the delivery and cost of greater educational opportunity for larger segments of the population seeking to extend their learning. In developing areas such as India, Pakistan, and China, the issue is cost and infrastructure needs combined with burgeoning populations whose basic educational needs are not currently being met. While both developed and developing countries will look to build new facilities to alleviate this problem, they will rely on technology to solve it.

One advantage that many countries have over the United States is experience and expertise in delivering large-scale distance learning. The "mega" Western Governors' University (WGU) is the first of its kind in the United States. Around the world there are a number of "mega universities," primarily distance learning providers with enrollments in excess of 100,000 students. The combined student enrollment of five of these schools, located in China, India, Pakistan, Korea, and Indonesia, is more than two million. Most of these are modeled after the Open University of the United Kingdom, which has an enrollment of 150,000 students, 20,000 of whom live in other countries. Readers may wish to review Figure 1.4 in Chapter 1 for a listing of large distance learning universities around the world.

The open universities around the world have used a variety of technologies including print materials, audiotapes, videotapes, and broadcast television to deliver distance learning to large numbers of students. Internet technology is still relatively new or unaffordable in many parts of the world. However, as Internet technology does become available and affordable, students seem to "value greatly" the chance it provides to communicate with instructors and other students (Daniel, 1997). At the Open University of the United Kingdom, the number of students enrolled in Internet-based distance learning has increased from 5,000 students to more than 30,000 in a three-year period from 1995 to 1997. In a paper titled *The Multimedia Mega University: The Hope for the 21st Century,* John Daniel (1997) uses this and observations of other open universities around the world as evidence of his basic thesis that large-scale, Internet-based distance learning universities are the only solution for meeting the unprecedented need and global demand for higher and adult education.

A possible harbinger of Daniel's vision is a plan developed by Sylvan Learning Systems, Incorporated, a for-profit provider of educational services in the United States, to establish a private, for-profit network of colleges around the world. Sylvan's specialties are computerized testing and remedial education. Leading this network will be Joseph Duffy, former director of the United States Information Agency, former president of American University in Washington, and former Chancellor of the University of Massachusetts at Amherst. Douglas Becker, Sylvan's president, hopes to invest between $50 and $100 million a year for the next ten years to acquire and build a network of ten or more international universities. In January 1999, Sylvan announced that it offered $29 million to acquire the University Europea, a for-profit private college in Madrid, Spain, which would be the first college in this network (Honan, 1999).

OTHER ISSUES TO CONSIDER FOR DISTANCE LEARNING IN THE TWENTY-FIRST CENTURY

The social, technological, and educational trends presented in this chapter will lead to the further development and expansion of distance learning in the twenty-first century. However, several issues should be discussed that could impede this development.

First, the level of quality in distance learning will continue to come under close scrutiny. While most of the research literature finds well-delivered distance learning in various forms on a par with traditional face-to-face instruction, skepticism will continue. The number of for-profit digital colleges and universities that have emerged in the 1990s is almost impossible to determine. Some of these are performing an important educational service and are an outgrowth of well-respected proprietary schools. Some are little more than "digital diploma mills." George Connick (1999), in a publication titled *The Distance Learner's Guide,* clearly alerts prospective students "to beware of diploma mills" and unscrupulous distance learning providers. In April 1998, the first *International Digital Diploma Mill Conference* was held at Harvey Mudd College in Claremont, California. David F. Noble, a history professor at York University in Toronto, who coined the phrase "digital diploma mills" in a critique, noted that last year he received so many invitations to speak on this topic across North America that he could not honor them all. At many of the speaking engagements he did attend, "he drew crowds in the hundreds, mostly college faculty members" (Mendels, 1999). Although a small minority, low or no-quality schools will cast a shadow on others. Distance learning providers and regional accrediting agencies will need to continue to be scrupulous in assuring the quality of courses and programs offered. Distance learning providers should publicize well all accreditation and reviews in their recruitment material.

Second, student access to technology was covered in Chapter 5 but deserves another consideration as we look to the future. This is an important issue worldwide in developed as well as developing countries. In the United States, concern has existed regarding the evolution of a nation of information "haves" and "have nots." In some countries such as Brazil, Germany, France, Spain, and China, the cost of accessing the Internet is so high that a number of "cyberstrikes" have been staged protesting government policy and lack of intervention (Richter, 1999). In the poorest developing countries, many do not yet have access to basic telephone services. Developing educational programs that are unaffordable and unattainable by large segments of poor populations is, and will continue to be, questioned. While the digital and communications technology industries offer excellent products for a reasonable cost, distance learning providers, particularly those supported by public subsidies, need to be mindful that these products do not exist in many poorer people's homes. Nations that cooperate and invest billions of dollars in building a space station need to exert the same effort in resolving or at least alleviating the inequity that exists regarding access to what is increasingly being seen as important educational technology.

Third, the issue of scalability discussed in Chapter 8 is becoming more important as schools and colleges experiment with new distance learning technology and attempt to broaden the scope or "scale" of programs. Many faculty in schools with little experience in distance learning have begun to experiment by offering one or two courses in selected programs. This is desirable and worthwhile experimentation. Once successful, the natural tendency is to try to expand these experiments into entire programs. Then, many of the issues (i.e., student services, academic support services, faculty workload, etc.) discussed in Chapter 7 will need to be addressed. Failure to do so will leave institutions, faculty, and students vulnerable to a number of logistical and policy problems that will be more difficult to resolve after a program has commenced. These problems, in turn, will lead to negative perceptions of the quality of the programs and will hinder their future development.

Lastly, given the complexity of the educational enterprise, educational policy makers and planners should ensure that a wide spectrum of expertise in designing, developing, and evaluating distance learning programs is sought. Care must be taken that distance learning is not seen as the quick, easy, or inexpensive way to provide education for growing student populations. Decisions involving new distance learning courses and programs should involve administrators, faculty, and students to assure that such offerings are well prepared. Administrators, elected officials, and corporate sponsors cannot simply embrace the new technology as a way of servicing many or all students at reduced costs. By the same token, faculty cannot embrace the traditional, face-to-face class as the "tried and true" and only method of teaching and learning. The classroom has been evolving for centuries and will continue to do so. Where modern technology can be effective, it should be used. If it is not effective, it should be adjusted or abandoned. Finding the proper fit of academic program, student need, and instructional tools is the essence of good educational planning. Earlier in this chapter, reference was made to William R. Noyes who leads the for-profit Internet-based Magellan University but who is a proponent of the conventional university setting for younger "18-year-old" students. Noyes' insight is essential to the successful planning and development of quality distance learning programs. Schools and colleges are not only places where teachers teach and students learn. The bottom line cannot simply be how well students performed on a test, or how many secured positions at prestigious firms, or were accepted by good graduate schools. The place called school is a microcosm of society where values are transferred and people, especially the young, are developed. Learning is not knowing how to do one or two things well, but understanding where one's knowledge fits in the broader context of life.

MAKING CONNECTIONS ACROSS VIRTUAL SPACE AND TIME: A FINAL COMMENT

Earlier in this chapter, reference was made to James Dunderstadt (1997) and his description of an "ubiquitous university" where the constraints of time and space—and perhaps of reality itself—are relaxed by digital networks. The essence of his vision is a "culture of learning in which people are surrounded by, immersed in, and absorbed in learning experiences." Dunderstadt's vision describes the next stop of humankind's quest for knowledge. Digital networking technology that will allow people to immerse themselves in learning, literally in any place and at any time, is rapidly evolving. Schools, colleges, universities, and other educational providers are in the privileged position to assist in this endeavor. While technology will provide our twenty-first century chariot, tall ship, or lunar module, the well-designed distance learning program will provide the map, chart, or flight plan.

SUMMARY

This chapter takes a look at the future and speculates on the possibilities and implications for distance learning. The future is defined as the early part of the twenty-first century wherein advances in computer, communications, and video technologies will extend distance learning further into people's lives.

In a section titled *Shaping Our World,* three major trends are discussed that form the basic framework of the future for distance learning. Population growth combined with demands for greater educational opportunity is already putting significant pressures on schools, colleges, and universities. In the early part of the twenty-first century, these pressures will reach crisis proportions. Information technologies have been advancing that are seen as part of the solution for alleviating this crisis. A convergence of computer, communications, and audio/video technologies will streamline all information storage and communications into a new global medium that will be even more conducive to developing distance learning applications.

As distance learning providers make greater use of the new technologies, new types of schools, structures, and enterprises will evolve. Four models (for-profit schools, for-profit subsidiaries, statewide coordinating bodies, and mega universities) are presented as examples.

One result of the end of the Cold War in the 1980s and 1990s, is that countries around the world are collaborating in political, economic, and cultural activities. Education will be a critical support for these activities in the twenty-first century. Many countries outside of the United States already make extensive use of large-scale distance learning programs that enroll hundreds of thousands of students every year. These large-scale distance learning programs will be seen as important vehicles for establishing and maintaining educational and other collaborative relationships.

While the chapter makes the case that distance learning will play a more significant role in the future, policy makers and planners should consider several issues that are pertinent to its progress: quality assurance, student access to technology, scalability issues, and rigorous planning.

The chapter concludes with a final word on making connections in virtual space and time.

CASE STUDY

Future University State System Year: 2014

Setting

The Future University State System (FUSS) is the administrative and governing body responsible for all publicly funded higher and adult education services in the state, including lifelong learning centers, community colleges, senior colleges, and one comprehensive university center. FUSS is also a charter member of the World Open University System (WOUS), which was established in 2010 to coordinate and act as a clearinghouse for all UNIVET-based distance learning courses taken around the world. UNIVET (Universal Network), which replaced the Internet in 2007, is the main Earth-based digital communications network. Almost 30 percent of the students at FUSS take one or more UNIVET-based courses each year to fulfill the requirements for degrees or to improve job and career skills. UNIVET-based (and its predecessor Internet) distance learning was a critical element of a plan conceived in 2003 to deal with unprecedented increases in the state's post-secondary enrollment.

The Issue

Carroll Linden, the chancellor of FUSS, has been requested to submit a special five-year facilities improvement plan. The cover letter provided by the Governor's Task Force on Finance, Facilities, and the Future states that FUSS can expect approximately $500 million per year over the next five years, or $2.5 billion in total. This is a welcome relief since major capital construction at FUSS has been deferred for the past three years due to budget crises. Chancellor Linden has been meeting with her senior staff and the presidents of all the colleges to develop the University's proposal. Four major priorities have emerged:

1. Fund a variety of campus-specific capital improvement projects (i.e., renovations, new buildings, deferred maintenance, etc.) totaling $1.5 billion.
2. Build a new senior college campus in the northeast part of the state, which has experienced significant population growth in the past seven years due to a large influx of new immigrants. Presently, all of the senior colleges are in the south and western portions of the state. Cost is $1.8 billion. Several state senators from the northeast section of the state have promised their support for the new college.
3. Install new high-speed communications technologies that were made available in 2007 when UNIVET was established. Faculty and students at the colleges (with the exception of the university center) are able to use UNIVET with the older Internet technologies but do not realize its full benefits, particularly in terms of speed, virtual reality, and holography features. The cost for upgrading and equipping new communications facilities at all of the colleges and centers is $600 million. This project is supported enthusiastically by the Council of College Presidents at FUSS.
4. Establish *Access to Knowledge Centers*. A major program titled *Access to Knowledge* (AK) has been discussed extensively and is a joint program with all the primary and secondary schools, libraries, hospitals, and community organizations to bring modern technology into every community and neighborhood. FUSS would establish the four geographically dispersed AK Centers to coordinate and fund a number of facilities and equipment-upgrade projects around the state to make sure that the organizations and agencies mentioned above are equipped with the latest technology and in turn can become centers of technical assistance in their locales. The Council of Deans of Professional (Business, Education, Health Sciences, Social Work) Programs at FUSS conceived the plan three years ago in response to concerns that approximately 30 percent of these agencies—most of which were in lower socio-economic areas—in the state did not have adequate access to the newer communications technologies. The federal government has a challenge grant program that will provide one-quarter of the funds needed. The cost for AK is approximately $400 million, of which $100 million will be provided by the federal government. Another $100 million is likely to come from private donations from several major businesses in the state, but there

is no commitment yet. The Chancellor's Office has been receiving numerous e-calls from local government officials voicing support for the *Access to Knowledge* program.

Assume you are Chancellor Linden. Develop a five-year priority plan for the Governor's Task Force on Finance, Facilities, and the Future outlining the costs and projects to be funded for each of the five years. You cannot ask for more than $500 million per year. Also assume that you will minimally request $600 million for campus-specific renovation projects mentioned in Item No. 1 on page 207.

REFERENCES

Arenson, K. (1998, October 7). N.Y.U. sees profits in virtual classes. *The New York Times*, p. B8.

Christman, B. (1998). *Information revolution fills space between the ears: Magellan abandons bricks and mortar.* http://www.magellan.edu/news/star.html

Connick, G. P. (Ed.). (1999). *The distance learner's guide.* Upper Saddle River, NJ: Prentice-Hall.

Connick, G. P. (1997). Issues and trends to take us into the twenty-first century. (T. E. Cyrs, Ed.). *Teaching and learning at a distance: What it takes to effectively design, deliver and evaluate programs.* San Francisco: Jossey-Bass Publishers.

Daniel, J. (1997). *The multimedia mega university: The hope for the 21st century.* Paper presented at the North of England Education Conference, Leeds, GB.

Dunderstadt, J. J. (1997). The future of the university in an age of knowledge. *Journal of Asynchronous Learning Networks, 1*(1), 78–88.

Fredricksen, E., Pickett, A., Pelz, W., Swan, K., & Shea, P. (1999, August). *Student satisfaction and perceived learning with on-line courses: Principles and examples from the SUNY Learning Network.* Paper presented at the Sloan ALN Summer Workshop, Urbana, Illinois.

Gibson, W. (1996, July 14). The Net is a waste of time and that's exactly what's right about it. *The New York Times Magazine*, pp. 30–31.

Honan, W. H. (1999, January 20). Sylvan plans overseas college network. *The New York Times*, p. B8.

Ibrahim, Y. (1997, January 20). As most wired nation, Finland has jump on 21st century. *The New York Times*, p. D1, D3.

Mendels, P. (1999, January 6). Universities embrace technology, but distance learning faces controversy. *The New York Times*, p. E1.

National Center for Education Statistics. (1997a). *A back to school special report on the baby boom echo: Here come the teenagers.* U.S. Department of Education. Office of Educational Research and Improvement. http://oeri.ed.gov/pubs/bbecho/

National Center for Education Statistics. (1997b). Integrated Postsecondary Education Data System, "Fall Enrollment, 1995" survey. (Prepared January 1997). U.S. Department of Education. http://nces.ed.gov/pubs/digest97/d97t176.html

Richter, M. (1999, January 14). Overseas Internet users protest high cost of access. *The New York Times*, p. G3.

Riley, R. W. (1998). *A back to school special report on the baby boom echo: America's schools are overcrowded and wearing out.* U.S. Department of Education. http://www.ed.gov/pubs/bbecho98/part2.html

Tapscott, D. (1998). *Growing up digital.* New York: McGraw-Hill.

A Guide to Designing a Web-Based Distance Learning Course

TECHNOLOGICALLY SIMPLE AND PEDAGOGICALLY POWERFUL

There are many books, articles, and Web sites available concerning the design of interesting, appealing, and effective Web sites. However, much of this material assumes that the purpose of a Web site is to attract Web navigators to a product, service, or information base. While a distance learning provider may utilize this material to design a college or university home page intended to encourage students to apply and enroll in a program, it is not necessarily helpful in creating a course Web site. Students accessing a course Web site are already enrolled and will prefer a clear, simple navigational layout designed to help them quickly access whatever they need to participate in the course. Technologically simple Web pages that are pedagogically powerful, that provide good content, and that engage students in active learning are needed. This being said, many designers and faculty are very creative in their use of color, in their choice of backgrounds, and in providing stimulating and provocative images and animation to attract student attention. While the efficient and simple course home page layout remains the primary goal, the creative talents of course designers are recognized and respected. Readers may wish to review the format, style, and contents of several course Web pages. The University of Texas maintains an excellent Web site titled, *The World Lecture Hall* (http://www.utexas.edu/world/lecture/index.html), which contains links to hundreds of pages created by faculty who are using the Web to deliver class materials.

The material presented in the following paragraphs is based on the Web-based distance learning model (see Figure 8.1) discussed in Chapter 8. Readers may wish to review this model before proceeding.

THE COURSE WEB SITE

Instructors throughout the world are using the Web in a variety of ways. Course home pages abound in every subject area. At the end of this guide is a series of figures illustrating examples of Web pages for a typical Web-based, asynchronous learning course. These examples will be referenced extensively in the following paragraphs. These examples are provided mainly to illustrate the *components* of Web-based courses and are not provided to illustrate the best design. As mentioned earlier, design is frequently in the eye of the beholder or in this case the faculty and students. Readers are encouraged to view and critique these examples in relation to their own preferences for Web page design and layout. Figure G.1 provides ten suggestions for course Web page design.

Figure G.2A is a simple, easy-to-navigate *Course Home Page*, where students can find all the basic information and resources they need to participate in the course. Included on the home page are a small school/course logo, course title, instructor's name, instructor's e-mail address, course description/theme, and links to the other pages on the Web site. The information provided at these links can vary depending on the needs of the students, the nature of the course, the style of the instructor, and the course management software available. However, designers will find that much of the information and resources provided at these links will need to be provided in a typical Web-based course.

The *Course Outline* page (see Figure G.2B) includes material found in most syllabi including a list of topics and associated activities such as readings and assignments. If the course is following a semester or other calendar schedule, the course outline should also include dates/weeks when topics will be covered in the course. If the course is to be completed at the student's own pace or on demand, then the outline might include suggested time allotments for each topic.

The *Reading List* page (see Figure G.2C) provides the bibliography of all required and recommended readings. If possible, this list should also include information about where readings can be located such as at a bookstore, Web Resources, or Library Resources. For traditional textbook materials, references or links to on-line book companies such as barnesandnoble.com or Amazon.com, are helpful.

Students in all courses are anxious to know what is required of them in the form of assignments. A link to a page (*Student Assignments/Evaluation*) that summarizes all assignments and tests and includes due dates is most helpful. Also on this page is a statement of how students will be evaluated for the course. This page should conclude with directions and logistics for submitting papers (e-mail, fax, regular mail) and taking tests (on-line, test site, proctoring center). Figure G.2D provides an excerpt from a *Student Assignments/Evaluation* page.

Topic Presentations (see Figure G.2E) is a simple page of links to the instructor's presentations of the topics in the course. In Figure G.2E, the topics are organized in tabular format to provide an overview for the entire course. Course designers may also consider providing these links as part of the *Course Outline* page described earlier. Figure G.2F provides an excerpt from a single topic (Week 3) presentation page.

Web Resources (see Figure G.2G) provides references to pertinent course material available at other Web sites. A brief description of each reference with a link to its Uniform Resource Locator (URL) is standard. These links can be referenced in the *Course Outline* or *Topics Presentation,* or on the electronic bulletin board as needed.

Library and Media Resources (see Figure G.2H) provides links to any library, video, audio, or image collection pertinent to the course that is available to students in on-line form. While the tendency for many distance learning instructors and librarians is to provide as much material as possible on-line, this is not always possible. Older books and periodicals may not be available in digital or computer-readable form. Where course material is available at a virtual library, they should be linked or easily accessed via this page.

The *Communications Center* (See Figure G.2I) is the link to the main communications facilities for the course including an electronic bulletin board or discussion group, group e-mail, individual e-mail, on-line or Internet Relay Chat (IRC), and telephone numbers of important contacts including the instructor, tutors, and technical assistance. Directions for using these facilities should be included on the Help Desk Page. A directory of the e-mail addresses of instructors, tutors, and other students could also be included at this site.

The *Archives* is a link to the important past activities in the course. It generally includes an on-line "search" facility (see Figure G.2J) for any phrase or topic already discussed on the bulletin board. A very popular feature of this page might be a link to a "Frequently Asked Questions" (FAQ) page.

Possibly the most important link on the course home page is the *Help Desk* (see Figure G.2K). Beginning students should find directions here for participating in the course and information about where they can seek assistance. The *Help Desk* should have a clearly designated area for "Getting Started" activities. A statement(s) should always be provided informing students of the expected response time to questions or comments.

TEACHING AND LEARNING IN VIRTUAL SPACE AND TIME

As indicated in Chapter 4, the interaction and communication between instructor and student, student and student, and student and content is of primary importance in all distance learning and especially in a Web-based or virtual model. Readers may wish to review the material in Chapter 4. Also please refer to the end of this guide for a script of an actual lesson (Figure G.2L). An excerpt of the interaction and communication derived from this script is provided in Figure G.2M.

Electronic bulletin boards, discussion groups, and e-mail systems are the most common vehicles for Web-based distance learning communications. Software such as *ListServ* (group e-mail); *Eudora* and *Pegasus* (individual e-mail); and, increasingly, Web-browser-based e-mail systems are reliable, easy to use, and fast. This makes them indispensable to a Web-based distance learning course. Students are becoming more familiar with these facilities as e-mail systems proliferate through-out the general population. However, while these systems provide the basic tech-nology for easy communication, designers should be sensitive to the fact that composing and reading many e-mail messages will put demands on the time of all participants. This can become problematic depending on the interaction level and the response expectation rate of teachers and students. Knox (1997) described his first unpleasant experience with Web-based learning that relied extensively on e-mail, "Student time is valuable and scarce . . . In creating a course when anything might be done at any time, I had created one where it appeared that everything needed to be done all the time."

In traditional classes and in some other distance learning models such as point-to-point videoconferencing, most communications are synchronous, that is, hap-pening at the same time if not also in the same place. An instructor asks an open-ended question in a traditional class. Student hands are raised, one or more students are called on to respond, and a discussion ensues. By the same token, a student who does not understand a point that an instructor has made raises his or her hand and asks a question, and the instructor responds immediately. In Web-based distance learning, the vast majority of the communications will be asyn-chronous, that is, happening at any time and in any place. Asynchronous communications, however, do not forfeit the responsibility of teacher or learner to respond promptly to questions and comments. If a student asks a question, an in-structor or tutor should try to respond as quickly as possible and vice versa. Hence, while the terms "any time" and "any place" learning have been popularized ex-tensively in this book and other distance learning sources, the term "any time" in practice has restrictions with respect to instructors and students responding to one another. Rather than any time, both teachers and students prefer and come to ex-pect prompt replies to inquiries.

In designing Web-based distance learning courses, response time standards should be considered. For example, if a student asks a question, how promptly should an instructor or tutor respond? In an hour, a day, two days, or a week? Most distance learner providers would say "the faster the better," but setting a standard of an hour or so could make e-mail slaves of instructors. On the other hand, if a stu-dent must wait a week or more, the learning moment might be lost for the student. A sensible standard is probably within twenty-four hours, depending on the in-structor and/or tutoring assistance available for the number of students enrolled.

Just as a standard should be established for instructors responding to students, the same should be considered for students responding to instructors. For the most part, the objectives of a lesson or learning activity determine this. If an instructor wants to develop an ongoing weekly bulletin board discussion with students, then all activities including responses and comments from students need to take place within the space of a week and, more likely, within days. In posing specific ques-tions for a weekly discussion, an instructor might establish a response time expec-tation of two days within which students should respond. On the other hand, if the instructor has assigned a group essay, position paper, or case analysis that might require extensive student-to-student interaction, then one, two, or more weeks depending on the extent of the assignment would be appropriate.

Distance learning providers generally find it easier to establish response time standards for the instructors and/or tutors than for students. Instructors frequently are part of the course design activity and help establish instructional goals and objectives including student interactions. Dedicated instructors in all instructional formats know the importance of asking and responding to questions and generally are conscientious about responding promptly. Establishing standards for students is more problematic. In traditional courses, some students answer more questions than others, some hand in assignments on time whereas others need extensions, and so on. The same is true in a Web-based environment. However, in a traditional class, students are physically present in a class to hear a discussion, and to hear questions and responses from the instructor and fellow students. In a Web-based environment, attendance is difficult to monitor, since to "hear" the discussion, students log on to the bulletin board or read their e-mail. To guarantee participation, some instructors may require students to post a minimum number of messages to a bulletin board on a weekly or other scheduled basis. Making such a requirement depends on a number of instructional factors such as the level of students, type of course, and number of tests or examinations. Designers and instructors should develop strategies that encourage all students to participate. Rotating and assigning weekly student facilitators is a good technique for sharing the responsibility and work associated with active participation in a bulletin board discussion. If all students are not encouraged to post messages and interact, the bulletin board discussions can easily become one-sided or the domain of just a few students.

Figure G.2M at the end of this guide shows an excerpt of an actual weekly bulletin board discussion (lesson) that follows the script in Figure G.2L. In reading the discussion, please note the following instructional techniques:

1. The forty-eight-hour interval between the instructor's postings allows students time to reflect on the material and questions.
2. The use of student first names to convey familiarity even though instructor and students never meet.
3. Encouragement and focus of discussion on student comments.
4. The development of dialogue in which students reference each other as well as the instructor.
5. Allowing students to "control" the discussion to a degree, while keeping students focused on the main themes of the lesson.

As mentioned earlier in this section, the type of information provided at a course Web site can vary depending on the needs of the students, the nature of the course, the style of the instructor, and the course management software available. The same is true of how this information will be communicated among all participants. The above represents one popular approach and technique.

SUGGESTED ACTIVITY

Readers may wish to view and critique several different course Web sites including the one presented in this *Guide.* As indicated earlier, The University of Texas maintains an excellent Web site titled *The World Lecture Hall* (see http://www.utexas.edu/world/lecture/index.html), which contains links to hundreds of course Web pages.

Readers may also wish to design their own course Web site and make determinations as to its components, design, style, etc.

A SAMPLE WEB-BASED COURSE

In the following pages, Figures G.2A through G.2M are presented to illustrate the features and content of a typical Web-based course. The main purpose of these illustrations is to show the reader one way to design such a course. Obviously, the World Wide Web can be used in a variety of ways for distance learning. The model presented here is for a course that would be conducted during a fifteen-week semester. Other models using self-paced instruction, or shorter or longer time allotments can easily be adapted from this model. While all names (school, instructor, students) have been changed, the course titled *Contemporary Issues of Education* has been conducted on the Web using materials similar to those presented on the following pages.

List of Figures

REFERENCES

Knox, E. L. (1997). The pedagogy of Web site design. *ALN Magazine, 1*(2). Available: http://www.aln.org/alnweb/magazine/issue2/knox.htm

FIGURE G.1 Ten Suggestions for Course Web Page Design

1. Identify the college, course, and instructor at the beginning of the course home page.
2. Use a consistent style for all pages and links at the Web site so that students become familiar with the location of important information and links.
3. Highlight course-related materials, not the computer systems or software being used.
4. Assume many home computer users have lower-end processors or slower modem-speed, so limit large audio/video files to what is pedagogically needed rather than providing a "show."
5. Avoid the electronic vanity plate syndrome with extensive photographs of one or two individuals.
6. Use easy-to-read fonts, preferably in dark colors on a light background.
7. Do not use intrusive background patterns or wallpaper that make it difficult to read text.
8. Avoid page clutter that makes it difficult to access important or needed information.
9. Edit all text for spelling and grammar.
10. Keep current events and links to pages current.

FIGURE G.2A Sample Course Home Page

National College, School of Education

EDUC 722—ISSUES IN CONTEMPORARY EDUCATION

Instructor: Dr. Lynne Jones, *e-mail address: ljones@national.edu*

Course Description

This course is designed to provide a forum wherein issues in contemporary education will be presented and discussed. It is also designed to provide future administrators with an appreciation of differences in points of view and to have them consider how they would approach issues that can be divisive in a school or community.

Below are the resources and information you need to participate in this course. If this is the first time you are accessing this Web page, please select "Getting Started/Help Desk."

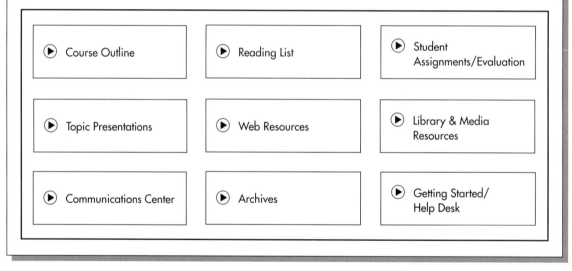

▶ Course Outline	▶ Reading List	▶ Student Assignments/Evaluation
▶ Topic Presentations	▶ Web Resources	▶ Library & Media Resources
▶ Communications Center	▶ Archives	▶ Getting Started/ Help Desk

FIGURE G.2B Sample Course Outline

National College, School of Education

HOME

EDUC 722—ISSUES IN CONTEMPORARY EDUCATION

Instructor: Dr. Lynne Jones, *e-mail address: ljones@national.edu*

Course Outline

- Week 1—August 30th
  - Topic: Orientation to Asynchronous Learning
  - Reads: See Materials at the Getting Started/Help Desk Web Page

- Week 2—Sept. 6th
  - Topic: Educational Issues - The Socio-Political Context
  - Reads: Traub (1998); Nelson et al., Chap. 1

- Week 3—Sept. 13th
  - Topic: Control of Schools
  - Reads: Nelson et al., Chap. 9; Also Review Report No. 4 at the Great City Schools Web Site

- Week 4—Sept. 20th
  - Topic: Equity in School Finance
  - Reads: Nelson et al., Chap. 4

- Week 5—Sept. 27th
  - Topic: Corporate America's Influence on Education
  - Reads: Nelson et al., Chap. 11
  - Open-Book Test

- Week 6—Oct. 4th
  - Topic: Privatization/School Choice
  - Reads: Nelson et al., Chap. 16

(continued)

- Week 7—Oct. 11th
  - Topic: Charter Schools
  - Reads: Manno et al. (1998)
  - Written Assignment No. 1 Due

- Week 8—Oct. 18th
  - Topic: School-Based Management/Shared Decision-Making
  - Reads: Nelson et al., Chap. 13

- Week 9—Oct. 25th
  - Topic: Teacher Unionization
  - Reads: Nelson et al., Chap. 15

- Week 10—Nov. 1st
  - Topic: Bilingual Education
  - Reads: Del Valle (1998)
  - Open-Book Test

- Week 11—Nov. 8th
  - Topic: Pluralism-Diversity-Multiculturalism in the Curriculum
  - Reads: Cornbleth (1998); Nelson et al., Chap. 8

- Week 12—Nov. 15th
  - Topic: Special Education
  - Reads: See Current Issue of Educational Leadership at American Assoc. for Supervision and Curriculum Development (ASCD) Web Site
  - Written Assignment No. 2 Due

- Week 13—Nov. 29th
  - Topic: Should Schools Teach Values?
  - Reads: Nelson et al., Chap. 10

- Week 14—Dec. 6th
  - Topic: School Reform: Excellence and Equity
  - Reads: Nelson et al., Chap. 18

- Week 15—Final Examination—Meet as a Class—Monday, Dec. 14th, 6:15 P.M. National College, 695 Park Avenue, New York, NY 10021, Room NC-1000.

FIGURE G.2C Sample Course Reading List

National College, School of Education

HOME

EDUC 722—ISSUES IN CONTEMPORARY EDUCATION

Instructor: Dr. Lynne Jones, *e-mail address: ljones@national.edu*

Reading List

Required Readings

Cornbleth, C. (1998, Summer). An American curriculum. *Teachers College Record, 99* (4), 622–646. Available: http://www.tcrecord.tc.columbia.edu

Del Valle, S. (1998, Summer). Bilingual education for Puerto Ricans in New York City: From hope to compromise. *Harvard Education Review, 68*(2), 193–217. Available: http://www.edreview.org

Manno, B. V., Finn, C. E., Bierlein, L. E., & Vanourek, G. (Spring, 1998). Charter schools: Accomplishments and dilemmas. *Teachers College Record, 99* (3), 537–558. Available: http://www.tcrecord.tc.columbia.edu

Nelson, J. L., Carlson, K., & Palonsky, S. B. (1996). *Critical issues in education: A dialectic approach.* New York: McGraw-Hill. Available: http://www.amazon.com

Traub, J. (1998, June 28). Nathan Glazer changes his mind, again. *New York Times Magazine.* Available: http://www.nytimes.com

In this course, students are also expected to keep current on local and national educational policy issues by reading newspapers (i.e., *N.Y. Times*) and professional journals (i.e., *Educational Leadership*).

Recommended Readings

Apple, M. W., & Beane, J. A. (Eds.). (1995). *Democratic schools.* Alexandria, VA: Association for Supervision and Curriculum Development.

Carol, L. N. et al. (1986). *School boards: Strengthening grassroots leadership.* Washington, DC: The Institute for Educational Leadership, Inc.

(continued)

FIGURE G.2C Sample Course Reading List *(concluded)*

Connell, R. W. (1994). Poverty and education. *Harvard Educational Review, 64*(2), 125–149.

Delpit, L. (1995). *Other people's children.: Cultural conflict in the classroom.* New York: New Press.

Educational Leadership. (1998). Volume 56(5). Entire issue dedicated to the theme: Strengthening the Teaching Profession.

Gardner, H. (1995). *Leading minds: An anatomy of leadership.* New York: Basic Books.

Lantieri, L., & Patti, J. (1996). *Waging peace in our schools.* Boston: Beacon Press.

Nieto, S. (1994). Lessons from students on creating a chance. *Harvard Educational Review, 64*(4), 392, 426.

Ramirez Smith, C. (1995). Stopping the cycle of failure: The Comer Model. *Educational Leadership, 52*(5), 14, 19.

Rossow, L. F. (1990). *The principalship: Dimensions in instructional leadership.* Englewood Cliffs, NJ: Prentice Hall, Inc.

Sarason, C. (1996). *Revisiting the culture of the school and the problem of change.* New York: Teachers College Press.

Sergiovanni, T. J. (1994). *Building community in schools.* San Francisco, CA: Jossey Bass.

Sergiovanni, T. J. (1987). *The principalship: A reflective practice approach.* Boston: Allyn and Bacon.

Short, P., & Greer, J. (1997). *Leadership and school change. Leadership in empowered schools: Themes from innovative efforts.* Englewood Cliffs, NJ: Prentice Hall, Inc. 17–32.

The New London Group. (1996). A pedagogy of multiliteracies: Designing social futures. *Harvard Educational Review, 66*(1), 60–92.

Thurow, L. (1996). *The future of capitalism.* New York: William Morrow and Co.

FIGURE G.2D Excerpt from a Sample Student Assignments/Evaluation Page

National College, School of Education

HOME

EDUC 722—ISSUES IN CONTEMPORARY EDUCATION

Instructor: Dr. Lynne Jones, *e-mail address: ljones@national.edu*

Student Assignments/Evaluation

-
-

Course Evaluation

Evaluation will be based on writing assignments, a semester project, and class participation. For this Internet-based course, student participation will be most important. Throughout the semester, each of you will take turns being a discussion facilitator on a class topic. These assignments will figure significantly into your class participation evaluation.

-
-

Written Assignments

Written Assignment #1

Assume you are an administrator working at the NYC Board of Education at 110 Livingston Street in the Office of Policy Analysis. During the past year, the NY State Legislature has been debating the merits of charter schools. The senate has already introduced a bill that would use public funds to establish such schools. Review the article by Manno, Finn, Bierlein, and Vanourek and any other materials that you deem appropriate and prepare a three-page position paper for the chancellor highlighting the pros and cons of charter schools. Most important, conclude the paper with a well-developed rationale and recommendation as to whether or not the chancellor should support the establishment of publicly funded charter schools.

Due: Prior to October 11. Be prepared to discuss your paper on-line during the week of October 11.

(continued)

FIGURE G.2D Excerpt from a Sample Student Assignments/Evaluation Page *(concluded)*

Assignment #2

You have just been appointed principal of P.S. 123. You have been requested by the superintendent in your district to consider adopting an inclusion program that would mainstream into regular classes most special education students currently housed at P.S. 123. Inclusion programs are broadly defined as combining special and regular education students in the same classes. Class size, which is currently thirty-five students for regular classes and eighteen students for special education classes, will be established and carefully monitored not to exceed twenty-six students. Each class will be team-taught with a regular teacher and a special education teacher. In discussions with the teaching staff, there is ambivalence at best and possibly hostility to the proposal. Regular teachers have indicated that the special education students will be too disruptive. Special education teachers are concerned that the needs of the special education students will be compromised in larger integrated (regular and special education students) classes.

Prepare a three-page memorandum outlining your position on this matter for the superintendent. Identify the strengths and weaknesses of the inclusion program based on the information provided above and any other information that you deem helpful. Conclude your paper with a well-developed argument/decision for accepting or rejecting the proposal.

Due prior to November 15. Be prepared to discuss your paper on-line during the week of November 15.

FIGURE G.2E   Sample Topic Presentations Page

National College, School of Education

HOME

EDUC 722—ISSUES IN CONTEMPORARY EDUCATION

Instructor: Dr. Lynne Jones, *e-mail address: ljones@national.edu*

Topic Presentations

The following topic presentations should be reviewed prior to the start of each week's discussion. They supplement much of the material provided in the required readings. If, for any reason, you receive a message that the requested URL cannot be found, please contact the Help Desk immediately.

- ▶ Week 1: Orientation to Asynchronous Learning
- ▶ Week 2: Educational Issues: The Socio-Political Context
- ▶ Week 3: Control of Schools
- ▶ Week 4: Equity in School Finance
- ▶ Week 5: Corporate America's Influence on Education
- ▶ Week 6: Privatization/School Choice
- ▶ Week 7: Charter Schools
- ▶ Week 8: School-Based Management/Shared Decision-Making
- ▶ Week 9: Teacher Unionization
- ▶ Week 10: Bilingual Education
- ▶ Week 11: Pluralism/Diversity/Multiculturalism
- ▶ Week 12: Special Education
- ▶ Week 13: Should Schools Teach Values?
- ▶ Week 14: School Reform: Excellence and Equity
- ▶ Week 15: Final Examination

FIGURE G.2F   Excerpt from a Topic Presentation

National College, School of Education

HOME

EDUC 722—ISSUES IN CONTEMPORARY EDUCATION

Instructor: Dr. Lynne Jones, *e-mail address: ljones@national.edu*

Week 3

Topic(s):

- Control of Schools

Readings:

- Nelson et al., Chap. 9

Key Questions:

- Where should the major control and authority for education exist?

- Would education be better served if the formulation of policies was done centrally (federal government) or locally (states, communities, schools)?

- What are the benefits/problems of a strong central system of education versus local control?

....

Topic Presentation

The United States is relatively unique in that the control of education is shared among several entities at the federal, state, and local levels of government. Most other countries have established the control of education as a power of the central or national government. In the United States, a good deal of power rests with the states and locally elected or appointed boards of education. These boards are generally made up of individuals with little if any professional experience in education. They represent their communities and are expected to act as important bridges between residents of the community and the schools.

One result of the separation of control of education has been a struggle/vying for power/influence among the various governmental entities. Unfortunately, much of this struggle takes place in a political arena and results in education being closely intertwined with political processes at all levels of government.

FIGURE G.2F *(concluded)*

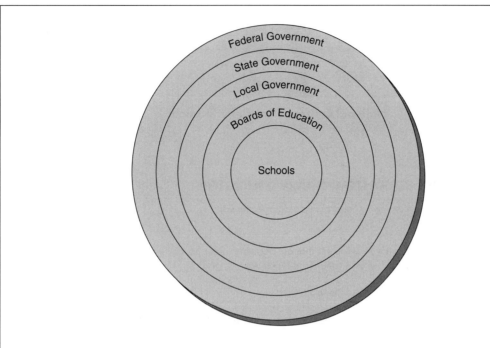

Central Control Versus Local Control?

- Arguments for Central Control

  - More Efficient—administration, curriculum, books, standards.
  - Standard Curriculum—students can easily transfer from one school to another—important consideration in a mobile society.
  - Financial Oversight—costs for education should be comparable.
  - National Cohesion—a diploma from any one school indicates that students have learned or at least been exposed to a given body of knowledge.

- Arguments for Local Control

  - Communities are different and have different needs.
  - U.S. Constitution recognized the diversity in the country and reserved the power to control schools to the states and localities.
  - Less bureaucratic and more responsive to the individual needs of students.

FIGURE G.2G Sample Web Resources Page

National College, School of Education

HOME

EDUC 722—ISSUES IN CONTEMPORARY EDUCATION

Instructor: Dr. Lynne Jones, *e-mail address: ljones@national.edu*

Links to Other Sites

The following links provide information resources that are pertinent to our course. If you receive a message that the requested URL cannot be found, please contact the Help Desk.

- ▶ American Association of School Administrators
- ▶ American Association for Supervision and Curriculum Development (ASCD)
- ▶ American Federation of Teachers
- ▶ Brown vs. Board of Education: Forty Years Later
- ▶ Council of Great City Schools
- ▶ Interstate School Leaders Licensure Consortium
- ▶ National Association of Elementary School Principals
- ▶ National Association of Secondary School Principals
- ▶ National Council Association of Teacher Education
- ▶ National Parent Teachers Association (PTA)
- ▶ Phi Delta Kappa
- ▶ U.S. Department of Education
- ▶ Yahoo Search Engine—Education

FIGURE G.2H Sample Library and Media Resources Page

National College, School of Education

HOME

EDUC 722—ISSUES IN CONTEMPORARY EDUCATION

Instructor: Dr. Lynne Jones, *e-mail address: ljones@national.edu*

Library and Media Resources

The following library and media resources provide information that is pertinent to our course. If, for any reason, you have a problem accessing any of these resources, please contact the Help Desk.

- ▶ Abstracts
- ▶ Articles (journals, newspapers)
- ▶ Diagrams and Illustrations
  - •
  - •
  - •
- ▶ ERIC Database
- ▶ Images and Photographs
- ▶ Movies
- ▶ Sound Files

FIGURE G.21 Sample Communications Center Page

National College, School of Education

EDUC 722—ISSUES IN CONTEMPORARY EDUCATION

Instructor: Dr. Lynne Jones, *e-mail address: ljones@national.edu*

Communications Center

The following communications facilities are available for all students participating in this course. If, for any reason, you have a problem posting messages, sending/receiving e-mail, or participating in an on-line chat, please contact the Help Desk as soon as possible.

- ▶ Announcements
- ▶ Bulletin Board/Discussion LIST
- ▶ Chat On-Line
- ▶ E-mail Center
- ▶ Faculty Biographies
- ▶ Student Biographies
- ▶ Telephone Contacts

FIGURE G.2J Sample Archives Page

National College, School of Education

HOME

EDUC 722—ISSUES IN CONTEMPORARY EDUCATION

Instructor: Dr. Lynne Jones, *e-mail address: ljones@national.edu*

EDUC-722 Bulletin Board Discussion Archives

Search For:

apple or pear
(green apple) or (red apple)

☐ *Substring search*

In messages where:

- The *subject* is or contains:

pie or cake

- The *author's address* is or contains:

granny

Since:

(date/time)

Until:

(date/time)

June 2000
2 May 2000

| Start the search! |

Help!

FIGURE G.2K Sample Help Desk Page

National College, School of Education

HOME

EDUC 722—ISSUES IN CONTEMPORARY EDUCATION

Instructor: Dr. Lynne Jones, *e-mail address: ljones@national.edu*

Help Desk

The following resources are available to assist you in participating in this course. Feel free to e-mail any questions or comments you might have regarding this course. Most questions are generally answered within six hours every day between the hours of 8:00 A.M. and 10:00 P.M. If any question cannot be answered easily via e-mail, you will receive the name and telephone number of a person who will assist you. If this is the first time you are taking a Web-based course, you should click on "Getting Started." If you wish to contact the Help Desk by telephone, the number is 1(800) 696-5000, and assistance is available every day from 8:00 A.M. to 10:00 P.M., Eastern Standard Time.

- ▶ Getting Started

- ▶ Course Tutors

- ▶ Frequently Asked Questions

- ▶ How to Participate in an Asynchronous Course

- ▶ How to Use the Communications Center

  •

  •

  •

- ▶ Student Counselors

- ▶ Technical Assistance

- ▶ Telephone Contacts

FIGURE G.2L Excerpt of a Script for an Asynchronous Learning Class

This excerpt is the script for an asynchronous learning session on the issue of the local control of schools. (See Figure G.2F for additional information on the content of the lesson.)

This class is conducted entirely in asynchronous mode over the Internet. Students access all material remotely via e-mail and the World Wide Web from their homes or in their places of business. The discussion session for each topic lasts one week beginning on Sunday evening and continuing through Saturday.

Friday	-	Remind student facilitators for the coming week's discussion via e-mail that they should have read all the material and be familiar with key questions.
Sunday	-	Initiate week's discussion on the Web-browser-based e-mail system by introducing the topic and concluding with the following open-ended questions:
		Where should the major control and authority for education rest?
		Would education be better served if the formulation of policies took place centrally (federal government) or locally (states, communities, schools)?
		Refer students to the material available at the class Web site for Week 3.
		Remind students that if they have any questions, they should feel free to e-mail the instructor at any time.
Monday	-	Monitor student comments and questions on the electronic bulletin board and individual e-mail.
Tuesday	-	Compliment students who made exceptionally good postings to the electronic bulletin board during the past forty-eight hours.
		Conclude with open-ended question:
		What are the benefits/problems of a strong central system of education versus local control?
		Remind students that if they have any questions, they should feel free to e-mail the instructor at any time.
Wednesday	-	Monitor student comments and questions on the electronic bulletin board and individual e-mail.
Thursday	-	Compliment and refer to students who made exceptionally good postings to the electronic bulletin board during the past forty-eight hours.
		Briefly review the discussion for the week.
		Use quote from John Stuart Mill to provoke further discussion:
		"A general State [national] education is a mere contrivance for molding people to be exactly like one another; and as the mold in which it casts them is that which pleases the predominant power in the government . . . it establishes a despotism of the mind."
		Remind students that if they have any questions, they should feel free to e-mail the instructor at any time.
Friday	-	Monitor student comments and questions on the electronic bulletin board and individual e-mail.
Saturday	-	Summarize the week's discussion and post same to the class's Web site later this evening.
		Thank student facilitators for their contribution to this week's discussion.
		Wish everybody a Happy Weekend!

FIGURE G.2M Excerpt of a Weekly Electronic Bulletin Board Discussion for an Asynchronous Learning Class

Dr. Jones

Week 03—Sunday (Message 01)

Before starting our discussion this evening, I would like to welcome two new students, Lyle _____ and Barbara _____, to our class. At some point, it would be helpful if Lyle and Barbara would post brief biographical sketches of themselves to our LIST.

Our topic this week is the control of education. The reading in Nelson et al. (Chapter 9) refers to the control of curriculum as a major source of conflict between national and local educational authorities. For our discussion this week, we need not limit ourselves to curriculum and are free to consider other aspects of control including policy, standards, budget, personnel, etc. As background, the United States is relatively unique in that the control of education is shared among several entities at the federal, state, and local levels of government. Most other countries have established the control of education as a power of the central or national government. In the United States, a good deal of power rests with the states and locally elected or appointed boards of education. These boards are generally made up of individuals with little if any professional experience in education. They represent their communities and are expected to act as important bridges between residents of the community and the schools. In New York City, major conflicts have occurred between the central board of education and local community boards. Even within school districts, school superintendents vie with principals and community groups for control of schools.

Over the years, I have heard many teachers and administrators express frustration in dealing with controls imposed by central boards of education, by the state, or by the federal government. As part of our discussion last week, Joe commented that

"Our new principal spent the entire 2 1/2 hour conference on Tuesday reading to us his fourteen pages of school rules and regulations (about 2 or 3 were new to us) and kept repeating the mantra of how accountable we are this year to carry out the English Language Arts standards mandated by the state and city. The teachers are accountable to the principal who is accountable to the superintendent who is accountable to the chancellor who is accountable to the mayor, etc."

On the other hand, Nelson quotes Albert Shanker, who spent a lifetime fighting for teacher rights and empowerment, and the American Federation of Teachers as supporting national [and central] control in matters of curriculum, standardized tests, teacher certification, etc. (see pp. 241–243).

My questions to you are as follows:

As educators, do you feel most of your colleagues resent central control of your schools and would rather have greater autonomy? If so, where should the major control and authority rest?

Also, was [is] Shanker and the AFT out of touch with its membership in calling for greater national control?

Brian _____ (Sunday)

Welcome to our two new class members!

All education is local, just like politics, to quote Tip O'Neil. I kept thinking of the name of our country when reading the Nelson Chapter: United States of America. It is local entities united by some national standards. Education offers one area of these national standards. . . .

So . . . isn't the point that behind closed classroom doors teachers still have the ultimate local control of teaching/education? All the talk, all the dialectics, all the standards don't really make anyone do anything in her/his classroom, as far as I've noticed, observed, and heard.

Rick _____ (Sunday)

As an educator, I feel that teachers in general resent central control of schools. Central control often involves administrators that are totally out of touch with the school population. They have not set foot in a classroom in twenty years and dictate from ivory towers. Teachers are in the trenches every day. They discover through trial and error what works well in a continually changing environment. They adapt, make changes, and grow as educators in the process. . . .

I like the AFT's idea about a national curriculum stabilizing what mobile students learn in any given geographic location. I'm just not sure if the price paid is worth the effort. For all classmates that made it through this extensive posting, I'm sorry for the length.

Naomi _____ (Monday)

I understand Rick's point about wanting autonomy in our schools and classroom. Yes, I want the freedom to be creative about my teaching. However, I don't feel that a national curriculum would necessarily take away my right to do so. (Wouldn't that depend on WHO sets the curriculum and who is in charge of how it is implemented?) Rather, I have in recent years (especially in my school) noticed a few things that actually lead me to argue in favor of a national curriculum. . . .

This leads me to believe that Shanker was not necessarily out of touch when he called for greater national control. I feel that national standards can provide CONTENT but they don't necessarily dictate METHOD. We can still teach how we want to. Many other industrialized, successful nations have core curriculums where standardized tests are based on content.

There are some problems with a national curriculum, as the authors noted. It may indeed minimize the number of choices that parents currently have about where their kids attend (if all schools are offering the "same" curriculum). In addition, there is the concern over just who would decide the national curriculum. If we were to head down this road, who do you think SHOULD be responsible for deciding? . . .

Dr. Jones

Week 03—Tuesday Message (02)

Our discussion is off to a good start. In reading our colleagues' comments, it is obvious that control of education is an issue that evokes differences of opinion. Naomi supports national control while Rick favors local/school control. Several of you (Brian, Sue, Lisa, Adele) are trying to find a compromise (dialectic) wherein the national standards/control can provide broad guidelines but implementation strategy/control will still reside within

(continued)

communities and schools. As Brian concluded, in the final analysis "behind closed classroom doors . . . teachers have the ultimate control."

. . . .

If we move to a more nationally controlled system, say in matters of curriculum, a critical issue as Naomi indicates is "who decides the curriculum?" My next question for you is: If we can support national curricula, will the debates/decisions on these matters focus on educational interests or will they be driven by political or economic interests?

The LIST is available for your comments. You are also free to continue to respond to my earlier questions from Sunday evening.

Stan _____ (Tuesday)

Most teachers in my school would love to have total control of what and how they teach. For some of them that would be a fabulous idea. For others, it would be a disaster. Because this country is so vast and different culturally, socially, etc., a "National Standard" could work, but only if the broadest possible guidelines are utilized. . . .

I agree with Naomi that content can be dictated (within the prescribed standards) but not method. Therefore, how it is taught could meet localized expectations. . . .

Naomi _____ (Tuesday)

One would hope that the discussions and decisions surrounding a national curriculum would center on educational interests and needs. But it would be naive to assume that this would happen. I think educational issues would become even more political—candidates would have to articulate their positions on educational issues more clearly and would be elected, in part, on their support of or ideas for a national curriculum.

My ideal group of people designing the national curriculum would be a diverse group made up of educators (first and foremost). It must be initiated and written through consensus—ideas drawn from educators in local districts, which are articulated by the state. Each local district could elect a panel of educators to meet with state educational officials, and each state could send several top educators to meet with U.S. Dept. of Education officials to enact a national curriculum.

Barbara_____ (Tuesday)

. . .

I think standards should be like a sonnet, a framework meant to be filled by the creativity and expertise of the teacher, the experiences of the students, the necessity for satisfying families and communities that children are being prepared to function in a world that we cannot anticipate.

Susan _____ (Wednesday)

I agree with Naomi. I would hope that the decisions would be in the best interest of the students. And teachers would have a large voice in this matter, but knowing how the system is now, this would be a more politically and economically driven curricula.

Unless we reform the vast education system and the bureaucracy, we will continue to have policies that are watered down or are so far away from the reality of the classroom, that national curricula will be ineffective.

Dr. Jones

Week 03—Thursday (Message 03)

Our discussion is progressing very well with many excellent comments and observations. In response to my questions, several of you (Naomi, Sue, Joe) conclude that the establishment of national standards would be the result of a political process rather than an educational process. Brian introduced the issue of school finances, which we will discuss in greater detail next week. Joseph reminds us that the diversity of our communities makes a national discussion of standards difficult if not impossible. Annamarie provides us with an example from higher education wherein local government officials have attempted to assume extensive control over a university's governance and faculty prerogatives. Barbara's comparison of standards to a sonnet is an appropriate metaphor for an approach that allows the governmental authorities to establish the framework/content and let the education professionals develop the methods.

To stir our discussion a bit for the remainder of the week, at the end of Chapter 9 in Nelson et al., John Stuart Mill, nineteenth century philosopher, is quoted as follows: "A general State [national] education is a mere contrivance for molding people to be exactly like one another; and as the mold in which it casts them is that which pleases the predominant power in the government . . . it establishes a despotism of the mind." In addition to the homogenizing of minds, an important element of Mill's comment here is that a national education standard/policy would change every time a new party is in [predominant] power. Do we not also have that at the state and local level? . . .

Are not politics inherent in any major publicly funded activity such as education and does it matter whether standards are decided nationally or locally since they will be part of a political process and not an educational process? And as a result, have educators assumed [or have been forced to assume] a professional responsibility to buffer children from the political philosophies of elected officials be they at the national, state, or local levels?

As we conclude this week's discussion, feel free to respond to the above or any other comment posted earlier.

Ingrid_____ (Thursday)

I am really surprised that so many of us are in favor of national curriculums. I agree with Joe S. that standards need to remain flexible so that the students' needs remain the focus of our work. I (and Joe, but he is in JHS) teach science in a state that has a very set curriculum. The expectations placed on me are not vague, as they are in

(continued)

Naomi's school. I teach to a test. Method is left to me, but content is not. I have no real freedom to include some new or interesting or topical unit that I feel would benefit my students. This can be very frustrating. On the other hand, when I taught in JHS I know now that I did not set my standards high enough. I like Rick's suggestion to raise the standards without dictating the specifics so that local issues don't get ignored. The problem is how can we create the sonnet standards Barbara spoke of? . . .

I disagree with Rick and Brian's contention that even with standards the teachers have ultimate control. My department and I get called into the principal's office every year if our results are not up to "the chancellor's standards." We are constantly challenged to explain what we are doing to "meet the standards. . . ."

Rick _____ (Thursday)

. . .

Ingrid, about meeting standards and the ultimate control being the teacher, I think that different curriculum departments in educational institutions are more accountable than others. You must realize that I am an art educator. I have written the curriculum for all my courses and have never in thirteen years been questioned on what I was doing. A mathematics instructor, teaching a regents level class, is going to be scrutinized more closely. I am not saying that I am a proponent of the "totally hands off" approach to my department that I have experienced. The arts now have standards that we must abide by. Fortunately, members of my department have been achieving results well above the standards for years. In 2001 there will be an exit exam for art. I think it's about time. Maybe the arts are finally being viewed as significant, vital, and important learning activities. More accountability? Bring it on!

In response to Dr. Jones: I think it does matter whether standards are decided nationally or locally. Even if they are motivated by political agendas. People need to be part of the process and this happens at the local level. If not asked to be part of the plan, many local schools will not "buy into" the standards and consequently they will not be followed. I would hate to see national and state funding being used as motivation for schools to come around to national standards participation and implementation. . . .

Naomi_____ (Friday)

John Stuart Mill's quote reflects the fear of a "big brother" type of government where all our students become mirror images of each other. As an advocate of a national curriculum, this of course would be my worst nightmare. Maybe I am being too idealistic, but I really don't believe that national standards would "mold people to be exactly like one another." I would hope that it would raise the current educational standards so that we teachers in turn would raise our expectations for our students.

Politics are, as Dr. Jones notes, "inherent in . . . education." One only has to read the *New York Times* headlines to bring that point home. . . .

FIGURE G.2M *(concluded)*

So yes, the concern exists that standards or issues regarding curriculum may change depending on the administration elected, but hopefully not to the point where it would lower standards. A "dialectic" approach would lead to a healthy and appropriate curriculum, and I would hope that educators would be involved in the decision-making process.

Dr. Jones

Week 03—Saturday (Message 04)

Summary

Our topic this week was the control of education. Please refer to my notes at our Web site for additional background material on this topic. The reading in Nelson et al. (Chapter 9) refers to the control of curriculum as a major source of conflict between national and local educational authorities. The United States is relatively unique in that the control of education is shared among several entities at the federal, state, and local levels of government including mayors, city councils, boards of education, and school superintendents.

The issue of control is complex and even among a group of experienced teachers such as yourselves, differences of opinion have been expressed. Rick made the case that schools would function much better with less central control and more local/teacher control. Brian, on the other hand, observes that in the final analysis, teachers have significant control "behind their classroom doors." Naomi pointed out that too much teacher control in her school has led to a curriculum that varies widely even among teachers who teach the same grade. "A lot of my colleagues feel that the expectations placed upon us are vague, and this in turn translates into vague expectations for our students. We are not necessarily laying a knowledge base that is built upon year after year." Naomi makes a good case here for more central control and specifically for national standards. Barbara's comparison of national standards to a sonnet is an appropriate metaphor for an approach that allows central governmental authorities to establish the overall framework/content while letting the local education professionals develop the methods.

If we were to support greater national control of education policies, another major question is who and how these policies will be established. There is great concern (Naomi, Sue, Joe) that national standards/policies will be determined not for educational reasons but for political reasons. Education would be even more politicized than it already is at the local and state levels. The issue of control and who decides education policies in the political arena which we call Washington, D.C. is a most difficult question without an answer. Stan commented, "I am totally stymied in trying to reach a conclusion."

So are most of the proponents and opponents of national control of education.

. . .

In closing, I thank Brian, Naomi, and Rick for the excellent job they did as facilitators of our discussion this week. Their comments were stimulating and provoked a good deal of thought by all of us.

Have a great weekend!

On-Line Sources of Information on Distance Learning

American Center for the Study of Distance Education (Penn State University)
http://www.ed.psu.edu/acsde/

American Distance Education Consortium
http://www.adec.edu/

American Journal of Distance Education
http://www.ed.psu.edu/acsde/Jour.html

Annenberg Corporation for Public Broadcasting Project
http://www.learner.org/aboutacpb/

Asynchronous Learning Magazine
http://www.aln.org/alnweb/magazine/maga_issue1.htm

Copyrights and Universities
http://arl.cni.org/scomm/copyright/UniCopy.html

Copyright and Fair Use (Stanford University)
http://fairuse.stanford.edu/

Council for Higher Education Accreditation
http://www.chea.org

Distance Education Training Council
http://www.detc.org

European Journal of Open and Distance Learning
http://www1.nks.no/eurodl/

Global Alliance for Transnational Education
http://www.edugate.org/

Institute for Distance Education (University of Maryland)
http://www.umuc.edu/ide/ide.html

Jones Education Company Website (formerly the Mind Extension University)
http://www.jec.edu/index.html

Journal of Asynchronous Learning Networks
http://www.aln.org/alnweb/journal/jaln_vol12issue1.htm

Journal of Distance Education (Canada)
http://www.hil.unb.ca/Texts/JDE/

Journal of Distance Learning Administration
http://www.westga.edu/~distance/jmain11.html

Journal of Library Services for Distance Education
http://www.westga.edu/library/jlsde/

Lucent Technologies Center for Excellence in Distance Learning
http://www.lucent.com/cedl/

Penn State World Campus
http://www.worldcampus.psu.edu/

Public Broadcasting System Adult Learning Services
http://www.pbs.org/adultlearning/als/about_als/

Star Schools Project
http://star.ucc.nau.edu/starschools/index.html

The Open University of the United Kingdom
http://open.ac.uk

The Web of Asynchronous Learning Networks
http://www.aln.org/alnweb/

Western Governors University
http://www.wgu.edu

United States Distance Learning Association
http://www.usdla.org

University of London External Programme
http://www.lon.ac.uk/external/

University of Wisconsin Distance Education Clearinghouse
http://www.uwex.edu/disted/home.html

Virtual University Journal
http://www.openhouse.org.uk/virtual-university-press/vuj/welcom.htm

World Intellectual Property Organization
http://www.wipo.org/

World Lecture Hall
http://www.utexas.edu/world/lecture/index.html

Yahoo Distance Learning Directory
http://dir.yahoo.com/Education/Distance_Learning/

Glossary

Advanced Research Projects Administration Network (ARPANET) A worldwide data communications network established by the U.S. Department of Defense in the 1960s that evolved into the Internet.

ALN See **Asynchronous Learning Network.**

Analog A general term used to refer to any continuous physical property such as voltage, current, fluid pressure, rotation, and so on.

Andragogy Referring to adult learning. Made popular by Malcolm Knowles in his theory of *andragogy* or adult learning.

ARPANET See **Advanced Research Projects Administration Network.**

ASCII An acronym for American Standard Code for Information Interchange. It is a coding scheme that represents letters of the alphabet, numerals, and special characters as a series of binary digits or numbers.

Asynchronous Happening at different times. Asynchronous communication, for instance, is characterized by time-independence, that is, the sender and receiver do not communicate at the same time. An example is electronic mail.

Asynchronous Learning Network (ALN) A form of distance learning that uses computer networking technology, especially the Internet, for instructional activities.

Audioconferencing The use of telephone message handling equipment to connect multiple parties simultaneously as is done in a conference telephone call.

Audiographics A form of audioconferencing that allows for limited graphics capability as might be provided by an electronic blackboard or document camera.

Authoring language A user-friendly programming language used to develop specific applications such as teaching presentations, computer-assisted instruction, and multimedia. Examples include HyperCard, Astound, ToolBook, PowerPoint, and Authorware.

Authoring system See **Authoring language.**

Bandwidth In communications, the frequencies within which signals can be transmitted and received. Bandwidth directly relates to data transfer speed. The greater the bandwidth, the faster the data transmission speed.

Binary digit   In the binary number system, the binary digit is either 0 or 1. See also **Bit.**

Bit   A binary digit. In the binary number system, the bit is either 0 or 1. In electronic storage, it represents the smallest unit of data and is characterized as being either "on" or "off." Groups of eight bits are combined to represent characters of data that are referred to as *bytes.*

Broadband   A high-capacity communications circuit that is capable of transmitting data at speeds up to millions of bits per second.

Browser software (Web browser)   Software that provides facilities for accessing Uniform Resource Locators (URLs) on the World Wide Web. Examples of Web browsers include Netscape Navigator and Microsoft's Internet Explorer.

Byte   The minimum amount of primary storage or memory needed to store a character (letter, numeral, special character) of information. It usually is eight binary digits or bits.

CD-ROM   An acronym for compact disc-read only memory. It is a form of high-capacity optical storage that uses laser technology.

Central file server   The central or host computer in a network that provides files and programs to other computers.

Central Processing Unit (CPU)   The part of a computer hardware system that directs all processing activities. It consists of electronic circuitry and includes a control unit, an arithmetic-logic unit, and a primary storage or memory unit. On large computers, the term is used to refer to the entire main computer console. On some microcomputers, it refers only to the control unit and the arithmetic-logic unit.

Client server system   A distributed data communications system in which computers perform two important functions either as "clients" or "servers." The "client" function makes requests for data (i.e., files) from the "server," which locates the data on the data communications system and processes the request for the client.

Clip media   Digital files or libraries containing images, video, sounds, and other media that can be readily incorporated into a multimedia program.

CMS   See **Course Management System.**

Codec   Coding/decoding equipment used to convert and compress analog video signals into digital formats and vice versa.

Communications control program   See **Communications controller.**

Communications controller   A data communications device that is used to send and receive messages from multiple sources. A multiplexor is an example of a communications controller. In some networks, communications controlling is performed by computer programs that also are referred to as *communications controllers.*

Compressed video   A computer software technique used to reduce the number of bits or bytes needed to store or transmit a video file. Formulae or algorithms are used to replace empty or duplicate bits or bytes in a video file with coded bits and bytes that are then used to reconstruct the original video file. Compressed video is used most frequently when data transmissions are slow or limited due to narrow bandwidth communications.

Computer   An electronic device that accepts input, processes it according to a set of instructions, and produces the results as output. Computers can be classified as supercomputers, mainframes, minicomputers, microcomputers, laptop computers, and so forth, depending on physical size, speed, and peripheral devices.

Computer-Assisted Instruction (CAI)   The use of the computer to assist in the instructional process. One of the earliest used terms to refer generically to computer applications in education, it is also used to refer to tutor-type applications such as drill and practice, and tutorials.

Computer-Managed Instruction (CMI)   The use of the computer in an instructional process in which student progress is monitored and recorded for subsequent instructions and review. Most CMI applications also are able to adjust material to each individual student's level of understanding.

Computer-Mediated Communications (CMC)   The use of computer systems that incorporate communications software such as e-mail or LISTSERVs to enhance distance learning and computer-managed instruction applications.

Connectivity   Refers to the communications facilities (i.e., coaxial or fiber optic cable, telephone systems, computer equipment) that enable users to *connect* to computer networks.

Constructivism   Theory of learning that stresses the importance of experiences, experimentation, problem-solving, and the construction of knowledge.

Course Management System (CMS)   A set of computer software tools designed to enable users to create Web-based courses. Examples include WEBCT, TopClass, and LearningSpace.

Cyberspace   Descriptive term for the Internet.

Data communications   The methods and media used to transfer data from one computer device to another. Common data communications media include coaxial cable, telephone, fiber optics, and satellite systems.

Desktop publishing   The use of computer equipment to develop text and graphics. It usually refers to software that provides enhanced facilities for displaying characters, pictures, and color.

Digital   Related to digits. Computers are considered digital because all data and instructions are represented as binary digits.

Digitizer   Any device used to convert analog (continuous physical property such as voltage or current) signals into binary or digital format.

Directory   A grouping or catalog of file names that reside on a secondary storage device such as a disk. A directory is also referred to as a *folder.*

Disk operating system   A generic term used to refer to any operating system that resides on a disk device and is loaded as needed into primary storage.

Disk Operating System   See **DOS.**

Distance education   A generic, all-inclusive term used to refer to the physical separation of teachers and learners.

Distance learning   A term for the physical separation of teachers and learners that has become popular in recent years, particularly in the United States. While used interchangeably with distance education, distance learning puts the emphasis on the learner and is especially appropriate when students take on greater responsibility for their learning as is frequently the case when doing so from a distance.

Distributed system   A form of computer processing that distributes and links hardware over some geographic area as in a network. It assumes that the local hardware can perform some tasks as well as expand its capabilities by connecting to other hardware.

DOS   An acronym for Disk Operating System, the most popular operating system for Intel-based microcomputers. It is also referred to as *Microsoft* or *MS-DOS* after the company that developed it.

Downlink   The transmission of data from a communications satellite to an earth station.

Download   In a computer network, the process of transferring a copy of a file from one computer, generally referred to as a *central file server,* to another, requesting computer.

E-mail   See **Electronic mail.**

Environmental scanning   A term used in planning that means engaging in activities to provide information outside of an organization or on the external *environment.*

Electronic bulletin board   A group e-mail or mailing list that allows all participants to post and read messages.

Electronic mail (e-mail)   The transmission of messages over a data communications network.

Ergonomics   The study of people and their characteristics in relation to their working environments (furnishings, equipment, lighting, etc.). The objective of ergonomics is to develop comfortable and safe conditions so as to improve worker morale and efficiency. Ergonomics is especially important in designing facilities such as electronic classrooms.

Fiber optics   A term used to describe the method of transmitting and receiving light beams along an optical fiber that is usually made of a thin strand of glass. Fiber optics are destined to change radically the speed and nature of communications throughout the world.

File Transfer Protocol (FTP)   A popular protocol used for transferring data files on the World Wide Web.

Folder   A grouping or cataloging of file names that reside on a secondary storage device such as a disk. It is the same as a *directory.*

Formative evaluation measures   Measures that provide information to help refine, improve, or extend a program or process.

Frame rate   The number of frames or images per second displayed on a video device. Thirty frames per second is the full-motion video standard.

FTP   See **File Transfer Protocol.**

Gopher   A database communications protocol used for locating data files on the World Wide Web.

Graphical User Interface (GUI)   The graphic display of software options in the form of icons and pictures that can be selected, usually by a pointing device such as a mouse. It is considered a feature of user-friendly software such as that provided with the Macintosh operating system, Microsoft Windows, and many application software packages.

GUI   See **Graphical User Interface.**

Hand-held computer   A small portable computer capable of being used (held) in one hand.

Hardware   The physical components of a system used to transmit, store, and receive information. Examples include the physical components of computer and communications systems.

HTML   See **HyperText Markup Language.**

HTTP   See **HyperText Transfer Control Protocol.**

Hypermedia   A computer-based information retrieval system for accessing sound, text, images, graphics, or video in a nonsequential or nonlinear format.

Hypertext   A computer-based text and document retrieval system that can be accessed in a nonsequential or nonlinear format.

HyperText Markup Language (HTML)   Software language used to establish data files for access on the World Wide Web.

HyperText Transfer Control Protocol (HTTP)   The most commonly used protocol on the World Wide Web. It runs in conjunction with *TCP/IP.*

ILS   See **Integrated Learning System.**

Information superhighway   Descriptive term for the Internet.

Instructional Television Fixed Service (ITFS)   Instructional television service that operates over a limited or *fixed* geographic area using a microwave transmitter. Special receiver antennae are required by the students to access the microwave transmission.

Integrated Learning System (ILS)   A single computer package for delivering instruction that combines hardware, software, curriculum, and management components. It is usually supplied by a single vendor.

Integrated Services Digital Network (ISDN)   A high-speed (128 kilobits per second) data communications network evolving from existing telephone services.

Interactive   Operating in an interactive or back-and-forth mode. It refers to user and machine dialogue or interaction in which both are active participants in a process.

Interactive video   Combining computer and video technologies to provide for an active video environment in which users can control and select options based on a given application. Interactive video is a major advancement over other video technologies such as film and television, which are considered passive.

Interface   The point at which two components meet. With computers, it is used for both hardware, when two physical devices connect to one another, and software, when two programs work with one another. It is also used to refer to points where people connect to computer devices such as with graphical user interfaces.

Internet   The network of networks that provides the basic protocol standard for allowing data communications systems to link themselves together throughout the world.

Internet Relay Chat (IRC)   Computer software that allows multiple parties to participate in synchronous (same-time) communications on the Internet.

Intranet   In data communications, the adoption of the standard Internet protocol and software tools for a local network or establishing a mini-Internet within a local system.

IRC   See **Internet Relay Chat.**

ISDN   See **Integrated Services Digital Network.**

ITFS   See **Instructional Television Fixed Service.**

Java   An object-oriented programming language that attempts to operate across software platforms.

Javascript   A programming language similar to Java that generally operates with World Wide Web browser software.

LAN   See **Local Area Network.**

Laptop   A type of portable computer that can easily be used by resting it on one's lap.

Laserdisc   An optical disc used to store video images and associated audio or sound information in analog format. Same as a videodisc.

Listserv   An e-mail program that allows multiple computer users to send and receive messages on a single system. Listserv software is frequently used to administer electronic bulletin boards.

Local Area Network (LAN)   Connecting computer equipment using data communications over a limited geographic area such as a room, building, or campus.

Logo   A high-level programming language developed by Seymour Papert in 1968. It is a very popular programming language for teaching young children to use a computer.

Mainframe   Large computer systems capable of processing extensive amounts of data and of controlling many peripheral devices.

Media   The plural of medium. Defined as the symbol systems used to communicate and convey messages and information, including the text in books and newspapers, sound in radio transmissions, and images on television or in a film.

Media distribution system   A computer-based system that integrates several media sources (videotape, videodisc, computer, document camera, etc.) and is able to distribute them to selected output devices.

Menu   A presentation of options available that a user can select or request from a program. Menu-driven software anticipates user options and presents them in the form of lists or icons.

Microcomputer   A small computer system that usually utilizes one central processing unit. The Apple Macintosh and IBM PC/PS are among the most popular microcomputers ever manufactured.

Microprocessor   A central processing unit used for most microcomputer systems capable of being integrated on a single chip.

Modem   See **Modulator-demodulator.**

Modulator-demodulator (modem)   A data communications device used to convert computer digital signals into a telephone frequency or analog signal and vice versa.

Multimedia   Combining sound, text, images, animation, and video. With computers, it refers to a variety of applications that utilize CD-ROM, videodisc, and audio equipment.

Multiplexor   A data communications device used to control many or multiple messages by funneling them into a smaller number of communication lines or ports.

Multipoint videoconferencing   See **Videoconferencing.**

Narrowband   A low-capacity communications circuit that is capable of transmitting data at speeds of up to 56,000 bits per second.

Network   A group of computer devices connected by a data communications system. Two major types of networks are local area networks (LANs) and wide area networks (WANs).

Notebook   A very lightweight portable computer, usually weighing less than ten pounds, that can be easily carried under one's arm.

Optical scanning device   An input device that uses light sensors to scan paper documents and convert images into digital format. Optical mark readers and optical character readers are types of optical scanning devices.

Pixel   Short for picture element. A point on a grid such as a video screen that represents a single dot of light. Text and images are developed by manipulating many pixels.

Plug-in   A dynamic computer code module that performs a specific task that generally is made available or functions with World Wide Web browser software.

Point-to-point videoconferencing   See **Videoconferencing.**

Portfolio assessment   An alternative to traditional testing that requires students to compile a *portfolio* of material (papers written, creative works developed, log of relevant activities, etc.) which is used to assess student accomplishment in a course of study.

Portable computer   Any computer designed to be carried and moved about. Laptop, notebook, and hand-held computers are examples of portable computers.

Protocol   A general term for a set of rules, procedures, or standards used to exchange information in data communications. Examples of these rules include a code or signal indicating the beginning of a message, a code or signal indicating the end of a message, or a code or signal indicating that a device is busy with another task. Computer manufacturers have established various protocols for exchanging information on their equipment.

Router   An intermediary device on a communications network that accepts and routes messages from one link (i.e., LAN) on the network to other links.

Search engine   Software that provides keyword and other search facilities for locating information on the World Wide Web. Examples include *Yahoo, Lycos,* and *Alta Vista.*

Simulation software   A form of software used to represent a real-life situation on a computer.

Socratic Method   A method of critical inquiry and instruction used by the Greek philosopher Socrates that relies on the ability to develop questions and elicit responses from students to arrive at conclusions.

Software   Computer programs and instructions that direct the physical components (hardware) of a computer system to perform tasks.

Sound capture   Term used for converting analog sound into a digital file.

Speech synthesis   Producing spoken words from computer-generated or controlled equipment.

Student-centered learning   An approach to teaching and learning that puts the student in the center of the instructional process.

Summative evaluation measures   Measures that provide information that tallies or *sums up* what has occurred in a program or process.

Synchronous Happening at the same time. Synchronous communication for, instance, is characterized by time-dependence, that is, the sender and receiver communicate at the same time. An example is a telephone conversation.

System A group of interrelated parts assembled to achieve some common goal or end. The three major components of most systems are input, process, and output. Examples of systems include computer systems, ecological systems, economic systems, political systems, and school systems.

T1 A dedicated digital circuit that uses broadband data communications to provide high-speed transmissions of data at the rate of up to 1.5 million bits per second.

TCP/IP See **Transmission Control Protocol/Internet Protocol.**

Technology infrastructure The digital networking facilities needed to deliver data, audio, and video signals at high speed and high capacity reliably throughout an organization or defined area.

Train the trainer An approach to staff development that relies on developing a cadre of well-trained individuals in an organization who train other staff.

Transfer rate The time it takes to transfer data from one location (device) to another. In computer hardware evaluation, transfer rate would be used to measure the performance of input and output devices.

Transmission Control Protocol/Internet Protocol (TCP/IP) The standard protocol used on the Internet. Originally developed by the U.S. Department of Defense for *ARPANET.*

UNIX A powerful multitasking operating system developed at Bell Laboratories in 1969 and written in the C programming language. Variations of UNIX exist that enable it to run on IBM, Apple, and other manufacturers' computers. The UNIX operating system is especially popular for supporting the "server" function in client-server environments such as the Internet.

Uniform Resource Locator (URL) An electronic address that identifies a unique location of a data file on the World Wide Web.

Uplink The transmission of data from an earth station to a communications satellite.

Upload In a computer network, the process of transmitting a copy of a file from a computer to a central file server.

URL See **Uniform Resource Locator.**

Video board A CPU component capable of accepting and generating video.

Video capture Term used for converting analog video into a digital video file.

Videoconferencing The use of analog or digital video technology to connect multiple parties simultaneously in a *conference* where participants can see and hear each other. Point-to-point videoconferencing refers to a two-party conference. Multipoint videoconferencing refers to a multiple (more than two) party conference.

Videodisc   An optical disc used to store video images and associated audio or sound information in analog format. Same as a laserdisc.

Virtual   Being functional and effective without existing in a traditional mode. Virtual learning, for example, is learning that can functionally and effectively occur in the absence of traditional classroom environments.

WAN   See **Wide Area Network.**

Wave format   Digital file format used to store sounds as a pattern of oscillatory periodic electronic signals.

Web browser   See **Browser.**

Wide Area Network (WAN)   Connecting computer equipment using data communications over a widespread geographic area such as a town, city, or country.

World Wide Web   The protocol and file format software incorporating hyper-text and multimedia capabilities for use on the Internet.

Index